What is Gender?

What is Gender?

Sociological Approaches

Mary Holmes

SAGE Publications
Los Angeles · London · New Delhi · Singapore

SAGE Publications Ltd
1 Oliver's Yard
55 City Road
London EC1Y 1SP

SAGE Publications Inc.
2455 Teller Road
Thousand Oaks, California 91320

SAGE Publications India Pvt Ltd
B 1/I 1 Mohan Cooperative Industrial Area
Mathura Road
New Delhi 110 044

SAGE Publications Asia-Pacific Pte Ltd
33 Pekin Street #02-01
Far East Square
Singapore 048763

Library of Congress Control Number: 2006939135

British Library Cataloguing in Publication data

A catalogue record for this book is available from the
British Library

ISBN 978-0-7619-4712-7
ISBN 978-0-7619-4713-4 (pbk)

Typeset by C&M Digitals (P) Ltd., Chennai, India
Printed in Great Britain by The Cromwell Press Ltd, Trowbridge, Wiltshire
Printed on paper from sustainable resources

Contents

Acknowledgements

Much of this book was written within the warmth of supportiveness of the sociology department at the University of Aberdeen. I am indebted to my colleagues there in so many ways and I continue to miss their laughter. The book was finished at Flinders University and I apologize for ruining some of our pleasant lunches by making everyone discuss things like symbolic capital. I am very grateful to colleagues at those and other universities who read draft chapters for me: Alex Howson, Karen O'Reilly, Chris Beasley, Paula Black, Jane Haggis, Heather Brook, and Mike Hepworth. Thank you to Carolyn Corkindale, the Department of Sociology's excellent research assistant at Flinders, for tracking down many of the references and doing much tidying up of the manuscript. The faults, of course, remain mine. I commend you to those faults as points where as readers you can engage with the text and say: 'Hang on a minute, I'm not so sure about that'. It is that engagement which will make the book useful.

I had no leave to help me complete this book, apart from a few weeks at the end of one semester, so I hope you all feel very sorry for me. Thank you to Brent for always feeling sorry for me when I needed it. I am glad that I was able to complete this book and writing it reminded me of all the students I have taught and how much I learnt from them. So thank you to them. For students or colleagues who might read this, email me and tell me if you like the book or hate it, or have questions. That is what I think it should be about.

Introduction to the sociology of gender

> Chris got up and went to the bathroom. Leaving pyjamas on the floor and turning on the shower, Chris stepped into the water. It was not a hair-washing day, so after a quick rub with the soap it was time to get out and dry off. After towelling and applying hair putty to the new short haircut, Chris dabbed on some moisturising lotion and went to get dressed. Nothing special was happening today so jeans and a T-shirt would be fine. The only choice really to be made was between basketball boots or sandals.

This is a paragraph I made up. When you read it I imagine that you assumed either that Chris was a woman, or that Chris was a man. Yet Chris is a shortened name which both Christophers and Christines use and I have not used any pronouns to indicate sex. There is nothing in this description that definitively identifies masculinity or femininity. You may protest that 'real' men do not use moisturiser, or that women are less likely to have short hair. Nevertheless, most people know of men who are into face creams and other such products and women who have short hair. Your decision is not defensible, but the point is that you made a decision. We do not know how to think about people as neutral; we always think about them as women or as men and we interact with them accordingly. If you decided Chris was a woman, go back and read the paragraph again and imagine Chris is a man. Does that change how you read it or what you think about Chris? Do you think it 'typical' of a man just to leave his pyjamas on the floor; do you feel a little titillated by imagining a naked man in the shower? Try to continue describing Chris's day without giving away whether Chris is a man or a woman. It is very difficult to do.

We live in a world which is organized around the idea that women and men have different bodies, different capabilities, and different needs and desires. This book examines these assumptions, drawing on sociological and related approaches to understand how and why the social world is arranged around such gender distinctions. This introduction begins that task by defining key terms, then looking briefly at the history of gender within sociology. In some senses the rest of this chapter outlines what the book is not about – or, to put it more positively, why I focus on the issues that appear in the book and not on facts about inequalities or on media images of gender. I want to explain why I say so little about these things because long experience of teaching this topic tells me that people come to it with a strong sense of what is important. Many assume that women and men are equal now and that the media are most crucial in how we now behave as women and men. I want to establish some of the bare facts about inequalities and discuss why the media may not be as all powerful as they initially appear. I will then be able to turn to my central project of explaining the cultural turn within sociological and feminist approaches to gender. When the sociology of gender emerged, inequalities between women and men were the focus. Discussion of women's relative lack of access to wealth and other resources was gradually overtaken by concerns with language and meaning. The promise and problems of this shift within ideas about gender are the subject of following chapters. Those chapters will make more sense if the key terms used are clearly understood.

Defining terms

Key words are highlighted throughout the text in bold.

The sociology of gender and related knowledge sometimes uses language that may be unfamiliar or have different meanings to those used in everyday life. Terminology and jargon are the same thing depending on whether you understand them or not. Having specific terms with specific meanings is useful as a shorthand way of dealing with ideas that can otherwise take some time to explain. Defining the most crucial terms can serve as a way to introduce the kinds of things with which this book is concerned. The first thing to deal with is the distinction sociologists have made since the 1970s between **sex** (biological differences between males and females) and **gender** (socially produced differences between being feminine and being masculine). Later the book will return to the question of how distinct gender is from sex. However, it is generally agreed that gender differences are to be understood as a central feature of **patriarchy**, a social system in which men have come to be dominant in relation to women. There are, as we shall see, questions around to what extent gender is imposed on individuals as a result of the material conditions and social structures in which they live. Within sociology, '**material**' has meant various things. Karl Marx, whose thought forms a good deal of the foundations of sociology, was particularly concerned with how societies were organized, or structured, around meeting material needs, such as the need for food and shelter. He argues that people's lives were determined by how a society organized the production of the things needed to survive. This was an emphasis on the **economic**, meaning the producing, managing and distributing of resources within society. Marx argued that industrialization instituted a new economic system called **capitalism** based on employers exploiting workers' labour (only paying a wage not a share of the profits) and accumulating for themselves the wealth resulting from selling things. However, material is a term that has taken on broader meanings in more recent years, especially with regard to gender. Now it is maintained that the **material** may include a wider range of things, not just the things we need to survive but our bodies as things (Rahman and Witz, 2003). Yet widening what is meant by material has been only part of the story of developing understandings of gender. For sociologists the key has been to see gender as **a social construction** (something created by the social environment). An appreciation of how material conditions produce gender will be discussed but this book also looks at the importance of **discourses** (systematized ways of talking and thinking) in how gender operates. Medical and scientific discourses, for example, have been important in constructing gender. It is important to understand the part that ideas and meanings play in the social construction of femininity and masculinity. There are of course sociological discourses on gender and our discussion begins with a history of these ideas.

The history of gender

Classic sociology and other social theory contain little attention to the social differences between women and men. Marx, Weber and Durkheim are not noted for their insights into 'sex' inequality (the word gender was not known to them in its present usage) and in fact tended mostly to consider women's subordinate social role as a natural 'given' (Sydie, 1987). Durkheim thought of modernity's greater distinction between 'sex roles' as a functional, biologically based evolution resulting from the progressive forces of a shift to organic solidarity. To translate, he argued that as society became more complex, more distinct differences in body and mind emerged between women and men; they specialized in their roles and this made the division of labour more efficient and society stronger. Weber also saw women's dependent social position as fundamentally determined by 'the normal superiority of the physical and intellectual energies of the male' (Weber cited in Sydie, 1987: 59). This marred an otherwise interesting analysis of traditional power as patriarchal – in the pre-feminist sense of older males exercising traditional domination through the family (Sydie, 1987: 51–87). It seems slightly odd that these thinkers should view 'sex roles' as naturally determined, given that they were busy stressing how social forces affected everything else. It also seems a little odd given that Weber's wife Marianne was a notable German feminist and Marx's daughter Eleanor was involved in feminist politics. Nevertheless these thinkers failed to examine 'sex' as an important social division and this view was long dominant within sociology (Oakley, 1974). However, this does not mean that inequalities between women and men were entirely ignored. Marx recognized inequality between the sexes as a problem, albeit a problem of secondary importance to capitalist exploitation of workers. Marx's friend and collaborator Frederick Engels did attempt a Marxist explanation of women's subordination (see Chapter 4). There was also a tradition of women writing about women's social position. There was Mary Wollstonecraft (1985/1792) in the eighteenth century (see Chapter 4), and Harriet Martineau, in the nineteenth century, who also produced the first book on sociological methods (see Hill and Hoecker-Drysdale, 2001). In addition the highly influential Chicago School of sociology contained at least a dozen women from its establishment in the 1890s, including the well-known sociologist Jane Addams. These women were professional sociologists actively researching and writing on a range of issues, including many relating to women's place in society (Delamont, 1990: 139–159). Yet little or no reference is made to these women and more recent understandings of gender are often seen as beginning with Simone de Beauvoir's (1988/1949) philosophically based treatise, *The Second Sex*. In her famous statement that '[o]ne is not born, but rather becomes, a woman' (de Beauvoir, 1988/1949: 295), she established a core principle of most subsequent efforts to understand gender inequalities. It was not nature but society or 'culture' that made women (and men) what they were.

In the 1950s and early 1960s **Functionalism** was largely dominant within sociology and it contributed to sociological understandings of differences between women and men as socially constructed. While **social construction** involves structures such as class systems and institutions, the term principally refers to the processes by which ideas about how things should work are made into social reality. Before the concept of 'gender' came into sociological usage in the 1970s, mid-century functionalists talked about 'sex role differences'. Their argument could be summarized as claiming that sex role differences continue to exist because they function to promote social stability. Whether this was an intended (manifest) or unintended (latent) function of sex role differences did not seem to be of major interest to functionalists.

The focus of functionalist work was on understanding the 'complementary roles' performed by women and men as they function to keep society running smoothly. American sociologist Talcott Parsons is the major figure within twentieth century functionalism. It is Parsons's (see Parsons and Bales, 1956) views of women and men's 'complementary roles' that are taken as the key statement of functionalist ideas about gender. Writing in the 1950s, Parsons argues that modern social life, and in particular the modern organization of work as separate from home, means that someone needs to stay home to care for young children and perform the important early socialization of human infants. For highly complex and not entirely clear reasons associated with the workings of social groups, this emotional 'expressive' role is assigned to women and the rational and 'instrumental' (goal-focused) role of paid work is associated with men. These different 'sex roles' become the social norms and Parsons carefully describes how children become socialized into them. Therefore, Parsons's theory is very much sociological in looking not to nature but to social groups and social processes such as socialization to explain women's and men's different social positions. In the 1950s and 1960s, others using his work to understand sex roles tended to ignore this sociological position and assume that the expressive/instrumental dichotomy was in some form an expression of natural differences (Connell, 2002: 123). Though Parsons may have gone beyond this, his work offered more of a description of current gender expectations than an explication of the inequalities accompanying the differing sex roles. Parsons describes the ideal American family of the 1950s and does so in a way that justifies, rather than is critical of, this very historically and culturally specific example of gender roles. Parsons implies that this is the best way of organizing family life in response to modern social conditions, but for whom is it best? Since Parsons, much sociology of the family has focused more on how the breadwinner/housewife model of family life has been restrictive for many women. For others, it has remained a luxury they cannot afford because only those families where the men earn high wages could afford for the wife to stay at home. Other alternatives to the nuclear family are similarly ignored or devalued. Although Parsons himself does not discuss other cultures in any detail, he draws on the work of fellow contributors to the book to back his claim that a nuclear-style family still seems to function well and maintain social stability within many other societies (Parsons and Bales, 1956). The fact that the content of sex roles is different in other cultures does not necessarily challenge Parsons's overall argument that it is complementarity – the fact that one sex is assigned opposite tasks to the other – which is functional. However, as discussed in Chapters 1 and 2, anthropological research can illustrate that in some other cultures women's and men's roles are similar not opposite (for example both women and men may contribute to child rearing), and such an arrangement can also support stability. Parsons's focus on the way in which the sexes complement each other also fails to consider how and why the different roles have come to be valued differently. Functionalism does not explain why instrumental roles are more highly regarded within modern western society. The need for social stability was seen as justification of the continuance of such sex roles, and though changes in those roles were explored they were often construed as threatening that stability. The idea that 'stability' may not be beneficial to women constrained within traditional roles did not seem to occur to the functionalists. The importance attached to social stability prevented functionalists from developing a real analysis of how some social actors and groups might not benefit from the continuance of the sharply defined roles identified. Various feminist sociologists began systematically to examine differences between women and men as socially produced. It is from this key departure point in the 1970s that this book begins its travels.

It is hard for today's students of gender, faced with mountains of relevant books, to imagine the paucity of decent literature about women thirty to forty years ago. Into this void the new 'wave' of feminists began to launch their considerations of the causes and state of inequalities between women and men (see Chapter 4 and Chapter 6). It is also often difficult to comprehend how many changes have taken place for women even since the 1960s. Equal Pay legislation has been passed, women have more control over if and when they reproduce, a university education is more than a way for middle class women to meet a husband, job opportunities have improved, and so on. But are women and men equal now?

Material inequalities: are women and men equal now?

If you are a young woman you may feel that you have a lot of choice about what you do with your life. It probably seems like you will have more or less the same opportunities in life as your brothers and/or male friends. Young men reading this might feel that women can do whatever they want to these days and that talking about inequalities is out of date. Certainly the world has changed. Read some history or talk to your mothers and grandmothers and you will quickly appreciate that young women today are likely to have more education, better job opportunities and more independence than young women did forty or fifty years ago. Young women may be partly right in suggesting that they have much the same opportunities as men their age.

In terms of education young women are likely to have completed secondary school and probably did better than the boys. At university or college you are likely to see as many undergraduate women on campus as men, with women continuing to do slightly better. In the United

Kingdom, for example, six times more women enrolled in higher education in 2003/04 than in 1970/71, so that around 59 per cent of undergraduates are now women (Office for National Statistics, 2006: 38). While girls in wealthier nations are able to take advantage of at least a good basic education, in other areas of the world educational opportunity for girls can be limited. Non-formal, local and traditional forms of learning may exist in many places but formal westernized types of education are likely to bring greater status and social rewards. The amount of formal education varies greatly between different regions of Africa. Southern Africa has for some time demonstrated little difference between boys and girls in length of schooling. Early twenty-first century figures show boys getting 10.9 years and girls 10.4 years at school (African Development Bank, 2002: Table 1.8). However, in Western and Central Africa only 51 per cent of primary school age girls actually attend primary school compared to 59 per cent of boys. At secondary school this drops to just over one in five of secondary age girls attending, while one in four boys of secondary age attend (UNICEF, 2006: 121). India, on the whole, provides more education. Primary school is attended by 73 per cent of girls of primary school age, compared to 80 per cent for boys (UNICEF, 2006: 121). It has a strong formal educational tradition and, as with many western nations, women higher up the caste and class hierarchy tend to be well educated. In poorer families, however, girls will probably leave school fairly young, most likely to enter a marriage arranged for them. They will then become responsible for most of the domestic work in the home of their new parents-in-law. For such poorer families, manual work and the domestic support of that work may be crucial to survival and families need children to start bringing in money as soon as possible. But this does not explain why girls are expected to do the domestic work; that expectation is better understood in terms of a culture which values the welfare of the group and especially expects women to contribute to that group welfare rather than pursue individual goals. Thus caring roles at home are still promoted as the proper course for many less privileged women (Kodoth and Eapen, 2005; Mukhopadhyay and Seymour, 1994).

Among more privileged groups in the western world, university graduates of both sexes look forward to getting a 'good' job at the end of their degree. However, the subjects they take in doing their degrees are likely to differ and, therefore, their job options will differ. Have a look around a sociology class – I bet there are more women than men. Try visiting an English or history lecture and you will probably find fewer men there. Then go over to a physics lecture to see if the men outnumber the women, and finally pop in to the engineering department where you may be able to count the women on one hand (e.g. see Department of Education, Science and Training, 2005: 32; Equal

Employment Opportunities Commission, 2006: 8; National Science Board, 2006). These gender differences in choice of subject will affect what sorts of jobs graduates will be able to get. Although there are many good jobs that sociology and English graduates might end up with, it is not the same sort of direct route into high paying, high status work as studying engineering. The women who do engineering may not initially notice any difference between themselves and their male peers, but they may discover that the men in the class find it easier to get jobs than the women. Once in jobs it may become clear that the men are promoted ahead of women at a similar stage and with similar ability. Also women engineers may note that the men are not asked how they are going to combine a career with having a family. These are some of the factors in continuing pay gaps between women and men in science and engineering (Prokos and Padavic, 2005). Continuing beliefs about women's responsibility for their families play a part in determining to what extent women participate in paid work.

In most of South Asia, the Middle East and North Africa, women's economic participation rate is only around 30 per cent, compared to around 45 per cent in OECD (high income) countries (World Bank, 2006). This means that in most cases women are less likely to have a paid job than men. Even where women now form a large portion of the workforce they continue to work in different jobs, under different conditions and generally receive less pay. Sociologists refer to the dividing up of work into jobs thought of as 'men's jobs' and those thought of as 'women's jobs' as the sexual division of labour or (the more recent term) the **gendered division of labour**. The vertical division of labour by gender means that women are rare in the higher positions within occupations. This is especially true of influential managerial positions. In the Fortune 500 (America's top 500 companies) in 2005 only 16.4 per cent of all corporate officer (top management) positions were held by women. Over half of these companies had less than three women corporate officers in 2005 (Catalyst, 2006: 6, 9). The invisible barriers that seem to prevent women being promoted to upper management are referred to as 'the glass ceiling' (see Hymowitz and Schellhardt, 1986). Yet addressing and overcoming such barriers would not necessarily bring equality for all women because of the horizontal gender division of labour, which means that work is divided in gendered ways across occupations. This has obvious implications for how wealth is distributed between women and men.

Evidence indicates that women are poorer than men. They do not earn as much and generally have less access to the material rewards available in society. At the beginning of the twenty-first century in Western Europe, North America and Australasia, women earn around 75 to 90 per cent of the average man's wage. World wide the figure drops so that on a global level women earn around 60 per cent of the male average (Connell, 2002: 2; United Nations Statistics Division, 2005). Through a creative use of job titles, job descriptions and special 'bonuses' it is possible to evade equal pay legislation (where it exists) and to pay a man more than a woman who is, effectively, doing the same job. In poorer countries it is poverty rather than low pay that is the issue. The phrase **'feminization of poverty'** was conjured up by the United Nations to refer to an apparent trend in which an increasing number of those living in poverty are women, and that poverty is growing more severe. The reasons for such a trend are complex and debated. They may range from the costs of women's unpaid work, their related lack of educational and economic opportunities (including access to land and other resources), the rise of HIV/AIDS among women, and the ways in which globalization leads to new ways of exploiting women in developing countries (Barker, 2005).

Not everyone in developing countries is poor, and of course poverty exists in developed countries too. Women in developed and developing nations are more likely to be poor partly because of their caring responsibilities, which often make them reliant on social services. As these services are cut back women are often required to do more caring and yet there is less financial and other support available (Kehler, 2001). The feminization of poverty in wealthy nations may, however, be relative rather than absolute. **Absolute poverty** is about not being able to meet basic survival needs, for example not having enough food to eat. The most recent reliable statistics suggest that such poverty is still common in India, for example, where 36 per cent of women aged 15 to 49 were undernourished according to a 1998–99 survey (International Institute for Population Sciences and ORC Macro, 2000: 244). **Relative poverty** is more common in the West, where you may be able to eat, but do not have enough money to share in the other benefits your society has to offer. For example, you may not be able to afford a television or holidays; this makes you poor relative to those around you. And again it is mostly women who are poor, especially single mothers whether never married or divorced. When relationships break up it is usually the women who get custody of the children. Although welfare payments may offset some of the financial burdens women face after divorce, in most cases women are soon poorer than their ex-partners. Even where laws require a couple's assets to be halved and men to pay maintenance, men may fail to pay; never married and divorced women's earning opportunities are likely to be restricted by child care responsibilities, and their finances may be tight because they are bearing most of the cost of raising the children (for example, Uunk, 2004; Yamokoski and Keister, 2006).

The consequences of poverty for women range from the extreme case of starvation – or at very least severe ill health (Doyal, 2002) – to a more general lack of control over their lives. Women's lack of financial independence makes them vulnerable to the demands of their husbands, or other men with authority over them. When women have to rely on men to get what they need to survive they often do not have the luxury of saying no. In many nations, including wealthy ones, women lacking job skills and experience may be heavily reliant on men's financial support. This may be a key reason why women feel unable to leave violent partners (Dobash and Dobash, 1992). Women's poverty connects not only to sex and violence but is highly likely to constrain their choices about everything from the quality of their housing to what they eat. Where poverty is relative, attempts to feed and clothe children in the 'best' way may be funded by credit. Women take on much of this debt and may even hide it from male partners (where they are present). If this is the case, then women bear the stress of coping with debt payment, or trying to evade it when there is no money (Bridges and Disney, 2004; Parker, 1992). In addition, women's responsibility within families often goes beyond dealing with a lack of finance.

The difficulties for women of trying to combine paid work with family responsibilities have been extensively documented (see for example, Hochschild, 2003). Women continue to do most of the work at home and face a number of other problems associated with family life. Even where families are relatively happy, women continue to do more than their share of household labour. By the 1970s women had considerable equality compared with their position in the nineteenth century. Men have become more involved in family life, but Young and Willmott's (1973) picture of the newly emerging **'symmetrical family'** in which husband and wife perform similar work within the household seems overly optimistic. Ann Oakley's groundbreaking (1974) research into housework contested the symmetrical family argument and she argued that both men and women still saw housework as women's work. Her data suggest that men in the early 1970s did very little child care and less housework, with only a minority of husbands (15 per cent) involved to a high extent in housework. More recent studies (e.g. Crompton, 2005; Sullivan, 2000) suggest that there has been a barely perceptible rise in men's involvement, and women still do around twice as much housework as men. This means that for women doing both paid and unpaid work, tiredness, ill health and depression are routine (Hochschild, 2003). Political rights have been seen as crucial for allowing women to make changes to this position.

The achievement of equal voting rights with men is taken to be one of the major indicators of advances towards equality for women. The first nation state in which women received the vote was New Zealand in 1893. The franchise was awarded to British women over 30 in 1918, though they only got to vote on the same basis as men in 1928. In the United States women got the federal vote in 1920. Women in Switzerland could not vote until 1971. In Kuwait women were awarded the right to vote in 2005 (Inter-parliamentary Union, 2006). However, voting involves fairly limited political participation. Just having the vote does not guarantee women much influence within the decision-making processes in their society. There continues to be a lack of women in public politics and especially within parliament. Though not all parliaments are especially influential in key decision making, nationally or globally, female membership of them gives some indication of women's status. Rwanda is presently top of the list, as its lower house has very close to 50 per cent women. Nordic countries have long been the democratic nations with the highest proportion of women in parliament, and women currently fill around 40 per cent of their seats. The United Kingdom's parliament is less impressive with around 20 per cent of its members being women, although when a devolved Scottish Parliament was established in 1999 around 37 per cent of its seats were taken by women. The United States does not do well in this list, with only just over 15 per cent of its lower house seats being filled by women. This puts it below the world average of around 16 per cent of parliamentary seats being occupied by women. A handful of Arab nations and Pacific island states have no women representatives (Inter-parliamentary Union, 2006). There are questions, however, as to whether having more women in parliament necessarily means more attention to issues concerning women. This depends on believing that women will bring new ideas into decision making that will better encompass women's needs. Behind this is a belief that ideas or attitudes to women can and should be changed.

Though there are powerful points to be made about the continuance of gender inequalities, much of the way in which these have been discussed so far tends to cast women as victims of large social processes. This ignores privileged groups of women and underprivileged groups of men. Though women in many situations may lack control over their own lives, this does not mean they are totally without choices, or completely lacking in power to bring about change. The ability to make choices and changes is referred to as **agency**. Materialism has been criticized for ignoring agency because of its determinist tendencies. This means that it is criticized for the way in which its focus on material factors such as economic resources tends to assume that these entirely determine how people live their lives. What is missing here, according to the critics, such as post-structuralists (see Chapter 4), is an attempt to understand what kind of meanings people give to their own actions. In order to understand this, it is necessary to understand the role of ideas in the social construction of gender.

The symbolic: gender is a system of meanings

When students new to sociology are trying to make sense of why women and men act in the ways that they do, they often blame 'the media'. They suggest that the media might be responsible for anything from making women anorexic to encouraging men to be violent. But can this really explain the variety of ways in which gender is organized within social life? It is certainly worth considering how influential the media are in forming our ways of seeing the world. The media have become a huge part of people's lives, at least in wealthier nations and amongst more privileged groups in poorer nations. In particular the spread of television and computer media, such as games and the Internet, has brought huge changes in how people spend their leisure time and how they get news about the world around them. Jean Baudrillard (for example, 1983) is a French social theorist who builds on this basic fact to argue that the increasing importance of mass media has fundamentally changed the way that people see and understand their world. He goes so far as to suggest that the media *are* our reality. The media constantly present us with images, with models of the real that are always imitations or 'simulacra', as he calls them. However, we are so immersed in these imitations that we judge by them and distinctions between 'real' and 'simulated' break down. We exist therefore within a state of **hyperreality**. There is no longer any reality, only appearance. Meaning, media and politics become blurred, but arguably in highly gendered ways. It is only in a hyperreal world, we might argue, that Arnold Schwarzenegger could go from body builder to film star to Governor of California. People's decisions about voting for him were bound to be influenced by what they knew of him in the movies. Many probably thought it would be cool to have 'the Terminator' for Governor. Indeed when he entered the gubernatorial race, the media instantly gave him the title 'the Governator', linking the real politician with the fictional movie hero who is saviour of the human race. Obviously 'the Terminator' is a highly gendered image of muscular masculinity protecting us from harm. This is a version of the kind of macho leadership which has been popular within the US (Holmes, 2000b) and it did him no harm trading on that image. He was elected, despite having very little political experience and without his political views or policies being really known by most of the electorate. Likewise, in this hyperreal world people go on 'reality' television shows like *Big Brother* which are highly staged and artificial, in order to become celebrities; not for doing anything special but for doing something supposedly ordinary – pretending to 'be themselves'. The real and the fictional become mixed-up and confused. But Baudrillard has little to say about how this relates to gender.

Baudrillard can offer a way of seeing how people's decisions, including around how gender works, might be made on the basis of information communicated via mass media; but he assumes there is really no other way of getting information. People make decisions which are not strictly determined by what the media tell them, but by what they learnt from their family and at school. In addition, where people do draw ideas about gender from mass communication, they may be influenced not so much by the medium itself but by the way other people around them take up media reports and meanings (Fiske, 1989). There is also an assumption that the way women and men are presented in the media is negative. Sometimes, however, media texts might be empowering. They may offer visions of gender relations, for example, that are more egalitarian than in most people's real experience, promoting tolerance of diversity in sexual orientation or providing gender bending alternatives (Van Zoonen, 1995). Programmes such as *Queer as Folk*, *Ellen*, or *Will and Grace* are illustrations of some shows which challenge mainstream ideas about gender and sexuality. In this case it is possible that hyperreality could be understood as having emancipatory potential rather than necessarily being oppressive, as is usually insinuated. However, that assumes that images of femininity or masculinity presented in the media are clearly negative or clearly positive. In fact, that is a matter of interpretation. There is a wide variety of messages about gender and individuals do not just passively receive these as if from a hypodermic syringe (see Fiske, 1989). There is really no solid evidence that people model their behaviour on what they see in the media (Gauntlett, 2002: 28–33). Although the media may be increasingly important as a player in forming and influencing people, they are not the only way in which we learn about gender. Indeed, most students recognize what sociologists have long debated: that it is not entirely clear whether the media reflect already existing ideas, or create those ideas (see Gauntlett, 2002). Thus it is crucial to understand other possible sources from which gender is imposed and/or moulded.

Sitting on the fence? Economics and ideas?

There have been attempts to try and understand patriarchy and capitalism as intricately intertwined systems of both material and symbolic production. **Dual-systems theorists** (see Chapter 4) like Sylvia Walby, for example, concede that material and symbolic factors may have varying and unequal influence in the formation and shifting of inequalities. In her book *Theorizing Patriarchy* (Walby, 1990), she sets out a framework for understanding the patriarchal system and how it connects with capitalism. She argues that patriarchy is made up of six structures: paid work, household production, culture, sexuality, violence, and the state. Notice that she includes here not only economic arrangements (which she argues are currently capitalist) of paid and domestic work, but aspects materialists have struggled adequately to address such as culture and sexuality.

Later Walby (1996) develops her dual-systems approach and further investigates the extent of changes in gender relations in the last half of the twentieth century. In *Gender Transformations* she continues her earlier argument that western nations have moved from a system of **private (domestic) patriarchy** to **public patriarchy**. What she means is that prior to the mid-twentieth century women's lives were more likely to be controlled and constrained by the men within their immediate family. Women were dependent on fathers and then husbands. As women entered the workforce in greater numbers from World War II onwards, this gradually changed. Now, Walby argues, patriarchal domination of women operates chiefly within the public world of work and politics. Many women have financial independence, and may not need to rely on individual men to survive, but collective decisions affecting their lives are usually made by men. Politicians, who are nearly all men, make laws affecting them (like how much benefit single mothers can have); bosses who are mostly male adhere to policies that (either intentionally or unintentionally) discriminate against women. Both public and private patriarchy operate within contemporary society, but the dominant form is now public. The old domestic form excluded women from the public sphere, while the new 'public' form segregates them into particular jobs and into the lower levels of the hierarchy. Walby goes on to stress that young women's lives are more likely to be affected by public patriarchy. This is because younger women are more likely to have an education and to get jobs that allow a degree of independence from individual men. This may change as they get older and start families, though this depends on whether and how they continue to work. Many older women's lives still need to be understood in terms of the domestic system of patriarchy, which still operates for those who have not had the education, skills and work experience of the younger generation of women and who are still likely to be largely dependent upon husbands. Both types of patriarchy impact differently on different women depending on their class, age, position in the life course (for example before or after having children), and ethnicity.

Walby's approach is helpful in portraying the complexities and shifts in contemporary gender relations. However, her account of the relationship between the symbolic and the material production of gender inequalities is rather sketchy. Where cultural processes are considered they tend to be linked back to economics. Though the cultural is not independent of the economic, Walby needs to think more about why it is that discourses of equality coexist with manifest inequalities. In other words, many women (and men) appear to think that equality between the sexes has been achieved. Though she presents a great deal of evidence to show that gender inequalities continue to exist, she says little about why people might think all is equal now. Demonstrable changes in gender relations therefore need to be carefully considered within the context of how people make sense of those changes.

As noted earlier, young women who are social science and humanities students may see themselves as having the same opportunities as men. This may be because so far their experiences of the public world have been largely within the areas of the education sector where equality is well advanced. They expect to have autonomy, especially financially, and not to be controlled by fathers or husbands. Walby argues that for younger women gender inequalities are publicly located. But perhaps these inequalities are just more visible within the public sphere. For instance, in the area of work Walby emphasizes economic inequalities. She fails to consider, for example, the problems of women having to take on masculine values to succeed at work. Such cultural values may be a major factor in understanding the interweaving of capitalism and patriarchy. Perhaps the reason 'public' gender inequalities are more noticeable is because work, politics and other 'public' activities are what men take seriously and consider important. Therefore inequalities within the private sphere are rendered invisible and/or trivialized. So, according to Walby, women's social position has been improved (largely through women's political participation) but male resistance continues and the way in which gender inequalities operate has changed and shifted, becoming perhaps less obvious and less direct.

Walby's is just one account of how and why women's and men's lives and their relations to each other have changed, but it provides a big picture of women's place in social life that can be further explored within this book. This exploration will centre around questions as to what extent gender is a form of inequality that especially constrains women or whether it is an experience or practice in which women and men engage, and which is shaped by language and meaning.

How this book is organized

Initially the sociology of gender needed to separate bodies from their social fates (Oakley, 1997: 29). Chapter 2 examines why it was crucial to challenge common sense ideas about sex differences as 'natural' because these were used to justify inequalities between women and men. This involved taking on biological determinism and showing that the social environment was the key factor in shaping gender. Indeed 'sex' itself was not necessarily a clear demarcation between two types of bodies (male and female). Having established the importance of the social, Chapter 3 looks at how it is important to explicate the ways in which gender operated within social life. Influential in this respect were socialization theories and symbolic interactionism's attention to 'doing' gender.

These efforts to explain gender in sociologically satisfactory ways are best understood in the context of a broader range of theorizing on gender. Chapter 4 thus maps out gender theorizing, identifying major debates around the issues of equality versus difference and key approaches such as liberal, socialist and radical feminism. This map also charts the linguistic or cultural turn as a journey away from structuralism and towards post-structuralism. This turn eventually led many sociologists to feel a need for more materiality, whilst they were wary of returning to economic determinism. Instead there has been a return to other 'matter' in the form of bodies. Gender as a form of embodiment is thus extensively re-examined in Chapter 5 for its promise in thinking about both the systems of economics and of meanings as forming gender.

A dual attention to inequalities and meanings has been central to the politics of gender, as Chapter 6 explores. Feminist and masculinity politics have not only addressed material or economic disadvantage, but also put questions of identity and relationship to others onto the political agenda. Yet difficulties in dealing with what women's interests might be, given the diversity of persons in that category, made a feminist politics based on identity increasingly difficult to maintain. Intellectual attention to differences was productive, but for sociologists it was clear that differences around which social inequality was conducted should be the primary target. Although it might seem best to deal with the full range of social inequalities as they intersect with gender, in practice this would be a highly cumbersome analysis to execute. Therefore, like much of the literature I cover, I have focused my discussion around the relationship of gender to two major categories around which hierarchies operate.

Chapter 7 deals with the category of class and Chapter 8 with 'race'. Within accounts of the intertwining of class and gender we can most clearly see the cultural turn. From classifying women's class in economic terms, to adapting more sophisticated materialist analyses of women's oppression, scholars turned toward understandings of class as reproduced via symbolic meanings. The influence of Bourdieu in this matter is evaluated in terms of what kind of contribution it can make to understanding gender as both structural inequality and an individual practice over which people have some control. Similar debates are considered in relation to the relationships of gender to 'race' and ethnic identity, but there the constituting force of global histories of slavery and colonization are acknowledged. These are histories of both economic processes and of discourses as they produce formations of gender at global and local levels. From this we can see in what situations and how it might be desirable to combine materialist and 'cultural' approaches to understanding gender.

2

How different are women and men?

It used to be thought that a woman is a woman because of her ovaries alone. As we shall see later, there are many individuals with ovaries who are not women in the strict sense of the word and many with testes who are really feminine in many other respects. (Bell cited in Oudshoorn, 1994: 37)

This quotation may come as a surprise if you have always thought about the biological differences between women and men as clear and beyond question. Bell wrote this in 1916 in a scientific study about what came to be known as sex hormones. The quotation shows the emerging scientific awareness that sex differences were less straightforward than conventionally imagined. Indeed it is one illustration of the fact that how we understand differences between women and men changes historically. This is one indication for sociologists that those differences are not simply 'natural'. In order to question the naturalness of differences between women and men terminology became important. Initially the term **sex** described the anatomical and other physical differences. Later, as we will see in Chapter 3, sociologists of the 1970s adapted the term **gender** to be able to discuss femininity and masculinity as socially produced ways of acting.

To question the 'natural' basis of sex differences is to take part in a wider debate about whether human beings are a product of biological processes or of the social environment. This is known as the **nature/nurture debate**. Most people agree that both the natural and the social shape us as individuals but some suggest that the natural is more important while others, including most sociologists, argue that social factors are most influential in making us who we are. A sociological approach sets out to examine how differences between women and men are socially constructed; that is, how those differences are made and shaped by the social environment.

Social differences and the sociological imagination

The sociological imagination (Mills, 1959) is a way of thinking that is very useful in understanding all sorts of social phenomena, including the social construction of differences between women and men (Jackson, 1998a). This entire book is about the social construction of those differences, so what I say here will provide a framework to aid in placing and making sense of what follows in this and the following chapters. The book uses the sociological imagination as a way of thinking that seeks to make connections between the life of the individual and a wider historical and social context. According to Mills, imagining something sociologically involves striving to understand at what point private troubles are in fact public issues. For example, if one woman fails to become a politician this might be due to personal factors, but if hardly any political candidates are women then we begin to wonder if this is a public issue of discrimination. If one woman does not drive, that may be a personal choice; but if a law is passed forbidding women to drive, as in Saudi Arabia, that becomes a public issue. From a sociological viewpoint differences between women and men are largely the product of social forces.

Understanding the life of a woman or man involves understanding the history of the society in which they live (Mills, 1959). Changes in ideas about sex differences over time help illustrate the centrality of the social in determining what it means to be a woman or a man, as I discuss below. But by 'history' Mills means not just what happened in the past (although that is part of it), but the wider social context in which individuals live.

In locating the life of individuals in relation to wider social circumstances sociologists also often use cultural comparisons (Giddens, 1986: 13) because they help demonstrate that being born a woman (or man) can mean very different things depending on the social environment. Having a female body does not necessarily make you behave in a particular way. Cultural comparisons are usually drawn from anthropology. Information from different cultures helps sociologists question the importance of any physical or psychological differences between women and men and can be used to establish the extent to which those differences are socially constructed. The classic anthropological study of differences between women and men is Margaret Mead's (1962/1950) *Male and Female*, where she argued that whatever males do in a particular culture is always valued more than what the women do. Her early work on *Sex and Temperament in Three Primitive Societies* (Mead 1963/1935) argued that there was a range of different meanings of femininity and masculinity in different cultures. Some examples illustrate the variation of behaviours thought to be 'feminine' or 'masculine'. The Tchambuli tribe in New Guinea consider 'masculine' what most westerners regard as 'feminine'. In that tribe Mead observed that it is the men who adorn themselves. Tchambuli women are the dominant partners and men are emotionally dependent on them. In addition, not all peoples expect women and men to behave differently. Mead noted that the Arapesh of New Guinea regard both women and men as 'inherently gentle, responsive and co-operative' and that both women and men of the tribe take responsibility for child care (Mead, 1963/1935: 134). These are all traits that North Americans, Europeans and Australasians tend to see as 'feminine' characteristics. There is some debate within anthropology about the accuracy of Mead's findings on these particular cultures; some critics suggest she rather too conveniently found what she was looking for, while others suggest that her work is valuable in giving voice to women's as well as men's accounts of their culture (Lipset, 2003). Whilst many studies have gathered evidence of different meanings being associated with femininity and masculinity in different cultures (for example, see Oakley, 1972), this may slightly miss the point. It is important to recognize that the very tendency to categorize femininity and masculinity as opposite and mutually exclusive categories might be a western way of thinking. There are indeed cultures where there are more than two categories of sex/gender (Herdt, 1994). However, most cultures are not isolated from one another and many ideas about femininity and masculinity circulate around the globe via processes of colonization and globalization and the movement of peoples and ideas through, for example, religions and mass media. Therefore what is crucial is to examine patterns in the kinds of ideas that appear dominant, while also appreciating that there are alternatives and variations in these meanings, not only between cultures but within the same culture.

An appreciation of how differences between women and men are seen in varying ways can be part of an overall critical approach to gender (Giddens, 1986: 13). Being critical about the extent and significance of differences means not taking anything for granted. A critical approach means looking at the familiar world around you in a new way (Berger, 1963). This means always examining afresh why things are done the way they are, in your own society as well as in others. It is important to question ways of doing things, especially those that are taken for granted, such as practices of femininity and masculinity and what they reveal about the social character of differences between women and men. A crucial framework for this has been ideas about heteronormativity.

Heteronormativity

Contemporary society is based upon a **heteronormative** gender order: an order based on the idea that there are two opposite sexes that are attracted to each other. The gender order demands that we categorize people as women or men. People usually try to imitate what are perceived as 'normal' femininity or masculinity and the complex intersections between gender and sexuality are key to how this operates. Social rules about 'normal' gender and sexuality demand that you must be clear about who are boys and who are girls, so that boys and girls can grow up, fall in love with each other, and have more little boys and girls. French feminist (see Chapter 7) Monique Wittig (1992: 66) argues that '[t]he category of sex is a political category that founds society as heterosexual', sexual difference is socially produced in this way in order to oblige women to reproduce the species. Crucial in this production is men's appropriation of women's productive and reproductive powers and their bodies through the marriage contract.

Judith Butler (1990; 1993; 2004) has developed Wittig's ideas about heteronormativity (see Chapters 3 and 5) and **queer theory** generally (see Chapter 4 and Jagose, 1996; Seidman, 1996) has continued to explore connections between gender and sexuality and the implications of thinking about gay identities. Other texts deal with these connections in detail (for example, Beasley, 2005). The key issues are how gender relates to whom we desire, but also how desire corresponds to perceived differences between men's and women's bodies. In order to examine the social character of those differences sociologists need to engage with scientific understandings of 'sex' as rooted in physical biology, including psychological dispositions.

Physical differences

If there is one thing people like to feel certain about it is whether a newborn child is a girl or a boy. Until we have that piece of information it is difficult to think about a baby as a person at all and we do not know how to treat 'it'. How people think about a new human being immediately depends on the sex of the baby. The incredibly important decision about sex is made, in most cases, by a midwife or doctor taking a quick look at the newly arrived person to see if they have a penis or a vagina.

Having either a penis or a vagina is usually seen as the fundamental difference between sexes. Other parts of the reproductive system, such as wombs, ovaries, testes and scrotums, also supposedly separate women (female) from men (male). In addition, there are arguments about sex differences in skeletons, amounts of fat, muscles, ribs, bodily hair and physical strength. Men and women apparently also differ chromosomally and, to a slight degree, hormonally (Hird, 2004; Oudshoorn, 1994). But what you can see on the outside does not always match up with the other indicators of sex and there is a lot more biological variation than the simple categories 'male' and 'female' describe. To understand this it helps to begin by looking at how present scientific accounts of sex have developed.

The changing science of sex

In western science and common parlance prior to around 1700, women and men were understood not as anatomically different but as two variations of the same sex. In the scientific version of this 'one-sex' model women were supposedly 'imperfect' versions of men, their genitalia were described as being the same as men's, but on the inside rather than outside. The ovaries were seen as internal testes while the shaft of the vagina tipped by the clitoris was thought equivalent to the penis. In other words, women's reproductive organs were understood as like men's, except folded up inside. Just because women and men were understood as being similar does not mean that they were thought equal. Woman's 'unopened' genitalia were thought to reflect their incompleteness in comparison to man's godly perfection (Laqueur, 1990). This one-sex model is rather different to a more recent obsession with distinguishing males from females as completely different types of body that develop in the womb and emerge from it as distinct. The one-sex view placed less social boundaries upon bodies because individuals were not seen as inherently feminine or masculine. Femininity and masculinity were seen as shades of everyone's being, rather than oppositions. This view lent itself to conceptions of social status as something that should be used to control bodies. The higher your place in the social hierarchy the more you were expected to control your body, for example how and what you ate or the manner of blowing your nose (Elias, 2000/1939). More modern ideas differ in assuming that biological differences form a 'natural' basis for a person's position in the social hierarchy. For example, the idea that people with black skin were 'naturally' inferior was used to justify their low status within the apartheid system in South Africa in the late twentieth century. Similarly, the idea that women's reproductive systems made them irrational was, and sometimes still is, used to argue that they are not 'naturally' suited to the serious business of ruling the world. If social status is thought to be based on particular physical characteristics, then those characteristics become seen as significant. Not all physical differences take on such importance; for example eye colour is usually neither a help nor a hindrance to social success. On the other hand, the kinds of physical difference supposed to exist between women and men are thought to be of major significance in determining what kinds of lives individuals will lead. This view emerged as the dominant model used to understand sex difference, shifting from a one-sex to a two-sex basis from the eighteenth century onwards.

Understandings of sex that developed in the twentieth century suggest that foetuses start out the same, but gradually start to take different paths in developing sexed bodies, chromosomes and hormones. John Money is a psychologist whose explanations of how a foetus develops sex were very influential, especially in the early sociology of gender (for example, Oakley, 1972). John Money and Patricia Tucker (1975) explain how sex develops in terms of ten steps. First, they argue that chromosomal sex emerges as either an X or a Y chromosome becomes present. Females are XX and males are XY. Secondly, gonadal sex is established when the X or Y chromosome 'instructs' the fetal gonad to develop into a testis or an ovary. Thirdly, fetal hormonal sex is decided when the testis or ovary produces a 'male' (more testosterone) or 'female' (more oestrogen and progesterone) balance of hormones. Money argues that these differences in hormonal balance influence the following steps. The fourth step he identifies occurs when internal morphological sex (the development of bodily differences inside the body – for example a womb) is produced by hormonal action. In the fifth step external morphological sex (anatomical differences on the outside of the body – for example a penis) develops. According to Money the sixth step establishes brain sex (the development of potentialities such as a tendency to 'like strenuous physical activity' (Money and Tucker, 1975: 70) laid down by the mix of prenatal sex hormones an individual received). All the steps – but especially external morphological sex – are used once the child is born to determine the seventh step, which is sex of assignment and rearing. Money then thinks that to become 'properly' male or female a person must develop pubertal hormonal sex (as increased production of either testosterone or oestrogen starts turning boys into men and girls into women), an appropriate gender identity and role, and lastly have the ability to procreate (procreative sex) (Fausto-Sterling, 2004: 343). However this is now considered a rather simple story of sex development.

The two-sex model in which female and male foetuses 'fork off' from each other is open to a number of criticisms. First, this story of sex development fails to acknowledge that chromosomes are no guarantee of sex. The presence or absence of a hormonal substance called testis-determining factor (TDF), not the chromosome alone, determines whether gonads become testes or ovaries. Also there are other variations of chromosomal 'sex', such as XXY, XXYY and many more (Hird, 2004: 47–8), which need to be thought of not simply as 'detours' (Money and Tucker, 1975: 49). As for hormonal sex, while there is typically a difference between women and men in the balance of the different types of hormones, the differences are very slight. Women and men have the same hormones in very similar amounts. Women have testosterone among other hormones and men have oestrogen. Women tend to produce more oestrogen and progesterone, while men usually produce more testosterone and androgens (Oudshoorn, 1994). To call some hormones 'male sex hormones' and others 'female sex hormones' is misleading given that we all have them both and some women (for example some post-menopausal women) may have more testosterone than some men. The key thing is that the families of hormones previously labeled by scientists as 'female' or 'male' (they later added androgens which were thought 'bisexual'), are all extremely chemically similar (as Money admits). What is most noticeable is the similarity in our hormonal make up. Hormones play a part in sex development, but it is unlikely that they determine 'masculine' or 'feminine' behaviour as directly as Money implies, or in the crude way people often assume within everyday talk about testosterone-fuelled aggression, or the supposed irrationality of women boosted by their hormonal cycles. Overall there are problems with the idea of sex determination as a straightforward process in which male bodies distinctly fork off from female bodies and take on masculinity and femininity respectively (Fausto-Sterling, 2000; 2004).

Feminist biologists such as Linda Birke (1999), Nellie Oudshoorn (1994), and Ann Fausto-Sterling (2000; 2004) all point out that scientists have to interpret what they see and that their own social understandings of what it means to be male or female influence those interpretations. Oudshoorn (1994), for example, argues that early twentieth century discussions of sex differences continued to be influenced by long-standing common sense views of sex as an either/or opposition. These made it difficult to account for new evidence that emerged suggesting that women's and men's hormonal makeup was similar. Oudshoorn argues that there is no natural truth to the body but only interpretations of it. Although interpretations are crucial, this does not quite account for why scientists would bother to change their interpretations unless they had discovered something new when looking at bodies. However, what they see is usually limited by their fragmented approach. Scientists are typically looking at bits of bodies – cells, genes, chromosomes, or hormones in isolation. And what scientists are able to 'see' will depend upon the frameworks in which they are working. Nevertheless, in trying to understand things that do not make sense within that framework, interpretations – and indeed the framework itself – can change. Knowledge is often advanced by scientists debating the best way to interpret scientific findings. For example, Ann Fausto-Sterling (2004) is sceptical about geneticists' claims that there is a master sex-determining gene on the Y chromosome (called SDY) and when this is present a male is formed. Fausto-Sterling argues that the language used in this interpretation implies that in the absence of SDY females 'just naturally happen'. In this interpretation maleness comes across as an active presence but one always in danger of not successfully completing the steps needed to become male. Fausto-Sterling (2004) points out that this interpretation reflects social stereotypes about women as passive and men as active.

Interpretations of the link between homosexuality and biology also reflect stereotypes about gender. There are many putative associations between homosexuality and hormones, and questions about whether there is a homosexual gene. A lot of studies have been done on the relationship between hormonal levels and sexual orientation, but most are affected by the scientists' cultural assumptions. Having looked at many of these studies, Hird (2004: 40–2) notes that in some of them male homosexuals have been mistakenly assumed to be 'feminine' and female homosexuals 'masculine'. The scientists then set up hypotheses that gay men will have less testosterone than heterosexual men and gay women will have more testosterone than straight women. Most of the studies have found this not to be the case and she asserts that no association between hormonal levels and homosexuality has been proven. What this illustrates is that although scientists may strive to be objective, socio-culturally specific assumptions about how the world works can become entangled in their interpretations of sex.

Intersex

'Nature' actually produces a variation of combinations of female and male sex characteristics (Fausto-Sterling, 2002a; Hird, 2004; Oudshoorn, 1994). Some individuals have a genetic sex that is different from their hormonal and/or anatomical sex. For example a child might be genetically female (have two X chromosomes and no Y), but have male genitalia. Accurate estimates are difficult but anything from 1 in 2000 babies, to 17 in 1000 infants are born with some form of 'intersex' condition (Fausto-Sterling, 2002b: 20; Hird, 2004: 15) and this has prompted the slightly tongue in cheek suggestion that five sex categories would more accurately describe what occurs 'in nature' (Fausto-Sterling, 2002a; 2002b). Just because individuals whose genetic, hormonal and anatomical sex match are more common than the many other combinations does not mean those other combinations are not 'natural'. They are genetic variations and variations are important in maintaining the biodiversity which promotes life (Hird, 2004). However, society is organized around the idea that female or male are the only options, and it is very difficult for those whose sex is unclear to do anything within such a society or for others to know how to deal with them. From everyday matters such as which public toilets to use or ticking either 'female' or 'male' boxes on official forms, to major decisions about who goes into the frontline of battles, the assumption is that men are men and women are women.

The way that intersex individuals are dealt with shows that the decision about what sex to label a child is a social decision (see Kessler and McKenna, 1978). Any development of sex within an individual that does not fit into the categories 'male' or 'female' is seen as a 'wrong turning', they are supposedly sexual abnormalities that have to be 'fixed'. For example, where a child has a very small penis, even if genetically male, it is recommended they should have surgery and be raised as a girl. Fausto-Sterling (2004: 344) argues that this shows that having a sizeable penis is seen as crucial to being masculine. Complicated 'corrective' surgery is performed on people who are healthy, although anatomically sexually ambiguous (Hird, 2004: 131–42). Such people do not make sense in terms of one of the most basic ways in which society is organized.

The problems of being uncertain of one's sex are noted by Melissa, who has an intersex condition. She was born with XX chromosomes (female) and internally a womb and ovaries, but had ambiguous genitalia that were identified as either an enlarged clitoris or a small penis. She did not know about her condition until she was 18 years old, only being aware that something was wrong 'down there'. Her mother told her to 'always use a cubicle to change at school' and that only doctors should ever touch her (Toomey, 2001: 37). Melissa and others like her have been routinely subjected to operations to try and 'normalize' their ambiguous sexual anatomy. They are very seldom told the real reason for these operations and are often unaware of their condition. The outcome of surgery is frequently unsatisfactory for the individual, but the medical establishment are profoundly caught up in the belief that social and individual confusion will result if the distinction between male and female is questioned. Therefore where a newborn human's sex is unclear a medical team will meet to decide, as soon as possible after the birth, what sex to *make* the baby (Toomey, 2001: 40, emphasis mine). This illustrates that sex is primarily a social category, although initially sociologists of gender (for example, Oakley, 1972) tended to bracket sex off as a biological and fixed fact onto which the social meanings constituting gender were imposed. Discussions about the advantages and limitations of such a move occur in Chapter 3, but here I want to focus on how intersex people challenge ideas of women and men as absolutely physically different.

Intersexuality puts the categories 'male' and 'female' into question and shows how for granted we take it that females will become feminine and males masculine, and all will perform the social tasks expected.

Intersexual people show that bodies are important in forming gender identity and that having an ambiguous body makes forming a gender identity complex, but only because of entrenched common sense ideas that if you have a female body you must become feminine and if you have a male body you should become masculine. The assumption is that gender identity simply emerges from sex. For those whose bodies do not clearly fit either sex category, gender identity is a problem. In fact, even those whose bodies can be clearly 'sexed' sometimes do not feel like their gender identity corresponds to their sex. For example, some men with penises feel like women trapped in men's bodies. Their gender identity is not connected to their biological sex. Conventional wisdom indicates that 'male' or 'female' are adequate labels and that any bodies which do not 'fit' just need to be 'correctly' assigned to one or the other, and maybe reassigned later if 'wrong'. These are essentialist arguments that assume we all have a 'true' or 'natural' identity which is either feminine or masculine. If we are born female we will become 'feminine' as long as nothing goes 'wrong'. If this is such a 'natural' thing then how do people whose sex and gender differ emerge, why do all women not behave in the same way, and how and why do ways of being feminine and masculine change? If femininity just 'naturally' develops from having a female body, what happens if someone has a body that cannot clearly be defined as either female or male? Intersex people illustrate how hard it is for all of us to think of 'people' without thinking of them as gendered. The construction of gender (femininity and masculinity) is based on an early decision about sex (Kessler and McKenna, 1978).

Biological variations in sex are commonly reduced into just two categories – male and female – because for someone to be of in-between or ambiguous sex threatens a social order based on there being only two sexes. There is a whole series of decisions about what we can and cannot do and be which is organized around knowing whether someone is a man or a woman. Sociologists focus on the argument that once the decision about which sex we are is made, it has significant effects on how we live our lives. Much early sociological attention to gender gave particular importance to deciding just how different women and men are and to what extent these differences were due to social and cultural practices rather than a 'natural' product of biology.

Physical strength

In proposing that differences between women and men are largely social, sociologists have challenged ideas such as those which suggest that men's social dominance is justified because they are physically stronger. Ideas about what sort of physical tasks women and men are suited for differ from one culture to another, suggesting that it is not the physical differences themselves, but the social significance attached to them that determines what women and men do. As Margaret Mead (1962/1950) famously observed: different cultures may have different ideas about what tasks women and men should do, but in all cultures whatever men do is considered more valuable. So in many African cultures women do most of the heavy carrying and other hard labour, but this is thought less important than the lighter tasks men typically perform (Oakley, 1972: 141). How different tasks are valued is important in determining how resources are allocated. Therefore if men's tasks are thought more valuable, then men are more likely to get what they need to grow big and strong. Women's lack of power and prestige has often meant they get, or are expected to take, less food than men (Whitehead, 1994). Perhaps if women had been eating the same quantity and quality of food as men over the last several centuries, sex differences in stature and strength would be all but non-existent. Also, the differences that do exist vary. Some women are stronger than some men; and there are different kinds of strength. There are short feats of strength such as lifting heavy weights, or there is having stamina to keep going under trying physical conditions such as the endurance of pain.

Different types of strength might have different levels of importance in different social conditions, and many accounts of how women and men differ look back to prehistory for explanations. Rather tired old arguments suggest that in early societies the kind of strength men supposedly had was essential in doing the heavy work – especially hunting – needed for people to survive and develop as humans (Washburn and Lancaster, 1968). But this ignored the importance of women's work to community survival. Feminist anthropologists of the 1970s, building on Margaret Mead's work of the 1940s, disputed that men are universally stronger, and were critical of claims that human groups have depended on brute strength for survival. Sally Slocum (1975), for example, questioned arguments that hunter–gatherer societies relied on the masculine strength needed for hunting wild animals to eat. She pointed out that those societies got most of their diet from the food gathered by women. Gathering was a constant and physically demanding task, and for most women this task was combined with bearing and caring for children. In some cases women also hunted small animals. In short, it seems clear that women have not simply depended on men (and male strength) for their survival, as has often been stated. While these stories are helpful in trying to understand sex differences, they are often based on guesses about the past made by looking at small traditional societies now. But these societies are not completely untouched by change and the modern world, so the guesses may be inaccurate. There may be discontinuities with the past that disappear if we try to see history as a smooth forward progression.

The search for some origin from which current differences between women and men emerged tends to hark back to a mythic state of nature in which differences between women and men were somehow untouched by social forces. This is a fruitless search because the defining feature of humanity is some form of social organization. Humans not only adapt to their environment but adapt their environment to live; they build dwellings, they cut down trees. People continue to adapt their environment and adapt to it, sometimes in fairly haphazard ways. As social change has accelerated there is not always time for our bodies to evolve to meet current needs. In technological societies, for example, brute physical strength is not (if it ever was) crucial to survival. In fact, social attitudes to physical sex differences are also struggling to keep up with new scientific developments in areas such as reproductive technology, genetic engineering and cybernetics (see Haraway, 1985).

If physical differences between women and men are as uncertain and blurred as it now appears, what can be said about arguments that differences in men and women's bodies affect how they think? Scientists (usually men) over the centuries have tried to show that there are significant biologically based differences in intelligence between the sexes. But what the differences are and what they mean are open to interpretation (Oakley, 1972: 79–98). Some nineteenth century Britons thought that women's reproductive systems made them unfit for serious intellectual activity. Supporters of this view argued that women should not be admitted to universities because the mental strain would make them infertile (Delamont, 1978). There have also been disputes about the relative importance of slight differences in brain size and ways of using different parts of the brain. Whether there are differences and whether they are significant continues to be debated. Nineteenth century scientists argued that the smaller size of women's brains compared to men's meant that women were 'naturally' intellectually inferior. Then it was pointed out that women were usually smaller and lighter than men; in relation to their body size women's brains were on average actually bigger than men's. At this point most male scientists then decided that maybe smaller brains were better! They also began to look at other differences in brains, which might prove what they wanted to prove – that men were smarter than women. Whatever they found they tended to interpret in ways favourable to men (Figes, 1978/1970: 126; Schiebinger, 1989). But even if there are physical differences in brains are there really significant differences in how women and men think and, if so, how do these come about?

Psychological similarities

What is most striking about so-called 'sex-differences' research within psychology is its failure to find any really significant differences between how women and men use their minds. Feminist sociologists in the past drew heavily on debates about the relationships between 'sex and intellect' within psychology (see Oakley, 1972: 79–98). Other disciplines have also drawn on psychological testing in considering to what extent there are gendered modes of thought; for example there are some interesting philosophical debates about whether or not women make moral decisions in different ways to men (see Benhabib, 1987). Connell (2002: 40–6) provides a well-considered, brief evaluation of the huge volume of psychological research intended to establish whether women and men think, talk and judge differently. All the careful testing and re-testing seems only to have confirmed that actually the genders are virtually identical in everything from mathematical ability to self-esteem to motivation to visual sensing. Therefore, after over a hundred years of research, involving thousands of studies, 'the main finding is that *women and men are psychologically very similar*, as groups' (Connell, 2002: 42, emphasis in the original). However, it is arguably the branch of psychology called psychoanalysis that has been most influential in approaches to 'sex differences' since the nineteenth century, although sociologists have only engaged with these ideas more recently.

Psychoanalysis and sexual difference

Psychoanalysis has made a huge impact on both common sense and academic arguments about how and why women and men might differ in the ways they come to make sense of themselves and of the world. Some sociologists (for example, Barrett, 1992) have found psychoanalytic explanations of gender differences useful in explaining how women and men develop a sense of themselves as gendered. Others like Stevi Jackson (1999) have remained critical of these Freudian ideas that suggest that the early meaning we give our anatomy determines our lives. Before evaluating the sociological debates we need to understand what Freud had to say about the differences between women and men.

Freud

Sigmund Freud thought that gender differences developed from the way in which individuals learned to give meaning to their anatomy and to 'repress' drives, especially the sex drive, in order to allow 'civilized' society to function. He was an Austrian who began developing what became known as psychoanalysis at the beginning of the twentieth century. Freud argued that the incest taboo (social rules against sex with relatives) started the process by which boys learned how to be masculine and girls learned to be feminine. The desire that infants have for physical pleasure must be shaped into socially acceptable, heterosexual forms of sexual expression as they mature. He claimed that the incest taboo, present in all societies, was the key mechanism through which the sexual drive was directed into 'normal' femininity and masculinity. There is no neutral selfhood for Freud; to develop an identity is to become gendered. He thought that we become 'women' and 'men' by gradually separating ourselves from our mother. For boys he called this the Oedipus complex (Freud, 1910). The argument was that all children desire pleasure, which involves gratification of their physical needs. The first source of pleasure for a baby is its mother, who satisfies its needs. This desire for the satisfaction of needs slowly develops into more specifically sexual desires focused on the genitals. But young boys learn that it is not acceptable for them to sexually desire their mothers because to do so would mean competing with their much more powerful fathers. Boys notice that they have a penis, like their father, and fear that if they continue to attach themselves to their mother they might end up lacking a penis like her. This fear of castration encourages boys to turn away from identifying with their mother and to align themselves with their fathers, who symbolically represent separate selfhood. As a result they try to be like their father and therefore learn to be masculine.

Freud's (1932) theory on how girls learn to be feminine is generally thought less satisfactory than his ideas about masculinity. The story goes like this. Girls realize that they lack a penis and are supposedly envious of that male organ. The incest taboo prohibits them from fulfilling their desire to 'have' their father's penis. They know that their mother cannot provide them with a penis, but perhaps if they become like their mother, and behave in a feminine way, they will be able to attract men and get what is supposedly a penis substitute – a baby. Now, this story can be read as not really being about women wanting to have an actual penis, but about girls recognizing that fathers are symbolic of men (those with penises) and that men represent a distinct selfhood, separate from mother (Beasley, 2005: 53). Such selfhood clearly carries status within the social world, but is not (easily) accessible to women.

Julia Kristeva

Julia Kristeva argues that the symbolic realm is patriarchal, so the 'feminine' is an otherness that cannot be named. Femininity lies within what she calls the semiotic and is closely linked to the maternal (Kristeva, 1982). Most psychoanalysts follow Jacques Lacan in using the term 'symbolic' to refer to all forms of signification (Oliver, 1997: xv). The **symbolic** for Kristeva refers to grammatically systemized verbal language or equivalents (for example, deaf sign language), while the **semiotic** refers to something beyond the linguistic, to the rhythm and intonations through which bodily drives are expressed in ways relevant to meaning without having meaning themselves. Semiotic does *not* mean the science of signs, as it does for Saussure (see Chapter 4). For Kristeva (1980a; 1980b), the *symbolic* is one part of the signifying process, inseparable from the other *semiotic* part. She is building on Freud's notion of drives that push us towards satisfying our desires for sex, death and so on. Freud (for example, 1910) thought that these drives had to be repressed in order for civilized society to be possible, however, he also noted that they would 'slip' out in verbal mistakes, jokes and subconscious fantasies. Kristeva suggests that such drives are discharged in non-linguistic ways and in fact that we have a bodily drive to communicate. Drives are not simply bodily or biological to her, being neither 'natural' nor symbolic but acting between bodily experience that cannot be put into words and a structured symbolic system based on words. The symbolic aspect provides structure so that we can make sense of our experiences to ourselves and to others. The semiotic motivates communication but threatens the symbolic and the symbolic provides stability in order for communication to take place. Thus there is a dialectic between the semiotic and the symbolic which is crucial to the signifying process.

Kristeva characterizes the relationship between the semiotic and the symbolic as highly gendered in casting sexual difference as masculine superiority versus feminine lack. She argues that the notion of the semiotic provides some space for the expression of a femininity that is not an essence, but constructed via non-linguistic or extra-linguistic processes. This is quite radical in connecting the biological aspects of the body with the social aspects of language, to help explain how the feminine becomes **abject**. As Grosz (1989: 70) explains, abjection is 'the subject's reaction to the failure of the subject/object opposition to express adequately the subject's corporeality and its tenuous bodily boundaries'. Abjection is about fearing becoming an object of disgust (and therefore a non-subject) by breaking bodily boundaries. One way Kristeva has of explaining the importance of abjection is to turn to the work of anthropologist Mary Douglas. In *Purity and Danger* (1978) Douglas sets out how social divisions are maintained via notions of bodies that pollute. Particular types of bodies are thought filthy if they are seen as without proper boundaries. Fluids that break out from bodily boundaries – for example faeces, blood, milk, sweat, tears – are dirty because they are 'matter out of place'. Kristeva argues that menstrual blood in particular signifies the danger of sexual difference, the otherness of women. However, excrement is defiling because it threatens to remind us of the way maternal authority was exercized, above all, through potty training. This authority, unlike the paternal law bringing the infant into the symbolic, shapes the body as a territory, through prohibitions. Symbolic law operates partly via separation from the maternal and the bodily. Identity and language are supposedly achieved, if you believe Freud and Lacan, by separating oneself from the mother and achieving some distance from one's body. Rituals surrounding pollution – especially menstrual and excremental – draw attention to this boundary between (feminine) bodies and language, and perhaps even shift it. The system of ritual exclusions of the maternal and the bodily, therefore becomes central to the signifying order. The feminine is both excluded from and necessary to meaning. However, femininity remains inexpressable within the structured symbolic, according to Kristeva's logic. Only as a kind of background presence, 'speaking' mutely through the body, do women really seem to exist.

Although the attempt to put women and their bodies back into theory is welcome (see Chapter 5), Kristeva's account of women as a kind of semiotic hum within systems of representations is very limiting. How can women actually 'say' anything about themselves, how can feminism, which has relied so much on rational arguments, be possible if that is so? Kristeva (1981) finds feminism negative and instead recommends a dissolution of binary identities, but assumes that women's position 'outside' the symbolic renders them passive and unable to achieve such a dissolution (Grosz, 1989: 67). Such an approach is the result of her uncritical adoption of psychoanalysis and its assumptions that femininity is an inferior, castrated subjectivity (Grosz, 1989: 63–5). Psychoanalysis assumes that men are 'normal' and women are lacking. Feminists criticize Freud's theory for thinking in ways that are **phallocentric** (organized around the phallus – the symbol of the penis) because he assumes that ideas about the penis are central not just to male identity but to female identity. With all these problems, why then has Freud been so influential?

What was arguably important about Freud was that he actually tried to think about differences between men and women at a time when many thinkers ignored women's experiences altogether. He also tried to think about the way we give meaning to our anatomy, which allows recognition of the importance of social processes. He thought that we learn to be feminine or masculine through early interactions with significant others. His ideas about the unconscious are also crucial to his continuing influence. He thought the unconscious was a part of the psyche involving what individuals repressed in order to conform to social norms of how to behave. This argument implies that learning what it means to be a woman or a man is not a matter of consciously thinking that you desire your mother or father and so on. Freud is trying to tell a story about the way unconscious fantasies – desires we are not aware of in direct ways – might shape our gender identity. However, when he said that anatomy was destiny he did imply that the way gender was shaped was more or less 'fixed' by your particular anatomy. For example, he thought that not having a penis meant being feminine and that meant accepting an inferior position in the world. He thought that if women tried to behave 'like men' it was because of penis envy and they needed to have therapy to enable them to properly take on a feminine identity. He was a product of his time in valuing men, their bodies and ways of doing things, more highly than women.

Nancy Chodorow

Nancy Chodorow (1978) later provided a more woman-centred alternative to the original Freudian understanding of the psychological differences between women and men. Chodorow shares the same framework as Freud but understands the development of femininity as a smooth process rather than as a kind of deviation from a male 'normality'. Chodorow suggests that because women are usually the most important carer, all babies bond with them. As children grow older, boys realize that to be masculine means not being like their mother, so they have to make some sort of break with her in order to take on a masculine identity. Having to break this strong bond with the mother is difficult for boys and means they have to distance themselves emotionally. This emotional distance, according to Chodorow, is therefore part of being masculine and means men are not good at forming other close relationships. They achieve their identity through fragmentation and emphasizing discontinuity with others. Girls meanwhile realize they are like their mother and can continue to identify with her. As a result they have a much more continuous sense of identity, but they learn what it means to be feminine from their mother in her role *as a mother*. Other ways of being feminine tend to get ignored. Chodorow thinks that girls learn, most of all, that being feminine means nurturing and caring for others. Being feminine therefore becomes confused with being a mother and the only way girls really know how to be feminine is to act like a mother. This whole process means that effectively mothers are socializing their daughters into being mothers, and Chodorow calls this 'the reproduction of mothering'. The reproduction of mothering can disadvantage women in a world that continues to value competitiveness, which requires separation from others rather than the practices of caring that women learn to see as central to their identity. Chodorow goes beyond Freud by challenging the idea that men are the standard to which women must be compared and she tries to explain, rather than merely accepting, women's inferior social position. Nevertheless, her explanation of gender differences still heavily relies, like Freud's, on a rather simple story of how individuals learn to understand what it means to have a particular type of biological body. There has been considerable debate amongst feminist sociologists about the utility of psychoanalytic ideas.

Critical debates about psychoanalysis and feminism

Juliet Mitchell's (1975) re-reading of how Freud was useful in under-standing sexual difference was very influential within feminist debates about psychoanalysis, but many of its assumptions are more accessibly outlined by Ros Coward (1978). Coward critically re-reads Freud as providing a fundamental critique of the notion of gender as an inbuilt part of identity. She argues that this reading makes his sexism irrelevant, because what is crucial are his ideas about gender as acquired through social learning and never fixed. She argues that psychoanalysis can be used to look at the connections between sexual and social forms of oppression. Coward explains that some feminists have seen it as a way to explain how ideology works. She says it shows 'how the categories of masculinity and femininity are constructed in a particular society' (1978: 43). Her re-reading of Freud is, as is Mitchell's, heavily based on the ideas of Jacques Lacan (for example, 1968), a French philosopher who developed Freud in ways that stressed the importance of language in forming sexed subjects. This brings out what she suggests is the anti-essentialist nature of Freud's ideas. Lacan argues that to enter society the child must acquire language and therefore the positions of masculinity and femininity which are an integral part of language. The child does this via a process of splitting: separating themselves from their sense of connection to the mother's body, and thereby separating conscious from unconscious thought. Desires and thoughts no longer allowable as a social being are tucked away in the unconscious. The process of splitting is precarious and never complete, so identity shifts and subjectivity is socially constructed.

The way in which splitting supposedly works in the 'normal' development of femininity implies that feminine subjectivity may be more precarious. According to Freud (Coward, 1978) boys split from their mothers and identify as masculine because they fear castration as a punishment if they continue to compete with the powerful father to stay closely connected to the mother. Freud is read as suggesting that the initially bisexual drives he argues characterize sexuality are then socially organized into the approved form of heterosexual reproduction. However, girls supposedly realize they are already castrated and have a continuing struggle to define their sexuality. Coward notes that Freud's account of the girl's development as an abandonment of active clitorial sexuality for the mature woman's passive vaginal sexuality is unconvincing. Why would girls give up their active sexuality in such a way? Freud posits that it is because they recognize their sexual organs as inferior, which assumes that penises are somehow naturally and inevitably better. Such phallocentric assumptions have been the target of much of the criticism of Freud (for example, Jackson, 1999). For Coward, Lacan's ideas help overcome this problem because he argues that a crucial part of the process of splitting which makes the child into a social being is the mirror phase, when the child becomes fascinated with its image in the mirror. They learn to see themselves from the point of view of others – as an object, an independent individual not dependent on the mother. Yet to sociologists this is no new idea, as Charles Cooley (1902) proposed something very similar in his concept of the looking glass self (see Howson, 2004: 15–16). However, what Coward stresses as particularly useful about Lacan is that he argues that what is important in the development of gendered sexuality is not the actual penis, but the concept of the penis. Lacan calls this symbolic representation of the penis: the **phallus**. The phallus represents difference, not because of any natural superiority it may have as a sexual organ, but because it is symbolic of the valuing of maleness in the existing social and cultural order. Learning to be masculine and feminine is about learning that those who are identified as masculine will be privileged and that being a woman will entail accepting some level of social (not inherent) inferiority. There are questions about whether this makes women passive victims.

Feminist psychoanalyst, Luce Irigaray, argues that it is precisely women's position 'outside' discourse that enables them to criticize it. In a similar vein to Kristeva, she notes the extreme difficulty women have in representing themselves and their experiences within a masculine dominated symbolic system. Women only have access to these 'male' systems of representation which distance them from themselves and other women (Irigaray, 1985: 85). She sees ideas about sexuality as fundamental to systems of representation. Women's sexuality is multiple, and does not fit the dominant phallocentric model of sexuality based on men. Irigaray argues that such sexual discourses try to capture women within a logic of sameness. But women have a far more plural sense of sexuality and, therefore, of subjectivity. This plurality arises, she thinks, because the two lips of women's genitalia constantly touch. Women can touch themselves without aid of an instrument (for example, hand, woman) (Irigaray, 1991: 58). Thus, her body is always-already active (sexually). However, this active fluidity is presently inexpressible and/or excessive in relation to patriarchal ways of thinking about sexuality and subjectivity. Women remain outside discourse, but unlike Kristeva, Irigaray argues that their excess can be a basis for agency. Kristeva argues that sexual differentiation needs to be overcome, but Irigaray argues that women must be recognized as autonomous and sexually specific (Grosz, 1989: 100–1). She proposes the possibility of thinking about bodies differently, of defying bodies and the boundedness of binaries such that the feminine is no longer divided from, but instead related to, the masculine (Irigaray, 1985). Social changes, and in particular women's entry into the workforce, are helping to produce such new possibilities. As women have entered 'the circuits of production' and have been potentially freed from the mother role by contraception and abortion, they have begun to take on 'that impossible role: being a woman' (Irigaray, 1985: 83).

In order for women to be recognized they need to be seen as something more than mothers, something more than a semiotic hum. They must be seen as 'a woman, a subject with a life, sex and desires of her own' (Grosz, 1989: 179). Admirable though this formulation is, its reliance on a conception of the sexualized specificity of women's bodies raises difficulties. A conception of action and, by implication, agency, emerges as something originating from the spaces of the body. This is arguably a form of essentialism (see Fuss, 1989) and therefore can limit appreciations of how femininity changes, but it does provide an idea of action as not fully controlled by actors. Beverley Brown and Parveen Adams, in a critique of Irigaray (and Kristeva), suggest that rather than the body as origin, 'sexuality determines the organisation of a body' (1979: 39; see also Weeks, 1989). Feminist sociologists remain sceptical, but not always dismissive, of psychoanalysis.

Michèle Barrett dislikes the way the psychoanalytic tradition emerging from Freud tends to make rather grand claims about its ability to explain why women and men think and act differently. She is also aware of common criticisms of psychoanalysis as excluding other factors (such as the influence of social institutions). Although careful to praise the intellectual scope and bravery of Juliet Mitchell's (1975) effort to defend psychoanalysis amongst feminists, with whom it was vastly unpopular, Barrett (1992) is critical of many of the claims Mitchell makes. However, Barrett thinks that, used critically, psychoanalytical theory has advantages for understanding gender because it is poised between a focus on the symbolic and the material. Mitchell (1975) for example argues that Freud is suggesting that it is the ideas about anatomy, rather than the anatomy itself, which are important. Barrett (1980: 55) disagrees, suggesting that Freud does talk about the superiority of the actual physical penis. However, Barrett is perhaps a little literal in her approach to Freud. I would argue that Mitchell is saying that, with a little help from Lacan, we can use Freud to focus on the way in which the penis symbolizes the power and privilege to which those who have one are heir.

Barrett does concede that Freud made a distinctive break with biological determinism by questioning any 'natural' connection between femaleness and passivity and between sexual desire and heterosexual penetrative sex (1980: 56). However, his account of gender development assumes that the 'proper' development of femininity means accepting a passive sexuality (Barrett, 1980: 56–7). But why is the active termed masculine? She argues that to answer this it is not sufficient to see Freud as a product of his times. Barrett claims that sexism is fundamental to Freud's account and cannot be glossed over as do Mitchell and, I would add, Coward.

Sociologists have criticized psychoanalytic approaches to gender not only for their grand claims and their sexism but for their reductive aspects – their tendency to boil everything down to what happened to you as a child coming to terms with having a particular type of body. Stevi Jackson (1999) is opposed to psychoanalytic tendencies to reduce the explanation of all manner of behaviour to biological differences (having or not having a penis). She argues that this biological reductionism makes psychoanalysis unhelpful in doing sociology. She is especially critical of Freud's analysis of how girls become women, seeing it as fundamentally sexist. She is not convinced that later Lacanian readings of Freud are any improvement, and would perhaps not share the enthusiasm many introductory sociology textbooks seem to have for other psychoanalytic accounts (such as Chodorow's) that are still based on most of Freud's assumptions. Even where sociologists do see some value in psychoanalytic approaches, they tend to use them in understanding how children develop into gendered adults, but then direct most of their concern to examining the ongoing social production of differences between women and men.

Conclusion

Generally speaking sociologists have tried critically to understand differences between women and men not as 'natural' but as socially constructed. Historical variations in the way sex and gender have been understood and lived help to establish that differences between women and men are not a simple outcome of having a female or male body. In fact bodies cannot always simply and clearly be placed into only those two categories. Other physical differences between the sexes are also open to interpretation, and there may be as many differences between two individual men as between a man and a woman. Nevertheless, social life continues to be organized along very gendered lines and the idea that physical differences between the sexes are significant is used to justify many injustices, especially injustices to women. Assumptions that women are also somehow less intelligent or are psychologically, as well as physically, 'lacking' have also been used to justify women's generally lower social position.

Central to sociological understandings of gender have been examinations of the lives of women and men as not just different, but as unequal. In particular, sociological approaches to gender have traditionally focused on how gender differences are produced by the way society is organized, by the social structure. In the following chapters we will see how major social institutions such as families, the education system, work, and politics, shape gender in contemporary society. Sociologists also see ideas as important in shaping gender and this book also explores sociological discussions of gender socialization, gender roles, gender stereotyping, and other more recent attempts to consider the importance of the meanings people give to their gender. Sociological theories of gender differences have both informed and responded to the collection of large amounts of empirical evidence by social scientists which suggest that – for women – being 'different' means being disadvantaged. In order to understand gender as a form of social inequality as well as a set of social meanings, it is necessary to first examine in more detail how sociologists think we become gendered. In the next chapter we therefore consider whether gender is something that we 'do' and how we learn to do it.

Key readings

Coward, R. (1978) 'Re-reading Freud: the making of the feminine', *Spare Rib*, 70: 43–6.

Fausto-Sterling, A. (2002b) 'The five sexes, revisited', *Sciences*, 40: 18–23.

Grosz, E. (1989) *Sexual Subversions: Three French Feminists*. Sydney: Allen and Unwin.

Hird, M. (2004) *Sex, Gender, and Science*. New York: Palgrave.

Kessler, S.J. and McKenna, W. (1978) *Gender: An Ethnomethodological Approach*. New York: Wiley.

3

Is gender something that we do?

All the time you've got to weigh everything up: is it too tarty? Will I look like a right slag in it, what will people think? It drives me mad that every time you go to put your clothes on you have to think 'do I look dead common? Is it rough? Do I look like a dog?' (Skeggs, 1997: 3)

This is a working class British woman talking about the difficulties she faces in trying to appear feminine, and it highlights how individuals make choices, but within the constraints of their society. **Structure** and **agency** are involved. Much sociology has reinforced a view of gender as something that we *become*; we are shaped into being feminine or masculine by powerful social structures. However, there are alternative arguments that focus more on the part that individuals play in making choices about how they behave. This individual ability to shape our own lives is referred to as **agency**. When sociologists use the term agency they are NOT saying that we can do whatever we want, or that it all depends on individual differences. They are saying that society is always organized in ways that constrain people, but that there are usually various possibilities within those constraints. To take the woman above, she could wear whatever she likes but she is afraid of being judged 'tarty' or 'common'. For working class women in the North of England, respectability is particularly important in how they present themselves to the world (Skeggs, 1997). She talks about having to 'weigh everything up' to avoid negative reactions. This implies that individual women have to make decisions about how they *do* gender, but the choices they have about how to do gender are made in relation to the broad patterns of femininity within particular times and places. In this case Skeggs argues that, typically, working class women will express their femininity in different ways to middle class women, but will know that middle class styles of femininity are more highly valued within society than their own ways of talking, dressing and being. They have agency but the way society is organized or structured has a major effect on the choices they can make and the results of those choices. Those structural constraints are something sociologists have suggested that individuals learn as they develop a sense of self. Gender socialization theories have extended the classic explanations of self development to focus on gender as determined by social structures. These theories were a shift away from thinking about biological sex as determining behaviour and towards the proposal that gender was learnt. However, they thought it was learnt early and, once established, was very entrenched. From the 1970s onwards more emphasis began to be put on agency and gender began to be understood as something that we *do*. This shift can be understood by looking back to the early twentieth century when George Herbert Mead developed ideas about the emergence of a socially constructed self.

Becoming gendered: the self and early socialization

Mead: the socially constructed self

The basic message of Mead's (1962) work is that we develop a sense of self, an understanding of who we are, by interacting with others (see Box 3.1 for a summary of the four stages in Mead's model). **Socialization** refers to the processes by which we learn what it means to be an adult human being within our society. Socialization operates through social institutions such as families, school, work, the media, and generally through social interaction. Children learn to see themselves and what they do in relation to the people around them. The first stage is imitation when babies start to learn how to be human by copying the actions of people around them. If someone smiles at them, they smile. As they get older children then begin to recognize the '**significant other**'. They learn to take on the roles of their primary carers (usually parents). Play is very important at this stage as children often learn by acting out what they think their parents do; so parents may have the possibly uncomfortable experience of recognizing themselves when they see their child playing 'mummies and daddies'. But at this point a child still has a fairly simple understanding of who they are which revolves around those most significant to them. Gradually they move to a slightly more sophisticated understanding of themselves in relation to others. They begin to be able to take on the role of several others at once in one situation. This means they can think about what other people might do in a certain situation. This ability is crucial in playing games that have rules. To be able to play cards, for example, you have to have some conception about what the other players might do, and think about what you want to do in relation to them. All sorts of games are an important part of how we learn to do this, according to Mead.

The final stage in developing an adult self is learning to take the role of '**the generalized other**'. This means being able to imagine being many others in many situations. Learning to take on the role of the generalized other means being able to see yourself from the point of view, not just of those close to you or playing a game with you, but from the point of view of others 'generally'. Rather than just understanding how your mother or your friends might react to what you do in particular situations, you become aware of what might be considered socially acceptable in a whole range of circumstances. Mead suggests that this is the most important stage in becoming a socialized human being. He thinks that from then on people engage throughout their lives in continuous internal conversations with themselves about what they want to do and what 'other' people will think. We take into account what is socially acceptable in deciding how to behave. Mead was arguing that who we are and how we behave are socially constructed, but he did not consider how girls and boys might be given different messages about what is acceptable behaviour. It took other sociologists to consider how the self might be gendered.

Box 3.1   Mead's model of how the self develops through social interaction

1.	Cannot take the role of the other	Imitation
2.	Can be one other in one situation	Play
3.	Can be many others in one situation	Games (with rules)
4.	Can take the role of the generalized other	Understand social conventions

---

Ann Oakley: gender socialization

Ann Oakley (1972) was one of the first sociologists to extend ideas about socialization to try to understand how gender is learned and how femininity and masculinity are socially constructed. She and other sociologists were suggesting that perhaps women and men were only as different as a society made them. Oakley started using the term **gender** in the early 1970s to distinguish biological sex from gender. The word gender was borrowed from the social psychologist Robert Stoller who worked on individuals with ambiguous genital sex (Jackson, 1998b: 33). Oakley adapted the term to refer to the social classifications of 'masculine' and 'feminine' (Oakley, 1985a: 16). Oakley (1972) assumes that sex (biological difference) is the basis of gender distinctions but disputes that biology is destiny. Boys and girls are treated and talked about differently from birth, with girls entering what Jessie Bernard (1981: 120) referred to as 'the "pink world" of those up to five years of age'. There are different expectations about what is 'normal' for girls and what is 'normal' for boys. In explaining gender socialization sociologists have argued that the messages about how to be a boy and how to be a girl are communicated through social institutions. Here I want to briefly explain how sociologists have understood the role of social institutions in the early stages of gender socialization. Leaving the role of work for discussion later in the chapter, how do families and schools 'make' gender differences?

Gender socialization in the family

Oakley argues children learn what it means to be feminine and masculine not just from their parents (significant others) but by looking at themselves and their parents in terms of wider social expectations about gender (the 'generalized other'). Oakley's (1972) efforts to provide evidence about the importance of nurture were limited because she had to draw largely on psychological literature, given that very little else about the learning of gender was available at the time. She argued, for example, that parents, especially mothers, condition their children's behaviour by treating girls and boys in accordance with social expectations. Oakley refers to one piece of research that suggests that girls are fussed over more by their mother and implies that the mother's behaviour will actually make the girls less independent. Cognitivists argue that the conditioning works because the child has already recognized their gender identity by about four years old, and wants to live up to it. Social learning theorists believe that the child learns their gender because they are rewarded for behaving in gender appropriate ways. Oakley does not think it is possible or important to decide in which order the process occurs and she points out that gender identities vary depending on the type of family a child lives in and how their parents treat them. However, she argues that children identify their parents not just as individuals but in terms of the social groups to which their parents belong. Children pick up on the age and gender and status of their parents and compare them to others. They quickly learn how men and women are expected to behave, even if those close to them do not always behave according to those expectations.

From a more current sociological viewpoint, this story of gender acquisition perhaps relies too heavily on the influence of parents in early childhood. Also, although it indicates that children learn about gender partly by comparing their parents to others, a lot of emphasis is put on the parents' role in transmitting gender to their offspring. Liz Stanley and Sue Wise (1983) have commented that the focus of many socialization theories is not just on families, or even parents, but on the role of mothers. The assumption is that mothers are responsible for teaching children social expectations about gendered behaviour, which children supposedly passively internalize. Yet gender expectations are extremely varied and often contradictory. Socialization models do not usually appreciate complexity and variation and assume that people are determined by a clear set of social norms. One possible implication is that if families raised children differently gender inequalities would disappear. The generation of parents influenced by feminism who tried to bring up their children in gender neutral ways, soon discovered that not giving your boys guns was not enough. Parents and their children do not live in a bubble and children are always exposed to a wider circle of people and expectations within their social world. Children have grandparents and other extended family, they spend time with friends, at nursery, kindergarten or school, and they watch television and videos. It may be that parents have most influence, but they are far from the only source from which children will get ideas about gender appropriate behaviour. In focusing on parental, and especially motherly, influence there is also an assumption that parents have clear ideas, and agree with each other, on how girls and boys should behave. It is also assumed that they consistently reward 'appropriate' behaviour and the messages will be clear to children. Children may sometimes get contradictory messages about how to behave, and although the overall gender pattern is likely to be fairly clear, girls and boys do not just passively accommodate to a fixed feminine or masculine template but play around with the possibilities to different degrees. So if Grandpa is telling a child that girls do not play rugby, but her older cousin is in a women's rugby team and often throws rugby balls with her, that girl will have to interpret these different ideas about gender and choose a path through and around them.

Gender socialization at school

Schooling has historically emphasized gender differences, with girls often disadvantaged because of the gendering of subjects, a lack of role models, sexist resources, and the way that classroom interaction operated to favour boys (Delamont, 1990). Formal education in many cultures has been available only to the privileged few until relatively recently.

Compulsory primary education was introduced in most western nations in the late nineteenth century, but well into the twentieth century even wealthy women usually had a much more limited education than their brothers (Woolf, 1929). For middle and working class girls, education was seen either as a threat to, or preparation for, their duties as wives and mothers (Delamont, 1978). Educational opportunities have considerably improved for women in the rich developed nations as will be discussed, but they are still limited for the majority of women in the world (see Chapter 1) and women in most nations are considerably more likely to be illiterate than men (UNICEF, 2006: 114). Even in nations where women do reach similar levels of education to men, the kind of education they have had is often quite different. Girls have continued to be less likely than men to take 'hard sciences' such as physics (for example, see Department of Education, Science and Training, 2005: 32; Equal Employment Opportunities Commission, 2006: 8; National Science Board, 2006). These curriculum choices have profound implications for the later career options of women. Many higher status and better-paid jobs require scientific knowledge. The lack of women in highly regarded and powerful social roles also means many girls see those roles as being for men, and do not aspire to them. The education sector itself does not provide many role models of powerful women for girls to identify with, as despite women occupying the majority of education jobs, men have continued to hold most of the senior positions (for example, see Engender, 2000: 8). As well as lacking role models, girls also have previously had to make do with learning resources that were not oriented to them and their experiences.

In the 1970s a considerable amount of research on gender issues in education focused on criticizing the negative way that readers and textbooks reinforced gender differences. Everything from early readers (see Lobban, 1975; Weitzmann et al., 1972), to maths and science textbooks (Berrill and Wallis, 1976; Taylor, 1979; Walford, 1981), were found to feature less women and to portray boys and girls in stereotyped ways. For example boys in early readers were often shown as active and strong leaders, while girls were mainly shown as inferior beings involved with nurturing or doing domestic work (Lobban, 1975). Schools also reinforced gender differences by other means.

Teachers appear to spend more time interacting with boys in the classroom, but the extent and effect of this are debated (Delamont, 1990: 11, 86). Dale Spender (1982) argued that classroom interaction made girls invisible, with teachers both encouraging and yet devaluing 'feminine' behaviour in girls. Girls were encouraged to be quiet and good but boys more often needed disciplining and so even when teachers tried not to they devoted more attention to boys. Although much of this attention to boys was negative, it nevertheless meant that girls were being ignored.

Also, in order to try and prevent boys behaving badly teachers might tailor material so that it would appeal to the boys' interests, which could make class work more boring and difficult to engage with for the girls. For example, when the football world cup is taking place, a maths teacher might design some problems based around the probability of each team winning. If many girls are uninterested in soccer this may make it harder for them to do the problem. However Spender's argument is based on her observations of only a small number of lessons; not really enough to support her generalizations about women's invisibility. Bossert (1981) suggests that overall the past research on classroom interaction showed that there are gender differences but it is not clear how much this affects the behaviour of students. While many of the classroom problems identified might still exist, girls and boys are not always aware of what is going on in the classroom and it is difficult to determine how much influence classroom interaction has on their gender identities (Delamont, 1990: 11, 86). There have also been changes in teaching practice and in other aspects of education, especially since the 1980s.

Changes in education appear to have altered how learning is gendered and girls in the West have for some time achieved better results at school than boys (for example, see Cortis and Newmarch, 2000; Freeman, 2004; Office for National Statistics, 2001b: 68). Some of these changes have been deliberately made as a result of feminist lobbying, which made use of some of the early research. Considerable change has occurred in relation to early reading books and other children's texts and literature. These may have since become more balanced in the way they present girl and boy characters and there is more discussion of children's ability to interpret this literature in varying ways (for example, Davies, 1993; Hubler, 2000). Various programmes, addressing classroom interaction and the other issues discussed above, were put in place from the 1970s to encourage girls in school. Although girls are still underrepresented in some subject areas such as physics, the programmes appear to have been effective.

Thus concern has shifted to why boys are performing relatively poorly at school (for example, see Cortis and Newmarch, 2000; Mac an Gahill, 1994). The need for male role models is much voiced, although previous research did not suggest that being taught by women necessarily helped girls. There have been explanations, fuelled by classic sociological studies such as Paul Willis's (1977) *Learning to Labour*, proposing that boys – especially working class boys – perceive school as a feminine environment and academic learning as being for 'cissies'. Despite Paul Willis's determination to understand the part that the boys play in their own academic failure, many of these explanations again emphasize gender socialization as being established early and then firmly entrenched. Gender is thought to be imposed by the school system, or at least by a simple rejection of that system.

Since the 1980s others have proposed, based on their research with children, that femininity and masculinity are not just imposed on children within the classroom, but actively 'done' by them in more complex ways, there and within the playground (for example, see Francis, 1998; Prendergast and Forrest, 1998; Thorne, 1993). These criticisms of ideas about gender as imposed by social structures can be extended to socialization theories more generally.

Criticisms of gender socialization theories

Oakley's efforts to get away from conventional thinking about women that focused on their bodies were important but she tended to see sexed bodies as a kind of blank slate on which social gender was written (Gatens, 1991). This distinction between sex as a clear 'natural' fact and gender as a shifting set of social meanings has since been subject to much criticism, (for example, Gatens, 1991; Stanley, 2001/1984), and Oakley (1985a: 5–7) herself later recognized some of the limitations of this early work.

One problem with the kind of constructionist approach exemplified by Oakley is that it often attributed a great deal of importance to early socialization within the family. In her chapter on 'The learning of gender roles', Oakley (1972) spends over 12 of 15 pages talking mostly about children under five. Oakley makes only very brief nods towards non-parental influences on children such as school textbooks and the mass media. In short there is little consideration of gender as something we continue to learn in a variety of ways.

If gender socialization was as powerful as the model sometimes implies then we would be much more similar. Social expectations are not always clear, and even if they are, not all women follow them in the same way. There are different ways of dressing, sitting and speaking amongst women and people think differently about what it means to be feminine. This does not simply mean that everyone is different. There are patterns of class and age (for example) to the variations above. However, socialization theories tend to imply that people who do not conform are in some sense failures. As Stanley and Wise (1983) note, it is assumed that such people are not properly socialized. This seems a rather impoverished way to account for human diversity and resistance to limiting gender stereotypes. Thus socialization theories are felt to be lacking because they overemphasize the power of social structures in shaping individuals' gender. The extent to which individuals are able to exercize some agency, or play a part, in how they become gendered is often under-recognized.

Sue Sharpe (1976) produced an alternative account of gender socialization, in which she tries to recognize that children have some, albeit limited, agency in the formation of gender identities. Her account of 'how girls become women', draws on questionnaires and interviews from 249 mostly working class schoolgirls in Britain, including Asian and West Indian girls. Like Oakley, Sharpe is outlining 'the situation of girls growing up' (Sharpe, 1976: 11) and how that situation is socially produced by a particular gendered history, by economic conditions, and by ideologies promoted by the media, the education system, and how work is organized. Sharpe seems even more eager than Oakley to bracket off bodies as not really important in becoming gendered, but she makes more use of girls' own voices in making sense of socialization. Oakley drew on and gave credit to women's experiences in her other work, but not in her general explication of gender socialization. Sharpe is therefore useful in giving empirical richness to statements about how social institutions perpetuate particular notions of femininity. However, although the girls' own ways of thinking are reported, this does not necessarily always reinforce their agency. Often their ideas about gender appear very conventional, for example, one girl says:

> I don't agree with the wife going out to work and the husband staying at home and looking after the kids. I'd rather stay at home all day if it was that way really. I think there's a certain bargain in the home and for the women, that's her children and they need her more than the father. (Sharpe, 1976: 223)

Especially for the working class girls Sharpe talks to, their boredom with school and desire to rush out into marriage and/or the workforce are seen as 'schooled' into them and their ability to shape a less 'narrow' life seen as limited. The implication is that these are not their own ways of thinking; they have been 'brainwashed' by society. Dominant structures and meanings will gender their lives, and that will mean following gender conventions in fairly predictable ways likely to perpetuate class and gender inequalities. The strength of this analysis is in challenging common-sense thinking that suggests people can get ahead if they want to, if they work hard. Sociological evidence outlined in Chapter 1 and throughout the book illustrates that it is harder for some women to succeed because of already existing inequalities. Therefore working class girls are unlikely to be successful because they do not have the same advantages as middle class girls, let alone middle class men. Yet emphasizing how present inequalities shape people makes it hard to see how things change and how some working class women do succeed.

The picture of British school life in the 1970s for both boys (Willis, 1977) and girls (Sharpe, 1976) is one of a system reinforcing not just gender, but class inequalities (see Connell et al., 1982 for a similar view of education in Australia). Given Sharpe's data, it seems that the 'cissies' whom Willis's lads think school is for are not working class girls, but middle class children. Whilst many gender inequalities at school appear to have been quite successfully addressed, the same may not be true of class inequalities. Yet as the quote at the beginning of this chapter illustrates, working class women (and by extension working class men) do not just passively submit to middle class definitions of gender (see Chapter 7) and may produce less dominant but important definitions of their own (Skeggs, 1997).

Socialization theories do not adequately account for contradictory messages about gender. We can illustrate this briefly by looking at Barbie dolls and GI Joe dolls and figures, to see if there may still be some validity in Oakley's argument that children prefer certain toys because they are socialized into seeing certain behaviour as appropriate for girls as opposed to boys (Oakley, 1985a: 52, 177–8). Barbie dolls do still appear to reinforce particular ideas about femininity: ideas of women as passive, pretty things, interested in how they look, not in doing things. Barbie is thin, has long blonde hair and the proportions of her body exaggerate her breasts. Mattel's (2005) website, Barbie.com, lists five categories of Barbies: 'Barbie Diaries, Fashion Fever, Fairytopia, Superstar Barbies and Princess Barbies'. None of these appear particularly active, and the accessories reinforce a rather passive picture of girls. You can buy a 'pillow and playset assortment' to go with your Barbie Diaries Barbie, in which 'the pink pillow unfolds to reveal Barbie® doll's bedroom from the movie, complete with a canopy bed!' Your 'very own tiara' can be purchased to match with the Princess Barbie, and there is a special hairstyling head for the Fairytopia Barbies. The most active accessories go with the superstar 'American Idol' Barbie who has her own recording studio and a Ford Mustang car. All of these suggest that girls are socialized into valuing beauty and encouraged to focus on fantasy lives in which their appearance is crucial. Where are the Working Woman Barbies and the Motorbike Barbies? And where are the GI Joe 'doing the housework' accessories? In contrast to Barbie, GI Joe dolls (Action Man in the British market) or the new 'Sigma 6' action figures are presented in ways that encourage boys to aspire to active, exciting, dangerous and perhaps even violent behaviour. This behaviour is what contemporary western societies associate with being masculine. Of the GI Joe Sigma 6 toys featured on the website, five are distinctly active sounding action figures called Duke, Snake Eyes, Heavy Duty, Spirit Iron-Knife and Storm Shadow. The other two toys are a 'Ninja Hovercycle' and a 'Switchfire Blaster'. The characters do not have 'accessories', but weapons cases, and you can buy the enemies they fight (Hasbro, 2005). These toys appear to send messages to boys that masculinity is about attacking enemies, embracing danger, destroying things, and speeding around in fast vehicles. Or is it more complex than that?

More recent theories, usually identified as postmodernist, have suggested that there is more than one way to 'read' (or interpret) cultural products like toys and what they might say about gender expectations. Although Barbie, for instance, can tell us a lot about the culture in which we live, different interpretations of Barbie exist (Rogers, 1999). For example, there are boyfriend dolls available to 'go with' Barbie, which you could argue are there to do what Barbie, or at least her owners, want them to do. Barbie/girls are in control. Barbie's men certainly portray rather different ideas about masculinity than does GI Joe. The boyfriends tend to be clothed to escort Barbie to social occasions, or be dressed as Princes in the kind of outfit young GI Joe owners would probably consider 'cissy'. One of the male dolls is simple called 'the handsome groom' (Mattel, 2005). These male dolls are made for girls, not boys, but they do suggest that wearing combat gear is not the only way to be a man. Young boys are probably more likely to prefer GI Joe to 'Prince Aidan', but that does not mean that all boys will grow up into camouflage-wearing, aggressive, militaristic speed freaks. By the same token, just because girls might show an early pining for all things pink and Barbie-like, it does not necessarily mean they will go through life following the stereotypes of traditional femininity. Children may sometimes employ alternative gender meanings when playing with toys, so girls might dress Barbie in their brother's GI Joe uniforms, or create stories for their Barbies which are more like *Charlie's Angels* or *Lara Croft, Tomb Raider*. Conventional meanings remain hard to resist, but children engage with dominant and alternative messages about gender that are transmitted through cultural products such as toys, although perhaps more importantly through social institutions.

Gender socialization continues, for example, when people enter the workforce. Oakley and Sharpe give no real account of this (see Sharpe, 1976: 159–81). Even Oakley pays little attention to work despite her book *Sex, Gender and Society* (1985a) having emerged out of her study of housework (Oakley, 1974). She found that she could not make sense of what she was finding out about how work was organized in society without 'going back to the beginning; that is to the nature versus nurture debate' (Oakley, 1985b: 218). Sociology has continued to be centrally interested in how social structures (the way society is organized), not just early socialization, determine gender.

Gender as structure: gender is done to us

This book will return often to explanations of how gender is done to us, or imposed on individuals, via social structures. Connells (2002: 55) defines social structures as 'the enduring or extensive patterns among social relations'. Chapter 1 outlined Walby's (1986; 1990) argument that gender is determined and gender inequalities are perpetuated through six structures: paid work, household production, culture, sexuality, violence, and the state. Alternatively, Connell (2002) argues that is done to us (and by us) via four main structures, which are not always *inherently* unequal. Thus relations of power, production, emotions and the symbolic create the gender regime which shapes people's lives. These four dimensions of gender will be expanded on throughout the book. Power features especially prominently in the discussions around how gender relations are bound up with class and racial inequalities. Emotional relations are addressed there, but they and symbolic aspects of gender will be discussed in Chapter 5 which rethinks the relationship between bodies and gender. Many parts of the book, particularly Chapter 7 on class, examine gender as a practice operating on people within production, where that usually means the paid workplace (see Martin, 2003). There are also other things to say about gender as a form of interactive work, something not only done to us, but something that we 'do'.

Gender is something we do: from symbolic interactionism to gender performativity

There are three ways in which gender can be thought of as something we 'do'. The first argues that to do gender is to perform it, as an actor performs a role. Secondly, to 'do' gender can mean that we have to work at it. This tends to emphasize that doing gender is more like work than play. Thirdly, gender can be understood as **performative**, which means gender is produced through the repetition of gender norms. This tries to get away from the idea of actors doing gender, without going back to the idea that our gender is a fixed part of who we are; but more of that later. Initially I want to explain the influence of a dramaturgical approach to gender.

Gender as a performed role: playing gender

The dramaturgical approach to gender suggests that we are all actors, trying to give a good performance of femininity or masculinity. We know what the gendered scripts (see Gagnon and Simon, 1973) are – we know how to play the part of a woman or a man but we might each play that part slightly differently. This approach is derived from symbolic interactionism, which emerged from Mead's (1962) work and is linked to early ethnomethodological examinations of gender as a performance (Garfinkel, 1967; Kessler and McKenna, 1978). A principle theorist in this tradition is Erving Goffman (for example, 1987/1959), who follows on from Mead's argument about how we learn to be social human beings through interacting with others. Mead offers a way of thinking about social expectations and how we learn what they are. He also suggests that how we act is influenced by our understanding of what other people expect in particular situations. Goffman argues that throughout our lives we continue to alter our behaviour according to how we think others might see us. We are actors, adapting social scripts in order to try and give the best impression of ourselves, depending on the social situation. We behave differently when at dinner with relatives compared to when out partying with friends. It has been argued that women are the epitome of actors in Goffman's sense: continually constructing their selves through the perceptions of others (Tseëlon, 1995).

Goffman (1979) details how gender is produced as an unequal relation and made to seem natural because of the way we display our gender. Gender is understood as 'the culturally established correlates of sex' (Goffman, 1979: 1). **Displays** are defined as events indicating the identity, mood, intent, expectations, and relative relations of actors. These displays have a structure. Goffman talks about the schedule of displays that constitute interaction, with most displays being at the beginning or end of activities. He calls them bracket rituals, indicating the start and end of interactions. So, for example, men used to stand up when a woman entered the room and you may know older men who still do this. Displays usually involve a statement and response and can be symmetrical or asymmetrical. So, for example, a woman might interact with her male friend in a relatively symmetrical way. However, a male boss might interact with his secretary in an asymmetrical way, displaying his dominance and her subordination. For instance, she might be referred to by her first name by him while she always has to use his title: *Mr* Bossman. There are also identificatory stylings that play a part in gender displays by showing who is to be dealt with. Thus women might wear their hair certain ways, women and men normally wear different clothing and use different tones of voice. This helps us decide how to interact, whether to stand up (a man for a woman), not swear (thought impolite in front of 'ladies'), or what to talk about (children to women or sport to men). He outlines the various ritualized indications of gender as produced in everyday life.

Displays of gender are conventional, stylized, formal or informal, and sometimes optional. Some displays are sincere, others are not. Gender displays are conventional in that they follow widely held ideas about what is the norm for women and men. Gender displays are stylized in that many of the things we do to express femininity and masculinity become slightly exaggerated and ritualized. A now rather old-fashioned example is a man lighting a woman's cigarette. Another example might be a 'feminine' gesture of flicking back long hair. There are both informal and formalized ways of displaying gender. An informal display might be women smiling at men demurely; a formalized display might be a man opening a door for a woman. Some forms of gender display appear optional and men opening doors for women is an example. This is becoming a tricky decision for men as some women might think them terribly rude if they do not open doors, and other women might find it very old-fashioned and perhaps even condescending to do so. Goffman also notes that these displays do not have to be sincere. To take the door opening again, I have had many a nice young man hold a door open for me in a sincere manner, but when I was at the University of Aberdeen certain of my male colleagues developed a rather more ironic approach. Having read Norbert Elias's (2000/1939) ideas on the civilizing process, they invoked exaggerated eighteenth century courtly etiquette in opening the door for me and other women colleagues. The door would be opened with a deep and profound bow, preferably (heaviness of door allowing) with a waving of one hand down a slightly outstretched leg. They opened the door, but they made it known that they did not sincerely think we needed doors opened and that it was a rather outmoded display. These colleagues had read their Goffman and they knew that gender displays reproduce gender inequalities.

Goffman analyzes advertisements in order to show how gender displays indicate and reinforce the unequal social position of women relative to men, and make that inequality appear 'natural'. Looking at individual displays is not enough, but he argues that if you look at the overall pattern you will see that women are displayed as inferior and deferential to men. What you see when you look at the advertisements is larger men, looking down on smaller women. Men are portrayed as active protectors, while women passively shelter in their arms. Yet there are women who are larger than some men. On the rare occasions where larger women are shown coupled with smaller men, it is usually made into a joke. Thus the cumulative effect of gender displays is to 'constitute the hierarchy' between men and women (Goffman, 1979: 6). We keep seeing men displaying themselves as strong and superior, and women displaying themselves as delicate and childlike. We come to believe that this is 'natural'. In fact, Goffman argues, it is an illusion. Gender is an illusion we create when we interact with each other. We follow scripts which lay down the gender norms about what our 'nature' as women and men should be. As Goffman (1979: 8) says: '[t]here is no gender identity … only a schedule for the portrayal of gender'. In other words, it is all made up; but the illusion of gender as natural remains a powerful one, reinforced through gender display. Therefore Goffman emphasizes gender as something we do, but presents it as acting out a part in interaction with others. He gives the impression that we follow these scripts without too much thought. West and Zimmerman, however, give us an indication of the work involved in the routine doing of gender.

Doing gender as a routine accomplishment: working at gender

West and Zimmerman's well-known (1987) article on 'doing gender' argues that gender is best understood as a routine we must work at in everyday interaction. This means that despite finding Goffman extremely useful, they think that the emphasis on display looks too much at gender as happening at the periphery of interactions (in bracket rituals) and fails to see how gender is central to all interaction. People take their cues on how to do gender from others and people are constantly held accountable for whether their performance of gender is 'appropriate'. However, they argue that the terminology surrounding gender needs to be more precisely defined.

West and Zimmerman suggest that '**gender**' refers to acting the part, to the work involved in behaving as feminine or masculine. They argue that 'gender' in this sense must be distinguished from 'sex' and from 'sex category'. '**Sex**' should denote biological criteria, such as chromosomes and genes, used to decide who is male and who female. However, these are things that ordinary people cannot see, therefore we need the term '**sex category**' to refer to the classification of someone's sex that we make based on them looking the part. For example, do they have a beard to help classify them as male? 'Gender' should therefore refer to how people manage being classified into a sex category, 'male' or 'female'. West and Zimmerman go on to argue that doing gender means constantly engaging with socially circulating ideas which encourage women and men to look and act in certain ways that declare their 'sex category'. There is considerable work involved in this, but this work is central to social interaction. Most of us find it almost impossible to know how to interact with individuals if we are unable to decide which 'sex category' they belong in. However, we usually very quickly make a decision, or get some information to convince us whether they are 'male' or 'female' so we can then 'do' gender in interacting with them.

West and Zimmerman therefore disagree with Goffman's argument that gender displays are optional. They illustrate much of this with reference to a well-known study by Garfinkel (1967) of a supposedly intersex person known as Agnes. In terms of sex Agnes was hard to define, she had a penis, but at puberty developed breasts, and hormonally appeared female. In terms of sex category, Agnes was 'passing' as a woman. She wore women's clothing and had a boyfriend. Agnes had to work particularly hard to do femininity, as she had spent most of her early years as a boy and could not take it for granted that she would get it 'right'. Yet as West and Zimmerman argue, Agnes was only doing more consciously what most women do without thinking (see also Kessler and

McKenna, 1978). Even where we feel clear about someone's gender, and indeed our own, we are always managing the classification. We are all constantly working at presenting ourselves as feminine or masculine in relation to others, and through this interactive work gender is produced.

Melissa Tyler and Pamela Abbott's (1998) research on 'ordinary' women such as flight attendants further illustrates the kind of work involved in 'doing' gender. They draw on West and Zimmerman's ideas to show that:

> the labour which is involved in performing and maintaining the appearance of a flight attendant is not perceived as work, but as an aspect of just "being a woman", from which women are deemed to derive both pleasure and a sense of identity. As such this labour is neither recognised nor remunerated. (Tyler and Abbott, 1998: 434)

They suggest that this commodification of women as bodies is an illustration of how women are subordinated throughout contemporary western societies. In respect of flight attendants, the women's bodies were seen to symbolically represent the airline and expected to embody the company image: for example, by looking sleek and efficient. Women flight attendants are expected to groom themselves and work on their bodies to maintain the standards of appearance that the airline dictates, and yet to make it look like they have put no effort into it, but are 'naturally' poised and feminine. Airlines routinely weighed their women attendants, but not male attendants or pilots. The women were told to lose weight if they did not fit the strict height to weight ratios. Men were expected only to be clean and neat. Women's uniforms and cosmetics were also checked. The women internalized these demands and disciplined their bodies to try to conform. They dieted, visited hairdressers and gyms, bought expensive make-up, but were given no more financial allowance for this than male peers. They were expected to look flawlessly professional yet constantly felt deficient compared to colleagues, and that they must therefore work harder to look and be feminine in the way dictated. One attendant thought her airline were keen to employ less attractive women, because they thought they would *'work harder* to be exactly what [the airline] want us to be. Not just looks-wise, but being nice to passengers and so on' (quoted in Tyler and Abbott, 1998: 447). Thus, trying to live up to expectations of feminine beauty and behaviour do not come 'naturally' but involve considerable amounts of work not just for flight attendants but for most women. Yet many believe that symbolic interactionism remains too descriptive and does not adequately account for why large-scale social inequalities (such as those between women and men) continue to be reproduced (for example, Crossley, 1995: 135). There are many who have suggested that more structural accounts of doing femininity and masculinity are needed in order to understand gender inequalities.

Doing masculinity

Stoltenberg is unusual within masculinity studies in arguing that it is impossible to be a man without subordinating women (Beasley, 2005: 202). Almost all those involved in masculinity studies are highly critical of dominant forms of masculinity. However, most have some sympathy for men and are keen to point out that not all men are privileged within patriarchal society. Stoltenberg (2000a/1989; 2000b/1993), on the other hand, argues that all men do enjoy privilege – and indeed are complicit – within patriarchy and that only by refusing to take on manhood can change be brought to the social order. This aligns him with radical feminists such as Dworkin and Mackinnon (Beasley, 2005: 199–201). Stoltenberg is a modernist, promoting liberation and adhering strongly to notions of men as a coherent group. The strength of his position lies in his willingness to focus relentlessly on the need to change the dominance of men over women and especially to protest the way in which violence is used to maintain masculine domination. Other masculinity theorists can tend to drift away from an agenda of social change (Messner, 1997), by cleaving to more sympathetic views of men as not all bad. However, while Stoltenberg's commitment to ending sexism is admirable, if men inevitably learn to do masculinity as a form of domination over women, how is it possible for him (and other men) to resist and to protest against their own privilege (Beasley, 2005: 204–5)? Also Stoltenberg's insistence on seeing manhood as a unified position of sexual dominance neglects more complex understandings of masculinity.

Although written in 1995, Connell's book *Masculinities* remains one of the best pieces of sociology on the diversity of ways in which masculinity is done. He maintains that to understand gender requires looking not just at discourse, but also at such things as production and consumption, institutions, and social struggle. Connell argues that masculinity is constructed in relation to what it is not, and that means especially, but not only, femininity. We understand what 'masculine' means by contrasting it to things we think of as 'not masculine'. He agrees with the 1970s work of Juliet Mitchell (1975) and Gayle Rubin (1975) who crafted an understanding of gender as a complex set of different logics that do not always make sense and could be overturned over time. However, as Connell suggests, there are some meanings associated with masculinity that gain dominance for a time (for example, see Kimmel (1996) for a history of manhood in the USA). These dominant meanings constitute **hegemonic masculinity**, where hegemony refers to the process by which a group is able to assert its way of seeing the world as *the* way of seeing the world. Other less powerful versions of doing the masculine are always compelled to refer to hegemonic masculinity. Very few men actually behave according to the hegemonic masculine pattern, although it is a standard to which all men are compared. This standard, and therefore surrounding meanings, change as society changes. Connell looks at the challenges in the late twentieth century facing those close to hegemonic versions of the masculine, in particular middle class men in new technical occupations. First he sets out how certain more marginal groups of men are under particular pressure because of changing discourses about masculinity. These groups include unemployed working class men, men in the environmental movement, and gay men.

Unemployed working class men are no longer able to 'be men' in the same ways as their forefathers. They have had to readjust their notions of how to be masculine, which were previously based on them being the 'breadwinner'. Unskilled, unable to get regular work, and perhaps dependent on women's wages, many fashion their identities in a form that Connell (1995) calls 'protest masculinity'. This is a version of masculinity that takes aspects of hegemonic masculinity and remakes them within a context of poverty. It is a lashing out against a world over which they have little control. Violence and an aggressive heterosexuality are usually key to such ways of doing masculinity, although there are variations. They are trying to conform to hegemonic masculine standards, as far as they are able, while also protesting against some of the more middle class 'niceness' of those standards. Others within the group try to find alternative ways to be masculine; Connell gives the example of one who becomes a crossdresser, trying to live life as a woman. However, these alternatives tend to be individualized projects focused on changing the self. There is not the collective struggle Connell argues is necessary actually to change the gender order. One might expect to find more focus on wider political and social change within another group of men engaged in the environmental movement.

Men in the environmental movement have been forced to confront traditional stereotypes of masculine behaviour because they are working with strongly feminist women and trying to respond to feminist demands for respect and more egalitarian roles. Men may therefore find that they have to learn new ways of interacting with women as equals. They learn to be pro-feminist, and try to value traits within themselves that might conventionally be labelled 'feminine'. However, this does not mean that they reject masculinity or a 'heterosexual sensibility' (1995: 124), as Barry Ryan, a nurse who is part of this group explains:

> I'm still really masculine and I feel definitely male and I like that too. I like some aspects of being male, the physical strength I really like, I really like my body; that sort of mental strength that men learn to have whereby they can choose to put aside their feelings for the moment, which I think is great. (Connell, 1995: 123)

Men in this group guiltily distance themselves from many aspects of hegemonic masculinity defined by their feminist political colleagues as oppressive. However Connell argues that they fail to find positive alternatives, focusing more on trying to not be too conventionally masculine, and again these are largely individual responses which do not address the need for wider social and political change.

Gay men are a group one might expect to be more politically aware in their attempts to rethink their masculinity. Masculinity is usually defined in terms of a particular heterosexual aggressiveness. Western culture assumes that opposites attract, so to be gay is thought to mean to be feminine in some way. Although the men Connell spoke to are attracted to other men, and this calls into question their masculinity, they do not really challenge norms about how to be men. That is, they behave in a fairly conventional masculine manner. As one of the gay men he spoke to explained:

> If you're a guy why don't you just act like a guy? You're not female, don't act like one. That's a fairly strong point. And leather and all this other jazz, I just don't understand it I suppose. That's all there is to it. I am a very straight gay. (quoted in Connell, 1995: 156)

All of these groups of men described above are struggling to define themselves as men in relation to hegemonic masculinity. Hegemonic versions of masculinity are closely tied into capitalist values of rationality, calculation, and self-interest, but Connell is clear that he does not think hegemonic masculinity simply maps onto capitalism. Hegemonic masculinity is defined against femininity and 'other' identities considered not properly masculine. It is a way of thinking about masculine identity in which rationality and authority have become central. Connell is critical of the hegemonic version of masculinity, and points out that it is largely a myth. He allows that dominant ideas about being a man have shifted from an emphasis on physical strength to an emphasis on bodily and emotional control, on a 'scientific' approach to the world, and on the exercize of authority. However he argues that reason has limits as a basis for legitimation of hegemonic masculinity. It is capable of being used to undermine masculine authority. Rational arguments about the need for gender equality and how it is better for business to appoint the best *person* for the job have become widely accepted. Yet they challenge masculine authority, especially for men whose lives and livelihoods are dependent on the new knowledge-based or 'technical' occupations founded on rational ways of thinking. However, even such supposedly highly rational workplaces are not entirely rational. He gives the example of a pilot called Charles Lawrence who, despite working within the highly rationalized aviation industry, is paradoxically very superstitious (Connell, 1995: 177). In addition Connell notes that rationality is always challenged for these men when they have to deal with body issues, sexuality, and emotion – aspects of life deemed irrational. Even those close to hegemonic masculinity struggle to 'be men'.

In his attention to how gender is constructed around changing discourses, Connell approaches postmodernism but he remains committed to a structural approach overall (Beasley, 2005: 226). That commitment to structuralism is present to some degree in even the more 'poststructuralist' versions of sociology. Such commitment does not, as the history of sociology has demonstrated, preclude an interest in meanings. Connell offers analysis of the part meanings and structures play in the shifting and divergent ways of practicing masculinity. Whilst it may allow men to be represented as victims (Beasley, 2005: 229), generally his insistence on gender as a set of ordered relations means that different masculinities are always understood in relation to other gender categories, especially femininities. The problem with Connell's work is perhaps that he becomes a little too immersed in the individual details of these complexities, at least when talking about the sets of life histories he collected. This can serve, ironically, to highlight men's experiences of the world in ways that again put women at the margins (Beasley, 2005: 230). Thus it may be that his approach is not entirely successful in deconstructing the masculine. This may be because of the problems associated with seeing gender as something people 'do'.

Limitations to seeing gender as 'done': gender performativity

The most influential current theories about gender by Judith Butler (for example, 1990), sound very similar to socialization theories (Hood-Williams and Harrison, 1998: 89) and to symbolic interactionist approaches about doing gender, but could more accurately be described as arguing that gender 'does us'. Her work has been important because she has outlined how 'sex', not just gender, is socially constructed and has made important contributions to debates about how gender and sexuality are connected. She argues that gender is not 'natural', it is a stylized repetition of acts (Butler, 1990). Butler is a political philosopher and is therefore working within a different intellectual tradition to the symbolic interactionists. Butler (1988) does refer to Goffman in some of her very early work, but in adopting J.L. Austin's notion of performatives branches off into what can be thought of as a more radical understanding of gender. **Performatives** are words that do things. They bring into being the thing of which they speak. The classic example of a performative is the phrase 'I do' within a wedding ceremony. Uttering this phrase 'performs' the wedding. It is part of the legal procedure that makes you married. Another example is the phrase 'I bet' which when you say it brings the bet into being. Expanding this idea beyond narrow linguistic bounds, Butler puts together a sophisticated argument about gender as performative.

Butler argues that as soon as new parents announce 'it's a girl' then the process of gendering begins. With that phrase the girling of the girl starts to be performed, and the femininity of that individual begins to be constructed. Girls and boys are made feminine and masculine by selecting from available meanings about gender. She describes the **citation** of gender norms as central to gender practices. This sounds like a good deal of agency is involved, but Butler (1993: x) is adamant that gender is not something you can choose to do in the way you choose what clothes to put on. There is, Butler argues no '"doer" behind the deed' (1990: 25). It seems slightly puzzling to say that gender is a matter of copying, with slight variations, existing ways of doing gender and yet to say that it is not something that we actively choose to 'do'. In many places Butler does seem to suggest that agency operates, that gender is done, but this seeming contradiction can perhaps operate with some usefulness because she has a slightly different view of the self and subjectivity to the Meadian one used by symbolic interactionists. Butler, like Goffman, thinks that there is no 'real' basis to gender identity. She describes gender as a kind of masquerade with no substance behind it. Femininity does not exist except as a constantly shifting set of symbolic acts. What is 'feminine' has no basis in women's bodies or experiences; it is made up, it consists only of a collection of ways of acting that are considered feminine. There is only the pretending. However, this pretending produces the illusion that gender is a fundamental part of who we are.

Butler arguably improves on symbolic interactionism by explaining how gender brings us into being as social individuals. Goffman and West and Zimmerman slide back into a vision of gender as something individual actors choose how to do, while Butler works hard to maintain a vision of gender as something that makes us who we are in an ongoing way. Gender is not performed, it is performative. We must attribute a gender to someone in order to make sense of them as a human being. Only as gendered beings are persons 'culturally intelligible' (Butler, 1990: 16–17). Yet gender constitutes us without ever becoming part of us. As gender meanings are cited in many different ways and always changing, then our gender is never 'fixed'.

Butler's fluid view of gender suggests breaking down, 'troubling' (Butler, 1990), or 'undoing' (Butler, 2004) the binary categories 'feminine' and 'masculine'. However, her attempts at this are not always thought successful, nor politically wise (Seidman, 1994). She suggests that gender is not fixed but does not seem to think it can be done away with (Jackson, 1998b). Is it really that radical to propose that 'women' and 'men' can behave in ways that upset gender norms? However, Butler can help us think further about something only hinted at in Goffman and West and Zimmerman: that gender is in some sense imposed, or done to us, but not in entirely predetermined ways. This is something I want briefly to consider in some final remarks on the tricky question of whether gender is something we do.

Conclusion: doing gender, gender being done to us, or gender doing us?

As a sociologist I am drawn to the idea that gender is something we do, although within social constraints. If people *do* gender they have to engage with ideas about how it 'should' be done, even if they find ways to do it differently. People also have to do gender within conditions not of their own making, so they have far from a free rein. One thing that is important about the symbolic interactionist approach is that it reminds us that we do gender in interaction with others. What this can mean is that sometimes people within structured social relations do our gender for us, in ways that we may not like. A boss might insist, for example, that a woman wears make-up when she goes to work; a school board might ban girls from wearing trousers; a woman with short hair might get called a dyke. And in this sense it seems that Butler has something to offer. We have to operate with the ideas about gender that currently exist, and we insist on understanding people in gendered terms. Gender does not just stop us doing things, it makes us do things – but in fluid and changing ways, in which others have had a hand. Like Butler, I do not think that gender is a thing we can put on and take off like clothes, and I appreciate her attempts to see how sex/gender binaries create us as subjects. Yet I want to maintain some idea of an actor (or subject), once brought into being by gender, as then engaging with it. I think Butler herself retains some such idea. From this we can make use of the most important insight arising from seeing gender as doing us and us doing gender. Both Butler and the symbolic interactionists allow us to see gender and its supposed relationship to sex as things that have been made to look 'natural', but are in fact 'made up'. Although the supposed naturalness of femininity and masculinity are powerful illusions, it is exciting to think of them as illusions. If they are illusions of our own making they can be remade, not easily or without trouble, but they can be remade.

Key readings

Butler, J. (1990) *Gender Trouble: Feminism and the Subversion of Identity*. London: Routledge.

Connell, R.W. (1995) *Masculinities*. Cambridge: Polity Press.

Goffman, E. (1979) 'Gender display', in *Gender Advertisements*. Basingstoke: Macmillan.

Oakley, A. (1972) *Sex, Gender and Society*. London: Temple Smith. Or 1985 edition: see Oakley (1985a).

West, C. and Zimmerman, D. (1987) 'Doing gender', *Gender and Society,* 1 (2): 125–51.

4

How can gender best be explained?

The word 'theory' can immediately strike fear into the heart, but a theory is really just an explanation, and the theories presented here are attempts to explain gender. We all theorize to some extent, trying to explain the world around us. Theorists do this too, but more systematically. There are various good books (for example, Beasley, 2005; see Jackson, 1998b) which provide in-depth discussion of gender theories. What I offer is a large-scale map of this theoretical territory, as an aid to exploration. To help you in making sense of and comparing different theoretical approaches I use tables outlining key aspects of different theories. This, in addition to reading the introductory chapter, should make you aware that a major aim of this book is to chart how the linguistic turn has affected understandings of gender.

Explanations of gender have taken a linguistic or cultural turn, shifting emphasis from the material or economic to the symbolic, or the sphere of meaning. As outlined in Chapter 1, 'material' can mean a number of things, which complicates any simple story of a shift away from it. Within traditional sociology '**material**' has conventionally described Marxist approaches which are based on historical materialism. These approaches argue that social organization is centred around the production of material goods, as this is crucial to meeting human needs. More recently, for example, the concept has been central in trying to consider the flesh and blood reality of bodies as 'material' in relation to social meanings (Rahman and Witz, 2003). However, it can still be said that there is a traceable shift away from an emphasis on how material (usually meaning economic) conditions shape gender towards an emphasis on meanings. But a cultural turn is only part of the story.

This chapter has two major parts. The first part deals with the broad context of ideas about gender and is subdivided into one section discussing structuralist and post-structuralist theories and another outlining the categorization of approaches and debates within feminism, major

Table 4.1   **Theoretical traditions on which feminists draw**

	Structuralism	**Linguistic structuralism**	**Post-structuralism**
Intellectual tradition	Marxism, developed in sociology especially in early 20th century	Saussure's theories of linguistics, which attempt to understand the structures of language	Reaction against Marxism (e.g. Foucault), influenced by linguistic structuralism, Austin: performatives
Central ideas	Social structures determine individuals & their lives	Societies are signifying systems based around structures of meaning relying on difference	Representation is everything. Differences are produced through language
Ideas applied to gender	Social structures construct gender differences; women oppressed under (capitalist) patriarchy	Binary structure of language implies men normal/women different	Gender is a performance with no real basis
Theorists	Sylvia Walby Ann Oakley	Barthes (semiotics) Lacan (psychoanalysis)	Judith Butler
Political alliance	socialism, liberalism, feminism?	Marxism, socialism, liberalism?	Radical, queer, apolitical?

theoretical shifts within sociology, and theoretical approaches within feminism as they deal with gender. The second part of the chapter focuses on the turn to culture – the cultural/linguistic turn. Table 4.1 outlines the theoretical approaches covered in this chapter in terms of the broader intellectual traditions on which they draw. This and the following tables will help you see how the different approaches relate, but the tables do not contain all the important information and will not make sense unless you read the whole chapter. For instance, one of the most important things I do is discuss the strengths and limitations of the theories in their efforts to explain gender differences. Appreciating the advantages and disadvantages of using a particular theory is crucial in developing the critical approach central to sociological and feminist understandings of gender. But simply listing the strengths and limitations as points on a table would not encourage you as readers to think about how convincing you find a specific perspective, and why you find it convincing. The first shift in perspectives covered is from structuralism to poststructuralism.

Structuralist/Post-structuralist Theories

Sociologists still argue over the effects and desirability of a move from structuralist attention to 'things' (the material) to post-structuralist attention to 'words' and meaning (the linguistic). They might refer to this shift as '**the cultural turn**' (Chaney, 1994; Nash, 2001) or '**the linguistic turn**' (Barrett, 1992). In order to understand this linguistic/cultural turn it helps to first consider what structuralism is and how post-structuralism differs.

Structuralism

Structuralism tries to understand society in terms of its social structures, its regular patterns and relationships, and usually is interested in how those structures benefit some groups more than others (see Table 4.2). There is some debate but, generally speaking, a structuralist approach is one that seeks for a hidden 'reality' underlying what seems

Table 4.2   Linguistic and Marxist structuralism

	Linguistic structuralism	Marxist structuralism
Intellectual tradition	Saussure's theories of linguistics, which attempt to understand the structures of language	Karl Marx's theories on society as organized around conflict between competing class interests and economic structures as determining how people can live
Central ideas	Societies are signifying systems based around structures of meaning. The connection between a sign and what it signifies is arbitrary, thus meaning is constructed through difference	Capitalism as a pursuit of profit structured around the exploitation of workers. Women's unpaid labour exploited within capitalism
Theorists	Barthes (semiotics), Lacan (psychoanalysis)	Marx, Engels and many later sociologists

obvious or apparent. By looking carefully at the deeper organizing principles of social life, structuralists believe they can discover the truth. Structuralists approach social theory like a jigsaw puzzle. They think society has a clear structure – or pattern – which, if they can put the pieces together correctly, they will be able to see. To varying degrees structuralists suggest that this social structure determines how we live our lives. This is called structural determinism. Arguably the most significant variant of structuralism for sociologists is that emerging from the work of Karl Marx.

Marxist structuralists have devoted much effort to explaining what types of structures underlie society and how those structures determine social relations, including gender relations. A capitalist society, Marxists argue, is one in which production of food and objects is organized for profit and produces class inequalities. They argue that the capitalists, or employers, who own the means of production (the machines, buildings and other equipment needed to make things) exploit the workers by only paying them a wage instead of sharing the profits that the workers' labour generates. However, this does not explain why women generally have an inferior social position to men. Marx saw paid productive work as central within capitalist society; it was left to his co-writer Engels (1985/1884) to explain a sexual division of labour in which women usually did the unpaid domestic labour, often as well as undertaking lower paid jobs outside the home. Feminists have tried to re-theorize these Marxist forms of structuralism to better explain women's position (see Chapter 7). In various forms most have argued that capitalist society is organized not just around the exploitation of paid productive labour but depends upon the unpaid labour of women in the home to feed and care for paid workers and reproduce a generation of new ones by having children. There is some argument as to whether women should therefore be considered a class (see Delphy, 1984), or whether women's position arises out of the ways in which capitalism and patriarchy interweave. The latter was sometimes called dual-systems theory, and Sylvia Walby's work (1986; 1990; 1996) provides an example. Yet these are not the only forms of structuralism which have had influence within sociology and feminist scholarship.

Linguistic structuralism has also played a part in explaining gender divisions by establishing the importance of language in creating our world. This form of structuralism emerged from the early twentieth-century work of the linguist Ferdinand de Saussure on the structures of language. Saussure (1983) wanted to understand how language worked as a system, and how it was a system that we were born into and had to use. People can use language in slightly different ways, but they have to follow the rules of language in order to be understood. There are agreed meanings for words and agreed ways of putting them together. So if I

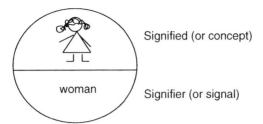

Figure 4.1   The sign

start referring to the sky as 'cabbage' people will not understand me and it will make social interaction very difficult. Saussure examined how language operated by breaking it down into what he thought was its basic unit: the sign (see Figure 4.1). The sign is made up of two parts that Saussure called the signified and the signifier, which are connected in an arbitrary way. The signified is the idea being represented (for example, the concept of female adult human being) and the signifier is what we use to represent that idea: in language this is a word (for example, the word 'woman'). In arguing that the sign is arbitrary, Saussure meant that there is no necessary connection between the concept (signified) and the word that stands for it. There is nothing in the word itself that tells us what it means. Everyone who speaks English agrees that the word 'woman' stands for the concept of female adult human being; they agree that because of tradition. Previous generations pass on what the word means. Different languages have different traditions and this shows that the connection between words and what they represent is arbitrary, and could be different. If this book was written in French then Figure 4.1 would have the same picture, but the signifier would be 'femme'. In saying that the sign is arbitrary, Saussure is taking part in a debate about where the meaning of words comes from. The other side of the debate suggests that words mean something because they refer to some material thing in the real world. Saussure argues that words refer not to actual things but to ideas about, or concepts of, things. He says that the meaning of words exists not in the words themselves, but in how they relate to other words within the system called language.

Within language meaning is constructed through difference (Saussure, 1983) and this argument has implications for understanding the way in which gender is constructed. We understand words by understanding how they relate to other words. So we understand a word because we know it is different to words with similar meanings and similar sounds. For example we understand the word cat by knowing it is different to words like lion and feline but also to words like mat and bat. We understand what is there by comparing it to what is absent. He argues, therefore, that binary oppositions are central to how we make sense of the world. So we can make sense of what black means because we understand it as what it is not – white. Cat makes sense as not dog, and so on. What Saussure also says is that the two terms in these sets of oppositions are not equal. It is not a case of A being understood in relation to B, but of A as opposed to not A. In other words meaning is established in terms of what is valued in society, as opposed to what is not valued, and this can be used to explain gender inequalities.

The way in which meaning is constructed within a male dominated society does not easily allow women to represent themselves except via rather limited patterns or images (see Kappeler, 1986). Women have performed a supporting function within masculine meaning systems, they have been defined as everything men are not (or do not wish to be). This means that women are viewed as 'other' and as lacking; but women are not always invisible. To reduce the threat men feel when confronted with their lack, women have been represented or encouraged to represent themselves as harmoniously beautiful. Their aesthetic perfection will disguise lack (Pollock, 1992: 147). Challenging the focus put on women's appearance, and the way in which women are stereotyped and sexualized, has been a central part of the feminist struggle. The difficulty has been in understanding how women play a part in constructing meaning; they do not simply consent to male definitions of them, which are in any case often contradictory. The ways in which binaries operate have been argued to play a large part in constructing gender differences.

If Saussure's ideas are extended in order to understand societies as 'signifying systems' based around structures of meaning (see Barthes, e.g. 1967 and Lacan, e.g. 1968, for instance), then gender operates as a symbolic distinction between masculine ('normal') as opposed to feminine (different and inferior). Gendered social life and relationships can be 'read' and interpreted in the same way that we read and interpret written texts. In order to read society as a text, linguistic structuralism reveals the hidden structures of meaning. Whether they focus on social structures or structures of meaning, structuralism emphasizes how individuals are constrained by wider social forces. Most classical, and indeed contemporary, sociology is structuralist in this sense.

As is evident from this brief account, there are feminists with structuralist leanings but some focus less on capitalism and instead argue that current social structures need to be primarily understood as patriarchal, or male dominated. Feminists who focus on patriarchy are often called radical feminists. This does not mean that radical feminists inevitably reject Marxist approaches and Christine Delphy could be described as a materialist radical feminist (Jackson, 1998b: 15). Feminists usually use the term patriarchal to describe societies in which men as a group are more likely to benefit from current social arrangements. There are disagreements about the definition and importance of patriarchy given that some individual men may be poorer and of lower status than some individual women, but most social scientists accept that societies are generally male dominated. One piece of evidence often used to support the argument that most so-called 'advanced' nations are still patriarchal is that women continue to earn less than men. Women in industrialized nations only earn about 75 to 80 per cent as much as men. Globally women's average incomes are just below 60 per cent of men's average incomes (Connell, 2002: 2; United Nations Statistics Division, 2005). Whilst helpful in supporting structuralist arguments about the importance of economic power, such statistics do not tell us much about the many different ways in which cultural meanings surrounding work might be important. However, there are other advantages to structuralist explanations of gender.

Advantages and disadvantages of the structuralist position in explaining gender

When applied to gender the advantages of the structuralist position are that it allows a discussion of gender relations in a way that makes it possible to argue that there are gender inequalities that need to be addressed politically. Women have just gained some status as subjects and need to speak out. There are still pressing issues regarding the unequal access of many women to resources (see Walby, 1996 and Chapter 1 above). Also a structuralist position is useful for criticizing conservative ideas about individualism, which suggest we can do whatever we want to and have only ourselves to blame if we do not succeed. Yet this approach has limitations in explaining gender relations.

There are several disadvantages to the structuralist position on gender. It can discourage us from thinking about diversity between women (see the problems with theoretical individualism outlined below). Structuralism's close connections with Marxism can mean economic factors are highlighted (for example, women get paid less) while cultural or symbolic factors (for example, a general devaluing of any tasks associated with women) are under-analyzed or ignored. Both Marxist and linguistic forms of structuralism have been accused of being overly deterministic, meaning they are thought to over-emphasize the extent to which people's lives are determined by social structure. Both are criticized for their assumption that individuals have very limited agency (power to act) to change social structures or social meanings.

Post-structralism

Post-structuralists are interested in fragmentation and fluidity. Post-structuralism is about rethinking linguistic structuralism rather than completely rejecting it. Most of post-structuralism goes against key structuralist assumptions (see discussion of the linguistic turn below). It proposes that there is no underlying 'truth' behind the appearances – the point is to analyze the 'appearances' (see Barthes, 1967, for example).

Foucault is one of the most influential figures in the move towards post-structuralism, especially for those interested in the sociology of gender. He has made critical use of insights from both linguistic and Marxist structuralism in ways that challenge both those perspectives and offer new ways of looking at the world. Interested both in 'things' and 'words', in both the material and meaning, Foucault sought to understand how the two connected, but in always shifting ways. He did not think there was one 'truth' to be discovered by looking at underlying rational structures. His work aimed to examine how changing **discourses** (systematically organized ways of making meaning such as psychiatric categorization) exert power upon human bodies. For example when he studied historical changes in systems of punishment, Foucault (1975/1979) argued that as imprisonment became the common form of punishment new ways of making meaning were also being established. Prisons were about watching people to make sure they behaved, but also were ideal places to collect information from observing people. This knowledge about people could then be used to design more efficient systems for controlling them. Foucault argued that a horribly efficient system of control was one in which prisoners could not be sure when or whether they were being watched. As a result prisoners had to assume they were being watched all the time and discipline, or control themselves, accordingly. Foucault argues that these discursive practices based around the idea of self-surveillance have become dominant not just within prisons, but within society as a whole. At school, for example, children learn to regulate their bodies and desires in order to fit into so-called 'normal' adult society. They learn to sit up straight, that it is preferable to go to the toilet in break time, and that they should be physically fit. Throughout our lives we learn to 'watch' ourselves, to constantly monitor our bodies and behaviour. Often we assume that we are doing what we want to do, but perhaps are merely doing what we think we 'should', because this internalized system of social control has become so effective. Feminists have found Foucault's ideas very useful, for example, in trying to understand how and why women discipline and shape their bodies in line with current discourses about what makes an attractive female body (see Chapter 5).

Foucault is important for the sociology of gender because he allows an understanding of how particular sets of ideas or meanings (discourses) have material effects upon bodies, but some of the pitfalls associated with structuralism remain. Much of Foucault's work is criticized for under-emphasizing agency and painting a picture of docile bodies determined

Table 4.3 **Structuralism and post-structuralism**

	Structuralism	post-structuralism
Intellectual tradition	Marxism & Saussure (see linguistic structuralism)	Reaction against Marxism (e.g. Foucault), influenced by linguistic structuralism, Austin: performatives
Central ideas applied to gender	Social structures construct gender differences. Women oppressed under (capitalist) patriarchy	Representation is everything. Gender differences are produced through language. 'Woman' is a social construction with no real basis
Feminist theorists	Sylvia Walby Ann Oakley	Denise Riley? Judith Butler?
Political leanings	Marxism, socialism, liberalism?	Radical, queer, apolitical?

if not by structures, then by the internalization of power. These pitfalls perhaps emerge because Foucault maintains an attachment to the world of material things, even if seeing it as shaped by meanings. This makes him a rather structural post-structuralist, but it also illustrates that materiality and meaning are not always so distinct. Links between ideas and economic or other forms of materiality have also been important within feminist thought, although distinctions can be made between 'materialist' feminism and a post-structuralist feminism interested in meaning.

Categorizing theoretical approaches within feminism

Feminism has a variety of forms as a political and an intellectual movement that has been concerned with inequalities as well as with the production of knowledge. It is therefore within the spirit of feminist enquiry that I want to raise some questions about how different ways of thinking within feminism are labelled. The labels 'liberal', 'socialist' and 'radical' are frequently used and it is helpful to know to what they might refer (for a summary see Table 4.4).

Liberal feminism

Liberal feminism emerged as part of **liberalism**: a political and intellectual doctrine promoting the ideals of equality of opportunity and the notion that individuals had certain rights. These included the right to liberty, the right to some say in who ruled them, and the right to pursue their own interests to achieve happiness – as long as this did not deliberately harm others. Liberalism was a child of the Enlightenment which occurred in eighteenth-century Europe. The **Enlightenment** was a major break with former ways of thinking based on tradition. It involved liberal thinkers such as John Locke, Thomas Hobbes and Jean-Jacques Rosseau. Central to this new intellectual understanding of the world were the ideas of reason and progress. Previously it was thought that society should be organized in the same way as in previous generations (according to tradition). But new thinkers proposed instead that it was time for social life to be determined by rational principles. In order for humanity to progress, it was argued, old beliefs had to be put aside. The light of science must be shone into the dark corners of ignorance and superstition. This decline in superstitious and religious belief is a process that Max Weber has described as 'disen-chantment' (Weber, 1968/1921; 1981/1927). If reason was to rule then old privileges could no longer be so easily justified as 'god-given' and, in the context of marked social changes, political upheaval followed. In the United States of America a war was fought to secure independence from British rule, and the resulting Declaration of Independence (1776) encapsulated many of the new ideas about individual rights to 'life, liberty, and the pursuit of happiness'. Shortly afterwards in France (1789), a revolution overthrew the monarchy and began principally the path to democracy. Other European and western nations were much affected by these events. Prior to the Enlightenment only men of property had polit-ical rights – Principally the right to vote – in these nations. Gradually, during the eighteenth and nineteenth century, voting and other rights were given to more of the population. But despite the protests of eighteenth-century women such as Mary Wollstonecraft, women (along with children, and indigenous and enslaved peoples) were not included.

Wollstonecraft's famous (1985) *Vindication of the Rights of Woman* was first published in 1792 and applies the liberal ideas of the Enlightenment to the situation of women. Wollstonecraft firmly supported the new emphasis on reason and used it to argue that women were the equals of men and the law should recognize them as such. Hers is a liberal call for independence – a call she applies to women, unlike others at that time. She is harshly critical of common and learned opinions about women's inferiority. Many books by 'great men' (and she names Rousseau) she thought aimed 'to degrade one half of the human species, and render women pleasing at the expense of every solid virtue' (Wollstonecraft, 1985: 104). Most of her argument is directed at demonstrating that women are creatures of reason and should have access to education. Through education, she thought, would come emancipation.

More recent liberal feminists follow Wollstonecraft in tending to accentuate the similarities between women and men, arguing that because women are fundamentally rational beings, like men, they should have the same opportunities and rights. Liberals believe that these rights can be obtained by reforming the present system, especially through changing legislation via democratic parliamentary channels. Current feminists arguably operating within the liberal tradition include Naomi Wolf and Martha Nussbaum (see Beasley, 2005).

Liberal feminists are mostly criticized for assuming that women can advance by being more like men and that this can be achieved via reform within the system. Such feminists tend to value competition, individual ambition and advancement through work in the public sphere. As Chris Beasley (2005: 34) puts it: '[i]f liberal feminism were a shirt it would probably be pinstriped and have shoulder-pads. It dresses for success'. However, some of these criticisms suggest that such qualities are simply 'male' and inevitably bad. Liberals would disagree, saying that women are capable of succeeding in the ways men have succeeded and this shows that such qualities do not belong to men and that things can change. They might suggest that if women enter the public world this will bring subtle alterations so that aggressive competition and other arguably less desirable features of the public sphere might become less valued. But usually, it is true that liberal feminism seems to assume that women have to fit into the present system, rather than that system changing. This provokes other feminists to criticize them for not going far enough in their demands. Evans (1995: 15) says liberal feminists can be understood as merely wanting women to have more chance of securing social rewards (for example, high paying jobs) given out in a hierarchical way. Liberals do not often seem interested in reorganizing how social rewards are distributed. Such an interest in reorganizing the social system in order to achieve a fairer distribution of social 'goodies' is what distinguishes socialism from liberalism.

Socialist and materialist feminism

Feminists starting from the socialist position of wanting to redistribute social rewards struggle to understand how class and gender might interrelate. Socialist and materialist feminists draw their political theory from Marxist materialism, which argues that 'the determining factor in history is, in the final instance, the production and reproduction of immediate life' (Engels cited in Kuhn and Wolpe, 1978: 7). They then worked to adapt this theory to (better) explain gender inequalities (see Chapter 7). Marxist feminists usually saw gender inequalities as caused by capitalism, while materialist feminists saw women as a class. In the former case they tried to use Marxist theories to understand women's domestic labour as essential to capitalism. Women have historically done the work of reproducing workers, both by giving birth to them and by feeding, clothing, and caring for them so that they can go out to work. The unpaid labour that this reproduction of paid labour involves has gone largely unrecognized. Because of this domestic role women have also formed a reserve army of cheap labour, used by capitalists whenever there is a shortage of men and then discarded at times of higher unemployment – often because of pressure from male-dominated trade unions. However, this argument fails to take account of the fact that women usually do different paid jobs to men, rather than simply standing in for them (Beechey, 1978). Marxist theory also does not explain why it is women that do domestic labour and, if that is unclear, it is also unclear why women should be the reserve army (see Jackson, 1998b: 16).

Those who understood women as a class focused on the way in which social relations were not simply capitalist, but also patriarchal. The French materialist feminist Christine Delphy (1984), for example, argued that the relation between husbands and wives could be seen as exploitative. Men, rather than recognizing women's work in the household by handing over a standard part of their income in return for their wives' domestic labour, only 'give' women enough for their basic needs (perhaps in the form of room and board or 'housekeeping'). Others such as Heidi Hartmann (1981) and Sylvia Walby (1986) developed a dual-systems theory that attempted to see capitalism and patriarchy as systems that connected through the labour market. Feminists tended to move towards a position in the 1980s where patriarchy was seen as existing not just within capitalism but within a range of historical conditions (Jackson, 1998b: 17–18). Yet the focus on materialism was felt by other feminists to be inadequate in explaining women's social position, leading to the emergence of radical feminism.

Radical feminism

Radical feminists argued that male control of women's sexuality was a key factor in women's oppression (see Dworkin, 1981; Kelly, 1988; MacKinnon, 1982). Kate Millet and Shulamith Firestone are the most visible of the first radical feminist theorists and certainly attended to sexuality, though Jackson (1998b: 19–20) suggests that Firestone is rather idiosyncratic. Millet's (1972/1970) book *Sexual Politics* was hugely influential and like other key feminists who published books in the same period (Firestone's *Dialectic of Sex*, 1972; Germaine Greer's *Female Eunuch*, 1970; Eva Figes's *Patriarchal Attitudes*, 1978/1970 – see Chapter 5 for what they said about bodies). Millet undertook the rather daunting task of explaining the causes of women's oppression. Her explanation took women's domination by men (patriarchy) as central to their social position. This inferior position, according to Millet, was not a product of 'natural' differences between women and men. Instead she rigorously examined the sociocultural production of women by redefining the concept of politics. Previously it was used to talk about decision-making in the public sphere. She broadened the definition, seeing politics as referring to 'power-structured relationships, arrangements whereby one group of persons is controlled by another' (Millet, 1972/1970: 23). This was part of a new understanding of the personal as political, which is discussed in Chapter 6. Millet provides a broad theory of how patriarchy operates through ideology (for example, myth & religion), institutions (for example, family, education, economy) and force (for example, wife-beating and rape). Although she recognizes class and race as variables in women's oppression, she tends to emphasize that all women are subject to oppression by men. For example, she argues that lower status males can use sex/violence over higher status women. She illustrates all of these ideas by looking at the literary reaction against women's emancipation as expressed in the work of D.H. Lawrence, Henry Miller and Norman Mailer. These texts exemplify the ways in which women are controlled and subjugated by being sexually objectified and physically dominated. This makes *Sexual Politics* far more than literary criticism, but Millet perhaps makes her theory too grand. There are doubts about whether patriarchy has the transhistorical character she claims. The argument that all women are oppressed is perhaps overgeneralized and commonalities between women overstated.

There were criticisms of radical feminism for assuming that 'women' shared relatively universally in the disadvantages reinforced by patriarchy, but this was arguably a feature of most male theorizing of the time. Most dominant thinking worked at large-scale philosophizing and universalized in ways that excluded 'others', such as women. Radical feminism attempted to highlight women's experiences by going beyond purely economic explanations of women's oppression to include ideology, and literary and other representations of women. In order to overcome that oppression radical feminists were not content to reform the present system, they envisaged a more revolutionary overturning of present ways of thinking about and organizing the world. However this perhaps oversimplifies the wide range of ideas which are sometimes forced under the radical feminist banner, and draws attention to problems with the classification of different types of feminism covered so far.

The typical labelling of feminists as liberal, socialist, or radical, best describes British feminism (Holmes, 1999), although these labels do have some relevance for feminism in other Commonwealth nations (Beasley, 1999). They can also be applied to American feminism but 'radical' will

Table 4.4   Feminist 'labels'

	Liberal feminism	Socialist/materialist feminism	Radical feminism
Intellectual tradition	Liberal modernism, Mary Wollstonecraft	Marxism, historical materialism	Marxism, liberation theory
Central ideas and views of women	Women are rational individuals entitled to the same social privileges as men	Women are oppressed because of capitalism or can be seen as a class, exploited through the capitalist sexual division of labour	Women are repressed within patriarchy, their sexuality controlled & experiences limited
Some theorists	Nussbaum, Woolf	Delphy, Rowbotham	Firestone, Millett, Jackson
Political goals	Reform within the system	Gender inequalities will disappear after revolution or socialist redistribution	Revalue 'feminine' values such as an ethic of care, feminist revolution

describe a slightly different political and theoretical approach to the one it applies to in Britain (Holmes, 1999). In America radical feminism is sometimes also called cultural feminism (Echols, 1989). Even within Britain and America these labels do not always fit all those involved in the feminist movement from the 1960s onwards and elsewhere the labels become even more difficult to apply. It is unclear, for instance, where those feminists interested in the intersections between racism and sexism might fit. The strong connection in America between the civil rights campaign to end racist segregation and legal discrimation in the USA can perhaps be covered by the 'liberal' label, but this does not fit other women's collective action against, say, the effects of colonization. So, for example, the thought and activities of black women/women of colour can become marginalized by this way of thinking about feminism. Also, to suggest that these are simply theoretical approaches ignores how they have been used in political action. Even those most intent on 'action' had some sense of why they thought women were oppressed, in order to decide what needed to be 'done'. This required rethinking whether feminists should focus on righting inequalities.

Equality/difference – the feminist debate

A debate emerged within feminism about whether its political goal was gender equality or whether women's differences, from men and each

Table 4.5   The equality/difference debate within feminism

	Equality	Difference
Central ideas	Rational individuals have certain rights that should be common to all	Women's difference (even if not 'natural') should be recognized and valued. Sometimes separatists
View of women	Women are equal, practically the same as men	Women are different, but not appreciated within patriarchy

other, needed to be valued. Although feminists can be grouped into those with equality or difference stances, this tends to oversimplify the way such ideas have been used within feminism. Often individual feminists might at different times employ both equality and difference arguments. For example, if campaigning for equal pay then their argument might be that women can do a job the same as a man and should be paid the same. However, when discussing maternity leave there may be a need to draw attention to women as different from men because of their ability to bear children. Claims that the workforce should allow for and value this difference might be politically appropriate (see Bacchi, 1990).

Arguably, however, those who consistently focus on equality are likely to be liberal feminists, while an attention to women's difference from men is typically part of a radical stance. Equality feminists are usually interested in reform within the present system. If the goal is equality of opportunity to compete for hierarchically distributed resources then there is likely to be little attention given to fostering equality for all women and radical social change is not contemplated (Evans, 1995: 15). In contrast, radicals are highly critical of present social systems in which women, and all associated with them, are devalued because of their difference from men. Men are seen as the standard, the norm against which women are measured and usually found lacking. But if women are different, of what does that difference consist? I will discuss elsewhere (especially in Chapters 2 and 5) debates about whether there is an essence common to all women, which distinguishes them from men. Claiming that women are different can fall into biological essentialism whereby bodies are supposed to determine ways of thinking and being. However, when feminists accentuate difference they rarely propose that anatomy is destiny. In most cases, while recognizing that female bodies may provide experiences (such as menstruation) that male bodies do not, the emphasis is usually on the way that these bodily (and other) experiences have been constructed within patriarchy. For example, a focus on women's generally smaller and lighter bodies might be seen not as 'natural' but as brought about by centuries of male domination in which women are typically allocated and expected to eat less food. The smallness of women may partly be passed on genetically but will be reinforced by sociocultural eating practices. Difference theorists might also question whether heaviness and largeness should be seen as superior, especially when the maintenance of such physiques and their power over the small might be used to continue to justify men's larger share of food resources. The problem with difference then is not difference itself, but the fact that under patriarchy women's supposed difference has been constructed as inferior. In order to bring about radical political change, it is argued that the entire patriarchal system needs to be overthrown. Competitiveness, aggression, individualism and other 'masculine' values are reinforced if women merely campaign for equality on men's terms. Rather, values associated with women, such as care, should be celebrated and encouraged in all people.

When difference is thought of as difference from men, this tends to universalize 'women' and remove them from specific historical and cultural contexts. Though the radical implications of celebrating 'womanly' virtues are seductive, the virtues recommended may be historically and culturally specific. What is 'womanly' in one culture or time may be 'manly' in another, as discussed in Chapter 2. The typical emphasis on care as a key womanly virtue in modern Western society can also be highly problematic given that this 'virtue' has been central to women's oppression and possibly produced by that oppression (Evans, 1995: 19). This does not mean it is bad that many women believe in caring for others and possibly devote themselves to doing so. It means that women are often compelled into taking on caring duties because other options are closed to them and because the pressure for them to do so is immense. Certainly within contemporary Western societies men benefit considerably from not having the expectation or the work of caring placed on them. So both a focus on equality and a focus on difference have their problems, but consideration of both has been crucial within feminism.

Equality and difference strands have existed throughout the feminist political movement and certainly in Western second-wave feminism, involved trying to understand differences between women. I do not accept that in the late 1960s and early 1970s there was a cosy sisterhood focused on changing the world for women, which was later broken up by naughty black, lesbian, working class and 'other' feminists who unhelpfully accentuated different identities and priorities among women (Holmes, 2004). Feminism has always been a debate, one overly dominated by white Western feminists, but one in which feminists of 'different' colours, sexual orientations, classes, abilities and so on have always participated. These identities often overlapped (if you were a black, working class lesbian for example) and did not automatically produce a particular approach to feminism, though they may lead women to prioritize different issues. And women from different backgrounds often shared common political approaches. What emerged from these debates was that the connection between inequalities and identity was by no

Table 4.6 Types of feminism

	Liberal feminism	Marxist/socialist feminist	Radical feminist	Equality	Difference
Intellectual tradition	Liberal modernism, Mary Wollstonecraft	Marxism	Marxism, liberation theory	Liberal modernist theory or socialism	Lacan and French feminism or lesbian political theory
Central ideas and views of women	Women are rational individuals entitled to the same social privileges as men	Women can be seen as a class, exploited through the capitalist sexual division of labour	Women are oppressed within patriarchy, especially through male control of sexuality	Rational individuals have certain rights that should be common to all	Women's difference (even if not 'natural') means they have special needs (feminine)
Some theorists	Friedan, Nussbaum Wolf	Delphy, Rowbotham	Millet, Jackson, Firestone	Beauvoir, Oakley	Irigaray, Young?
Political goals	Reform within the system	Gender inequalities will disappear after revolution, or socialist redistribution	Revalue 'feminine' values such as an ethic of care, feminist revolution	Redistribute wealth and social rewards	Difference should be recognized and valued

means clear and this prompted many feminists, and other scholars, to take a turn towards culture.

The Cultural/Linguistic Turn

In relation to explaining gender the cultural turn (sometimes called the linguistic turn) was a turn away from an emphasis on inequalities and towards more exploration of identity and meanings (see Table 4.7). Generally speaking the linguistic turn refers to a theoretical shift, across the humanities and social sciences, away from a focus on material things and towards concentration on language and representation. In sociology this 'cultural turn' moved away from the Marxist-influenced attention to structural and especially economic factors as determining social life and towards cultural studies' preoccupations with meaning (see Chaney, 1994). Michèle Barrett (1992) outlines four parts to the linguistic turn.

The first aspect of the linguistic turn was a critique of theoretical universalism. Theoretical universalism refers to the tendency of theorists to universalize, to make statements that seem to apply to everybody and everything (Barrett, 1992). Many classical sociological theories, for instance, have set out to try and find universal laws explaining how all of society works, but were basing their ideas on the experiences of white European men. More recent scholars – including Foucault and many feminists – were critical of such grand claims, and so were moving away from 'grand narratives' (large stories attempting to explain all) and towards more contextualized theorizing. Feminists also became critical of their own early theorizing that spoke about 'women's oppression' because this assumed that women are all the same. Trying to avoid theoretical universalism has been helpful in thinking about gender because it must be remembered that there are many different kinds of women. However, others argue that theorists need to make some generalizations if they are going to say anything, and especially if they are going to get people to work together towards political goals (see Chapter 6).

The second part of the linguistic turn, according to Barrett (1992), was the critique of rationalism and the subject. Rationality has historically been associated with masculinity and therefore feminist theorists needed to be critical of it. There is a long history to this association which I do not have space for here (see Lloyd, 1984), so I will confine myself to its more recent forms. Modern notions of reason and rational subjects (self-aware human actors) within Western thought developed most strongly from René Descartes' seventeenth-century declaration: 'I think therefore I am'. His philosophical understanding of what it means to exist as a human being established an oppositional hierarchy between the mind as the seat of reason, and the body as a disorderly vessel of sensation and emotion that must be kept under control. Women, due to their reproductive capacities, were thought closer to nature and to their bodies and thus deemed incapable of reason. These Western ideas about women's lack of rationality were long used to justify their inferior social status and deny them rights enjoyed by their brothers, such as the right to education and the right to vote (Bordo, 1987; Pateman, 1988). Post-structuralists criticized Cartesian (meaning 'following Descartes') ways of comprehending what it means to be human for assuming that we are always consciously aware of ourselves and in control of what we are doing. Post-structuralists instead think about the decentred subject. They argue that the self cannot form a basis for understanding human existence, because it is not the stable entity that Descartes assumed it to be. They argue that people have multiple selves and unconscious or irrational desires might often shape behaviour. Feminists were sympathetic to many of these criticisms of rationalism and the subject, but also reminded male poststructuralists that for women the problem had been them being thought irrational, when rationality was what was valued. That was one of the arguments Mary Wollstonecraft (1985/1792) made in the eighteenth century. Some status as rational subjects was tardily granted to different groups of women throughout the twentieth century. To suddenly declare that rationality was over-rated and that the subject is dead was frustrating in the extreme for many women, especially women of colour, who were only just finding a voice to exert a sense of subjectivity and speak of their experiences (see Chapters 6, 7 and 8). Yet feminists such as Denise Riley (1988) and Judith Butler (1992), advocating post-structuralist views of the subject, felt strongly that to continue to talk of women as subjects in the old way was to be caught again in the problems of falsely universalizing. Not all women are alike, and a notion of fragmented identities may have a lot to offer in thinking about how differences between women could be thought through. However, this recognition of diversity was combined with a need to consider women's general exclusion from the modernist project. This refers to the way in which the modern world was masculinized.

The third part of the linguistic turn involved highlighting this gendering of modernity (Barrett, 1992). Feminists directed their attention to the way in which the transition from a traditional agrarian into a complex modern industrial society has been associated with masculinity. The whole notion of the modern as reasoned scientific progress made the ideal 'modern' individual a male. Women continued to be thought of as irrational and ruled by emotions. Therefore feminists recognized that modernity was a project based on the exclusion of women. But feminism as a political project has relied hugely on modernist liberal ideas. Feminists are therefore aware of the gendered limitations of modernist thinking but often reluctant to abandon it totally. One crucial thread they did strive to rethink was what materialism might mean and what role the material might play in shaping society.

Barrett's (1992) outline of the linguistic turn looks fourthly and finally at the critique of materialism. This meant thinking through the limitations of analyses which focused on the material conditions of society such as how objects were made and the access of different groups to resources. This critique entailed relinquishing a materialist model of people, their lives and ideas as determined by the social structure. Other traditions of thought emphasizing experience and subjective interpretations were revitalized. These included phenomenology, which is discussed especially in relation to bodies in Chapter 5. In particular economic explanations were criticized and wider meanings of the 'material' beyond the economic were taken up (Rahman and Witz, 2003). One key example of how the linguistic turn shifted approaches to gender towards a concern with meaning was queer theory.

Queer theory

Queer theories further the disconnection of gender from sex and radically repudiate binary classifications of gender as identity. In queer theory social expectations that cast heterosexuality as the 'natural' and 'normal' form of sexuality are criticized. These forms of theory emerged from gay politics and therefore the dominance of heterosexuality rather than gender inequalities is emphasized (Beasley, 2005). Queer theorists often attend to practices they claim are ways of doing gender that transgress the binary divide. For queer theorists (for example, Jagose, 1996; Seidman, 1996) identities are multiple, fragmented and constantly shifting. Sexual preferences are not seen as fixed and desires are not static. Queer theory claims to be a celebration of radical diversity. It assumes that people can find space to play with and transform norms about sexuality that privilege heterosexuality and regard other forms of sexual practice as 'abnormal'. It can be argued that queer theory reflects the 'queer tendencies' of postmodernity, which has reorganized relations of sexuality. A full account of these queer tendencies would cover the self-critical nature of queer, the ways in which heterosexual relations have become less socially central, a move towards reflecting on heterosexuality as not necessarily self-evident, and the celebration of the queer within contemporary culture (Roseneil, 2000). This is not, however, the place for such a broad coverage. The key contribution of queer theory as an example of the linguistic turn in approaches to gender is that it provides 'a critical analysis of modern homo/heterosexual definition' (Sedgwick cited in Roseneil, 2000: 1).

In trying to understand gender we need to appreciate the centrality of heterosexuality in formulating identities and the socially approved relationships between identity categories. In other words, heterosexuality is crucial as a foundation for the categories 'woman' and 'man'. Convention has it that in the 'natural' course of things, boys will grow into men who will desire women. Man and woman will then reproduce and all will be as it 'should' be (Butler, 1993). To free desire and thereby sexuality it is therefore thought necessary to be free of such heterosexist stories. To this end Roseneil (2000) advocates merging elements of a queer perspective with sociological analysis of social changes relating to sexuality. This can expose the ways in which meanings and practices around sexuality have altered historically and thereby would help to denaturalize heterosexuality. In particular Roseneil (2000: 2.3) feels that there is much sociology can learn from queer theory's focus on culture, especially if this is understood within a recognition of the postmodern world as 'characterized by "economies of signs"'. What Roseneil is recommending is that by attending to meanings it is possible to understand and to challenge the central part that heterosexuality has played in perpetuating gender identities as fixed and as determining how we relate to whom.

There are others who feel that queer theory is over-optimistic in proposing the end of the gender binary man/woman. It can underestimate 'sedimented' gender patterns and their accompanying inequalities. Jeffrey Weeks (1985; 2000), for example, remains sceptical of the possibilities offered by the deconstructing of identities. He continues to advocate the need to reclaim gay and lesbian identities, albeit in flexible and diverse forms. Weeks (1985) argues that meanings surrounding homosexuality are not entirely open but a product of particular social and historical locations which tend to restrict non-heterosexuals. Beasley (2005: 157, 170) notes that others propose that the focus of queer theory on non-heterosexuals does not go far enough in undermining gender identity. Whilst discussing heterosexuality is clearly not always helpful in achieving a political shift towards the queer, it does seem contradictory if it is suggested that heterosexuality is somehow inherently non-subversive. It is also possible, as Connell (1995) has argued, that not all non-heterosexuals are inevitably subverting the gender order. Gender hierarchies can be reinforced not only by the way in which supposedly transgressive performances of gender play out (Jeffreys, 1996) but also by the way in which queer theory itself sometimes 'plays out'. But how does this relate to shifts from structuralism to post-structuralism in explaining how gender operates?

The explanations of structuralism and post-structuralism above broadly indicate that post-structuralism involves all four aspects of the linguistic turn in explaining gender. Most post-structuralist feminists still recognize that society is gendered. They focus on objecting to the way that binary structures always represent masculinity as superior. The critique of materialism involved in post-structuralism emphasizes words over things – deconstructing representations becomes the focus, rather than assuming that we need to search for an underlying social reality. This gives more attention to different ways in which people see their world, whereas structuralism does tend to assume that social scientists know best, or at least that ordinary people can be sadly mistaken in their interpretations. Yet post-structuralism has faults in addition to its possibilities.

Advantages and disadvantages of post-structuralism

Advantages of the post-structuralist position for thinking about gender are that it allows some consideration of to what extent we have freedom to choose, rather than implying that our lives are determined by our social surroundings. This might be especially beneficial for women, because they have historically been denied **agency** but have found ways to resist domination. Structuralism can make it difficult to get away from seeing women as victims and that can be disempowering for women hoping and acting for change. However, post-structuralism can reinforce ideas about individualism which are prominent in Western societies. These ideas imply that individuals are responsible for their own lives and if they do not succeed, it is their own fault. Such a view assumes that there is a level playing field on which all people engage, yet as we have seen there are many inequalities which can make it more difficult for some people to succeed than others. Nevertheless, post-structuralism can allow exploration of the contradictions and complexities of living gender because it is not so focused on economic structures. Also, because it focuses on the fluidity and fragmentation of the self it allows us to consider diversity in ways that are critical of a self versus other hierarchy. These are all issues that I will return to frequently in later chapters, but there are other faults to post-structuralism.

The principal disadvantage of the post-structuralist position is its **relativism**, which potentially means seeing different ways of doing gender as equally valid if understood relative to their own cultural context. Relativism tends to describe differences and see things as open to different interpretations, rather than to evaluate social practices against some underlying truth. This may have advantages in some situations, but can be politically naïve and critically lacking. If there is no 'Truth' does anything go? Or do we follow Foucault (e.g. 1963/1973) when he suggested that there are dominant discourses? If there are dominant discourses then I would argue that the responsibility of critical scholarship is to think about who these dominant discourses privilege and how? This can be done using post-structuralist ideas as long as the 'who' and the 'how' are not talked about as though they are fixed and unchanging. For example, dominant discourses are – among other things – arguably patriarchal. Those discourses operate within particular socio-historical conditions to

Table 4.7   The Linguistic turn

	The linguistic turn
Critique of theoretical universalism	Move away from the idea that theories can explain everything everywhere
Critique of rationality & the subject	Criticism of ideas about the self as conscious, rational and in control. Challenges the idea that conscious self-awareness can form the basis for understanding human existence
The gendering of modernity	Elaborating how the idea of modernity was associated with masculinity: rational progress, science, control etc
The critique of materialism	A questioning of ways of thinking that focus on things rather than on representation. Rejection of notion of social structure as determining all else (e.g. culture, beliefs)

create gender relationships that are unequal. The challenge is to analyze those shifting relationships without always seeing men as having power and women not.

The linguistic turn has its limitations in meeting the challenge of re-examining gendered power relations. Roseneil (1995) argues that within that turn, ideas already existing within feminism are reinvented and mystified. For example, the idea of 'woman' as a historical and shifting construction is not just Denise Riley's (1988), but was present within feminist thought formerly. Roseneil also proposes that those who have taken the cultural turn overemphasize fragmentation and ignore structural power. In addition she suggests that feminist thought has suffered from this intellectual shift because many scholars have lost touch with the materiality of gendered experience.

Conclusion

This chapter has endeavoured to map some of the key feminist theories in relation to their historical and intellectual context, in order to provide some guidance in reading the rest of this book. Those feminist theories are here located in relation to broad developments in social theory. Initially these developments are discussed in terms of the emergence of post-structuralism out of structuralism. A structuralist search for truth within the social or linguistic framework allowed attention to gender inequalities and their possible redress. Too much insistence on unitary gender identity was however exclusionary. This was replaced by a poststructuralist denial of any clear 'reality' and a focus on representation, which can perhaps provide the basis for a more radical undermining of the exclusionary nature of gender and other binaries. Yet this requires other shifts within feminism itself.

Feminist thought contained political goals of working towards equality, but also intellectual goals of better understanding gender differences. Commonly used categories describing feminism as liberal, socialist or radical, highlight that radical feminism was a challenge to existing political traditions in which equality was central. Liberals emphasized reform as the way to extend existing privileges to women, whilst socialists saw more revolutionary redistributions of those privileges as necessary. Radical feminists thought the meanings attached to women as different sexual beings needed attention and more positive recognition of their difference was thought crucial to achieving social change. However, such a story might imply that equality and difference were separately pursued by separate groups, rather than being strategies employed by all feminists as they thought appropriate. It was, however, perhaps partly the complexity of trying to establish to what extent women were different from men and from each other that prompted the cultural/linguistic turn towards an exploration of identity and meanings.

The linguistic turn in social theory was about a new focus on language and representation, the merits of which were hotly disputed by feminists and sociologists of gender. Whether it offers an escape from materialist determinism or merely an apolitical relativizing of gender as simply another kind of difference are questions that will be returned to elsewhere in the book. What this chapter has done is provide a large-scale view of the theoretical landscape in which sociological and feminist ideas about gender are located. This is intended to assist in evaluating – here and throughout the book – how gender might be best understood. Chapter 6 makes use of what has been learnt from the cultural turn to revisit the topic of bodies and the part they play in gendering.

Key readings

Barrett, M. (1992) 'Words and things: materialism and method in contemporary feminist analysis', in M. Barrett and A. Phillips (eds), *Destabilizing Theory: Contemporary Feminist Debates*. Cambridge: Polity Press.

Beasley, C. (2005) *Gender and Sexuality: Critical Theories, Critical Thinkers*. London: Sage.

Jackson, S. and Jones, J. (eds) (1998) *Contemporary Feminist Theories*. Edinburgh: Edinburgh University Press.

Roseneil, S. (1995) 'The coming of age of feminist sociology: Some issues of practice and theory for the next twenty years', *British Journal of Sociology*, 46 (2): 191–205.

5

Is gender about bodies?

> Even in the most simple body orientations of men and women as they sit, stand, and walk, one can observe a typical difference in body style and extension. Women are generally not as open with their bodies as men are in their gait and stride. Typically, the masculine stride is longer proportional to a man's body than is the feminine to a woman's. The man typically swings his arms in a more open and loose fashion than does a woman and typically has more up and down rhythm in his step. (Young, 1990: 145)

It is important to explode myths about the naturalness and fixity of sex differences (see Chapter 2), but this does not mean denying that bodies have any role in how gender is lived. This chapter is therefore an attempt to explain how sociologists, partly in response to the cultural turn, have tried to 'bring the body back in' to their understandings of gender. Sociological analysis of how bodies become gendered has focused on challenging essentialist approaches. Early second-wave feminism was extremely influential in providing insights into the social construction of women's (and men's) bodies as oppressed or resisting. In further exploring the ways in which the gendering of bodies is a social process, the importance of Foucault's work is examined. Alternative approaches such as corporeal feminism and phenomenology are then critically assessed. Overall this chapter centres around debates about the strengths and limitations of emphasizing the social construction of bodies and considers the possibilities of thinking of the body as both a material and a symbolic entity.

Gender and the sociology of the body

Only recently has 'the body' come to figure as a specific field within sociology (see Turner, 1984), but it crystallized many of the difficulties sociologists of gender had long grappled with in trying to understand women's bodies as something other than a problem to be overcome. First, there has been dissatisfaction with what some feminists have described as the 'masculinization of thought' entailed within the Enlightenment project in the West (Bordo, 1987). This has included dualistic conceptualizations of bodies originating from René Descartes' view of the self as a thinking self (I think therefore I am). Women have been thought problematically close to nature, while men were associated with cultured reason (Bordo, 1987; Lloyd, 1984; Riley, 1988: 20–1). Secondly there have been politically motivated attempts to better account for the social processes of power which define certain bodies (especially white men's) as 'normal' and others, such as women's, as 'abnormal'. Thirdly, the sociology of the body responded to recent social changes in which bodily appearance has become increasingly important (Blaikie et al., 2003). In addition, there has been a questioning of scientific and medical models of bodies that have been dominant since the eighteenth century. The 'two-sex model' of sexual difference (see Chapter 2) that emerged as part of the new Enlightenment worldview meant that women were totally defined by their bodies in a way they had not been in the past (Laqueur, 1990). The new biomedical models saw bodies as machines that are a collection of parts and doctors are like mechanics, tinkering around and repairing the faulty bits (Freund and Mcguire, 1999). Although this model of bodies may often be useful, such as when I break my leg and want it treated, it may not be such a useful way of diagnosing illnesses or understanding and treating more complex ailments such as chronic fatigue or cancer (Saks, 2001; Sointu, 2006). However, alternative therapies and remedies can also enforce the regulation of gendered bodies, which makes that sphere less challenging to consumerism and medicalization than it might initially appear (Sharma, 1996). The difficulty with all these ways of thinking about bodies is that women's bodies have been understood as deviant and problematic. Women have been thought unable to transcend their bodies in order to achieve 'proper' humanity. It is this 'problem' of woman's immanence that Simone de Beauvoir (1988/1949) struggles with in *The Second Sex*. Whether the body is necessarily a 'problem' for women has been rethought in the work of later feminists, who have challenged these historical associations of women with the body. I focus on the development of various ways of understanding bodies as socially constructed, all of which can be primarily defined as refutations of essentialism. Therefore I begin by explaining essentialism.

Essentialism: Gendered bodies are a reflection of 'natural' characteristics

Essentialism is the idea that there are identifiable necessary properties which define objects, for example it supposes that there is some essence (usually with a bodily basis) which is what makes a woman a woman. This might be the potential to bear children, a more caring attitude, or having a female body. Things like a caring attitude are defined as bodily in that they are thought to stem from women's childbearing capacities. Within essentialist thinking about gender the 'natural' or real body is understood to be the basis onto which social and cultural ideas about femininity and masculinity are imposed. There is thought to be an undeniability and authenticity to the body which are drawn on to build identity. For feminists who tend toward essentialism, the problem is that the essence of womanhood is not valued and difficult to express within a male-dominated society. American radical feminists Mary Daly and Adrienne Rich are often described as essentialists. Rich is perhaps less purely so, but then her work is perhaps more typical in that it shows a tendency toward essentialism without wholly ignoring the social.

Essentialism peeks through Rich's attempt to see motherhood as socially constructed. In *Of Woman Born* Rich (1986/1976) explores motherhood as a social institution and as an embodied and emotional experience. She critically explores the unrealistic social constructions of motherhood, discussing how guilty mothers feel when they cannot measure up to social expectations that they should always love their children single-mindedly and unconditionally. Rich argues that mothering is made difficult because women struggle to control their own bodies and thus their own lives. However, there is presumed to be some natural, 'free' body which can be recognized as liberating and beautiful. For example, the bond between mothers and children, whilst 'overlaid by social and traditional circumstances' is seen as 'always there from the first gaze between the mother and the infant at the breast' (Rich, 1986/1976: 32). For Rich the problem is that 'natural' bodily processes, including childbirth and rearing, are managed and/or dictated by men instead of women. The implication is that there is some core womanliness within the embodied experience of women, which can be freed from patriarchal distortions so that women can reconnect with it and move from passive suffering 'to a new active being' (Rich, 1986/1976: 129). With less male meddling women might come to see childbirth, and other embodied experiences they have as women, 'as one way of knowing and coming to terms with our bodies, of discovering our physical and psychic resources' (Rich, 1986/1976: 157). This assumes that there is some essence that can be discovered.

Most feminist writers, including Rich, are never wholly essentialist, appreciating that femininity is to some degree a social production (Fuss, 1989). However, Rich struggles to escape notions of a female body sending 'invisible messages of an urgency and restlessness which indeed cannot be appeased' (1986/1976: 284). Such an approach to the body is problematic for many feminists, and perhaps especially for sociologists who argue that bodies are socially constructed.

Constructionism: Bodies are gendered by social processes

Constructionist arguments oppose essentialism by proposing that gender is about conforming to social expectations. Goffman is a pioneer in considering the social construction of the body, especially in his work on stigma (Goffman, 1968), but his contribution to thinking about gendered bodies (Goffman, 1979) is sometimes overlooked (see Chapter 2). Goffman's work shows how distinctions between 'normal' and 'deviant' are crucial in how bodies are controlled and experienced. For Goffman gender is a form of tribal stigma, which marks half the population as having deviant bodies and determines that they must be interacted with in particular ways that reinforce the idea that men are 'naturally' superior. Yet he was not the first to consider that gender was a social rather than a 'natural' distinction.

Simone de Beauvoir (1988/1949), without the aid of the concept of gender, proclaimed in the 1940s what can be taken as the fundamental idea behind constructionism: that one *becomes* a woman. It is rather more recently that sociologists of gender have considered how one becomes a man (see Morgan, 1993). A classic example of early sociological thinking about gender as a social construction is Oakley's 1972 book *Sex, Gender and Society*, which is credited with bringing the term gender into the social sciences (Oakley, 1997: 32), although the concept does appear in some of the widely read classics of second wave feminist literature (see Greer, 1970; Millet, 1972/1970). Oakley's book is discussed in Chapter 3, but very briefly the key points on social construction are repeated here.

To say that gender is socially constructed was to resist ideas about women which assumed that differences between women and men were biological and therefore unchangeable. There was the need for 'a way of separating the bodies of human beings from their social fates' (Oakley, 1997: 29). Oakley did this by distinguishing 'sex' as 'the biological differences between male and female: the visible difference in genitalia, the related difference in procreative function. "Gender" however is a matter of culture: it refers to the social classification into masculine and feminine' (Oakley, 1972: 16). Gender as a concept therefore focused initially on how social factors, not bodies, determined people's behaviour. This involved investigating to what extent the sexes are physically different, and whether those differences are a product of environment (see Chapter 2). Evidence is presented of different ways of expressing femininity and masculinity across history and cultures. Oakley (1972: 30) refers to many studies, one being Geoffrey Gorer's accounts of the similarities between men's and women's bodies in Bali. She also notes the huge range of anthropological work indicating that in most cultures women do the bulk of the work, usually including the carrying of heavy burdens. Biological accounts which see how women and men use their bodies as the result of innate, 'natural', biological forces cannot explain such variation. For constructionists, social context is crucial in producing gendered bodies.

Constructionism might explain variations in how gender is done in different cultures as a product of different socialization and social institutions, but it can struggle to account for variations within the same culture. Sometimes biology is simply replaced by social environment as the all-powerful determining factor in how bodies are gendered. Too much focus on gender socialization, especially in the early years, assumes children passively accept gender norms and tends to cast those who do not as imperfectly socialized, rather than resisting (Stanley and Wise, 1983). Socialization theory also fails to deal effectively with the part that bodies play in the social construction of gender. Sociologists took up that challenge, initially through symbolic interactionism, as was discussed in Chapter 3. However, I would argue that the most important ideas about how gendered bodies are socially constructed emerged within second-wave feminist literature, as insights produced there continue to appear in the work of feminist sociologists of the body.

Gendered Bodies: From oppression, to social construction to discipline

Key feminist books published around 1970, by Betty Friedan, Kate Millet, Germaine Greer and Shulamith Firestone contained theorizing about bodies as socially constructed, not naturally given. Eva Figes' (1978/1970) book *Patriarchal Attitudes* could also be included in this list, but has little to say about bodies, determinedly focusing on such social factors as constructing gender. These women are not sociologists and their books were bestsellers, not academic tomes. Their books were widely read, and although seldom directly acknowledged (but see Howson, 2005; Oakley, 1972; Spender, 1985; Sydie, 1987), I would argue that they were hugely influential in shaping the thinking of feminists scholars. In particular it is well worth examining what they have to say about bodies. Second-wave insights on bodies involve varying views of social construction. First there is the acknowledgement that women's oppression within patriarchy impacts on, or is caused by, their bodies.

Secondly, the idea emerges that women and men have some agency in resisting gendered constructions of their bodies. Thirdly, there is work which discusses how bodies are 'disciplined' in line with patriarchal dictates about femininity and masculinity. The second and third viewpoints are very similar, but the utility of separating resisting bodies from disciplined bodies will become clear.

Oppressed bodies?

The language of oppression may seem outdated but second-wave feminists presented powerful accounts of some of the ways in which male dominance can constrain and (mis)shape women's bodies. In Friedan's (1965) iconic call to arms for feminism, *The Feminine Mystique*, first published in 1963, she bears testimony to the embodiment of 'the problem with no name'. The problem was that educated married women were feeling dissatisfied with 'the feminine mystique', an ideal promoted by women's magazines in the 1950s proposing that women should find fulfilment as wives and mothers. Many did not, and yet had no name for what they were feeling. Friedan's account of the problem is mired in a liberal, dualistic, and ethnocentric view of a 'civilized' society as 'one in which instinct and environment are increasingly controlled and transformed by the human mind' (Friedan, 1965: 124). Yet there are interesting claims about what 'the feminine mystique' does to bodies:

> A number of women told me about great bleeding blisters that break out on their hands and arms. 'I call it the housewives' blight' said a family doctor in Pennsylvania. 'I see it so often lately in these young women with four, five and six children, who bury themselves in their dishpans. But it isn't caused by detergent and it isn't cured by cortisone.' (Friedan, 1965: 16)

She also notes the extreme tiredness many young housewives experience, somewhat 'matronizingly' claiming that this is not real fatigue, but a result of boredom (Friedan, 1965: 27–8). Nevertheless, such ideas were insightful and feminist sociology has continued to deal with 'material' ways in which women's bodies are made ill (for example, Doyal, 2002), starved (for example, MacSween, 1993; Whitehead, 1994) and damaged, for example by sexual violence (for example, Kelly, 1988), within patriarchy. Many of these now taken for granted aspects of feminist thinking can be seen in fledgling form in Kate Millet's (1972/1970) *Sexual Politics*.

Millet's brilliant argument establishes that relations between women and men are socially constructed power relationships that oppress women, partly via myths about women's bodily weakness. She dismisses the idea that men's supposedly superior strength has produced male supremacy. Male muscles may have some biological basis, but have also been 'culturally encouraged, through breeding, diet, and exercise' and physical strength is no longer really politically relevant within 'civilization' (Millet, 1972/1970: 27). Millet is aware of gender as a concept that describes the cultural character of differences between women and men. The concept came from the work of Robert Stoller on gender reassignment and she takes his examples as evidence of the socially constructed nature of gender. So strong is this construction that a gender identity may form that is contrary to one's sex (Millet, 1972/1970: 30). This is a spurious argument based on substituting social for biological determinism. Gender as a concept arises precisely to describe disjunctions between sexed bodies and the socially enacted gender expressed through bodies, but to say that an identity may form contrary to one's sex assumes that 'normally' femaleness leads to femininity and maleness to masculinity. Only with a lot of social effort will other identities emerge, and often a realigning of bodies will be demanded to make the body fit the identity. There was little thinking on these matters at the time and these limitations do not detract from her central point that ideologies of women's weakness maintain patriarchy as power-structured relationships which oppress women. Other classic work more directly connects this oppression to women's bodies.

Shulamith Firestone argues that recognition of women only as bodies, not as rounded individuals, causes their oppression and this can only be overcome by artificial reproduction. Firestone wants to understand the historic conditions from which conflict between women and men has arisen, by extending Marx and Engels' methods to develop 'a materialist view of history based on sex itself' (Firestone, 1972: 15). In this endeavour she adapts Freudian psychology, proposing that children learn that a woman's embodiment limits her, while the father embodies – or his body symbolizes – the valued world of travel and adventure. Such views are promoted through racism, a culture of romance, and indeed culture generally. Following de Beauvoir, Firestone (1972: 149) argues that men's point of view is seen as the universal point of view, but sexism is fundamentally about seeing women as sexualized bodies available to men, and the concentration on women as bodies means a lack of recognition of women's individuality, of which the physical is only one part. Thus in order to bring about a revolution that will liberate women she argues it is necessary 'to free humanity from the tyranny of its biology' (Firestone, 1972: 183) so that women no longer need to suffer pregnancy and childbirth. Most feminists have tended to be sceptical of reproductive technologies as placing too much control in the hands of the male-dominated medical profession (for example, Corea, 1985;

Oakley, 1980; Stanworth, 1987). In contrast, Firestone thinks that if women no longer bear the children childcare will become shared and women and children will be fully integrated into society. Doing away with the biological family could allow a return to polymorphous perversity, a free flow of desire around anyone or anything that Freud argues young infants enjoy. But her solution is based on a dualism which assumes that individuality is mostly in the mind. Firestone seems to fall victim to the very tendency to view men as the standard of individuality of which she is critical. Like de Beauvoir, she often presents the female body as disgusting, for example employing a poorly evidenced essentialist argument about pregnancy as 'barbaric' and ugly, claiming that '[t]he child's first response, "What's wrong with that Fat Lady?"; the husband's guilty waning of sexual desire; the woman's tears in front of the mirror at eight months – are all gut reactions, not to be dismissed as cultural habits' (Firestone, 1972: 188). Yet in recent years pregnancy has arguably come to be considered very sexy. For example, a very pregnant Demi Moore appeared naked on the cover of *Vanity Fair* in 1991. This suggests that attitudes to pregnancy might be 'cultural habits'. Firestone describes pregnancy as 'the temporary deformation of the body of the individual for the sake of the species' (Firestone, 1972: 188), but most feminist work on reproductive bodies tries to challenge representations of pregnant or menstruating bodies as ill, hideous, or 'abnormal' (see for example, Laws, 1990; Martin, 1984; Shildrick, 1997). Despite these pieces of essentialism, Firestone is radically constructionist. If we construct a society in which women no longer have babies, then new ways for women and men to relate to each other as individuals will arise. Change social conditions and relations between people will change – that is her dialectic of sex. Yet Juliet Mitchell (1973: 89) argues that it is not a true dialectic because it is based on a dichotomous view of a conflict between male and female, whereas dialectic materialism understands conflict in terms of more complex contradictions between all aspects of a structure. Also, Firestone returns at crucial points to a classic liberal (and dualist) position which implies that the ideal individual is one free from bodily distractions. This is a position of which other feminists have been critical.

Resisting bodies?

Germaine Greer (1970) contests the disembodied liberal notion of the individual and in fact regards it as responsible for dubious ideas about femaleness as 'naturally' inferior. Her highly constructionist view of bodies draws on what evidence was available to her thirty-five years ago to make many of the points we covered in Chapter 2. She concludes that the female/male dichotomy is central to our way of thinking, not our way of being (Greer, 1970: 25). Biological differences between the sexes are in fact minimal, she claims, and open to interpretation. She even uses the term 'gender' in achieving this, but there is little direct discussion of what gender might mean and how it might differ from 'sex'. Nevertheless, she outlines ideas that were later detailed more thoroughly by Oakley and other social scientists:

> The 'normal' sex roles that we learn to play from our infancy are no more natural than the antics of a transvestite. In order to approximate those shapes and attitudes which are considered normal and desirable, both sexes deform themselves, justifying the process by referring to the primary, genetic difference between the sexes. (Greer, 1970: 29)

She argues that any sex differences that do exist are tiny and that bodily variations associated with males and females are probably largely created by the different social practices in which men and women engage. Bones are shaped by the different work and dress of women and men; curves arise from the conditions of women's lives and are displayed by feminine modes of dress. Her arguments are seductive and indeed sociologists exploring everything from education (for example, Thorne, 1993), to work (for example, Adkins, 1995; Tyler and Abbott, 1998), to fashion (for example, Finkelstein, 1991), engage with very similar claims about the social shaping of gendered bodies and the extent to which people can resist.

Greer is adamant that women can resist, that they can live for themselves and not for men. However, she recommends individual resistance. More radical feminists tended to analyze women as a group or class who could be freed from the tyranny of beauty and other bodily oppressions only by broad social change (Spender, 1985: 58). Nevertheless, Greer's polemic is fabulous, and at times evidence is presented and a careful analysis made. At other times she makes grand claims which are convincing but lack support. Her insights into the way that gender is socially constructed through bodies predict much of what a later sociology of the body will have to say, but these insights are often relatively undeveloped. For example she is rather selective in the social practices she refers to when illustrating the way gendered bodies are shaped. She talks of dress and cosmetics and work, but not of medicine or formal schooling. While her argument is compelling, it is neither as systematic, nor as carefully supported as sociological arguments, and therefore it is not entirely surprising that scholars would turn not to Greer but to later material on the social construction of bodies that has more detailed versions of some of the insights offered and is based on more rigorous analysis of empirical research or theorizing (see Brook, 1999; Howson, 2005). That is not to demean second-wave feminist knowledge on bodies.

Second-wave feminist understandings of bodies arose from a criticism of male dominance as natural, and a concern by women to gain knowledge about and better control of their bodies. As such, in addition to the ideas discussed above, second-wave feminists formed women's health groups highly critical of medical models of the body. They offered alternatives to thinking about the body, ones that relied largely on women's own embodied experiences. Such alternative knowledge was gathered in classic books such as the Boston Women's Health Book Collective *Our Bodies Ourselves* (Howson, 2004: 130–2). It was understandable given the lower status of women within society that political movement should focus on trying to remedy the inequalities to which women were subject, and that men's bodies should be largely ignored. However, it was sometimes implied that men were unconcerned with their bodily appearance and that masculinity was given and unchanging. Such implications have since been challenged.

Resisting embodiment? Men's bodies

Men achieved their political power by representing themselves as disembodied and casting women as disordered, irrational bodies (Bordo, 1987; Pateman, 1989). However, this denial of the importance of the body remains a privilege available only to powerful men, usually middle and upper class, who conform to particular dominant ideas about how to be a man. David Morgan (1993), for example, has distinguished between male bodies represented as classical (like eighteenth century aristocrats) and those represented as grotesque (like peasants). The line between these types is now more blurred, but working class men continue to be represented as having grotesque bodies, lacking in control. However they have some symbolic power via association with the natural and certain respect given to their capacity for violence. Current examples of 'classical' male bodies might be the controlled besuitedness of men such as George Clooney, or the suaveness of Ralph Fiennes. Although he is not real, Homer Simpson is perhaps the ultimate characterization of the working class man with a grotesque body that does not measure up to dominant ideals.

Hardly any individual measures up to the hegemonic ideal of male rationality and control over their bodies and emotions (Connell, 1995). However, all men have to struggle with that ideal in varying ways, which involve different relationships to embodiment. For male labourers and manual workers, for example, their bodies are what they use to make their living and they are simultaneously hyper–masculinized in displaying the kind of muscular body that is supposedly the ultimate marker of masculinity, and yet also femininized because they are objectified as bodies and treated like children in the way their bodies are regulated at work. As one welder said: 'How would you like to go up to someone, and say "I would like to go to the bathroom"'? If the foreman doesn't like you, he'll make you hold it, just ignore you' (Stallings cited in Donaldson, 1991: 12). Such workers complain that they are not treated 'like men' because they do not have autonomy over their bodies and their work, which is the mark of hegemonic maleness. Connell (1995) argues that masculinity is particularly constituted through bodily performance. Masculine identity is threatened if a man cannot perform, if he cannot display control over his body. Clearly the amount of control over his body a man is able to display depends on other factors such as class, age and ablebodiedness (see for example Seymour, 1998). Therefore it is not a simple matter of men being disembodied, and there appears to be a growing commodification of men's bodies and related increases in masculine body modification (for example, see Faludi, 1999). In addressing some of these issues sociologists have been heavily influenced by the work of French historian of ideas Michel Foucault, but similar ideas about bodies as disciplined can also be found in second–wave feminism.

Man-made bodies? Disciplined women and men?

Both Friedan (1965) and Greer (1970) argue that women are encouraged, cajoled and sometimes coerced into making their bodies conform to male dictated ideals. Intrinsic to the feminine mystique is that women are taught to find fulfilment through their bodies. They are encouraged to find themselves by dyeing their hair or having another baby (Friedan, 1965: 55). They are taught to remove their body hair because it is associated with animality and aggressive sexuality; they learn to be ashamed of menstruating. Women become objects of display, showing the status of their men. And the frustration of this position manifests itself in bodily disorders, in wrinkles and excess weight, as women are forced to deny their sexuality and thus become female eunuchs (Greer, 1970). Women's embodiment is characterized as one of 'passivity and sexlessness'. However, unlike de Beauvoir, Greer will not regard the female body as disgusting but instead is vituperative about men's loathing of women, which reduces women to despised bodies. She says a woman is regarded by men as 'a receptacle into which he has emptied his sperm, a kind of human spitoon' (Greer, 1970: 254). Greer plays to the gallery; she likes to shock, but that does not mean that there is not some truth to what she says. More recent feminist development of ideas about women's involvement in shaping their bodies has tended to make use of Foucault's ideas.

Foucault argues that modern forms of power produce certain kinds of embodied individuals, using visibility as one of a number of techniques. Unlike Freud, Foucault does not see power as simply repressive. Systems of power are not simply about saying no to bodily desires (Foucault, 1990/1976) but have come to operate around gaining knowledge of people's bodies, desires and behaviour and using that knowledge to control populations. To illustrate this he did detailed studies on the development of psychiatry (1967/1961), modern medicine (1973/ 1963), the prison (1979/1975), and sexuality (1990/1976). He argues that power changed from something the sovereign possessed and exercized directly on people and their bodies, to something that operated more subtley as a force which people internalized. For example, in *Discipline and Punish: The Birth of the Prison* (1979/1975) he elaborates the shift from monarchs inflicting pain and death on the bodies of those who strayed from the law, to a system of punishment in which people are imprisoned so they can be observed and reformed. Through observation of prisoners, new knowledge about what was 'abnormal' could be gained, and knowing that they were watched meant inmates would gradually internalize the rules about 'normal' behaviour and discipline themselves to conform to these rules. As Foucault (1979/1975: 233) puts it: 'penal imprisonment from the beginning of the nineteenth century, covered both the deprivation of liberty and the technical transformation of individuals'. Prisons were designed, both literally and figuratively, in ways that embodied the new principles of power. Foucault outlines how nineteenth-century architect Jeremy Bentham's designs for a panopticon can be seen as a blueprint for how to construct buildings that would make it easy to control people through an architecture that enforces visibility:

> at the centre, a tower; this tower is pierced with wide windows that open onto the inner side of the ring; the peripheric building is divided into cells, each of which extend the whole width of the building; they have two windows, one on the inside, corresponding to the windows of the tower; the other, on the outside, allows the light to cross the cell from one end to the other. All that is needed, then, is to place a supervisor in a central tower and to shut up in each cell a madman, a patient, a condemned man, a worker or a schoolboy. By the effect of backlighting, one can observe from the tower, standing out precisely against the light, the small captive shadows in the cells of the periphery. They are like so many cages, so many small theatres, in which each actor is alone, perfectly individualized and constantly visible. (Foucault, 1979/1975: 200)

The gaze is therefore central in disciplining bodies, even if not inevitably a 'male' gaze (Tseëlon, 1995). All this knowledge, gained by observation, could be used to 'better' control people. New forms of power are thus less brutal, but more all-encompassing and wholly entangled with forms of knowledge.

People discipline themselves and their bodies in accordance with powerful ways of thinking and talking about what is 'normal'. These dominant **discourses** arose from new 'scientific' ways of observing human beings. The development of a medical gaze, in particular, had vast effects (Foucault, 1973/1963). People diet and exercize to try and conform to medically endorsed notions of healthy bodies (for example, see Gimlin, 2001), while psychiatry classifies and defines what divides 'normal' sexuality and behaviour from deviant (Foucault, 1967/1961). People's self-definitions are influenced by the way they internalize and embody social norms. Yet Foucault only rather tangentially deals with gender. In his work on the development of psychiatry and of medicine he touches on the way in which discourses tend to produce women's bodies as hysterical and faulty compared to a masculine standard of normality (Foucault, 1967/1961; 1973/1963). Others have extended his work to deal more fully with issues of gender.

Bryan Turner's pioneering (1984) book, *The Body and Society,* is heavily influenced by Foucault (and Weber) but he differs in identifying patriarchal control of women's bodies as a key issue in the sociology of the body. This makes sense given that Turner's argument restates the central sociological problem of social order (how society remains relatively controlled and peaceful) as 'the problem of the government of the body' (Turner, 1984: 2). He argues that society has four tasks: the reproduction of populations over time, regulating bodies in space, disciplining interior bodies, and representing exterior bodies. The disorders women suffer in patriarchy are a sign of the problem of control, and relate to these tasks. Drawing on Foucault, Turner argues that knowledge about these new disorders is used to try and control women's sexuality in the service of order. Hysteria was an illness much talked of at the beginning of the twentieth century. It was a label given to women thought to be acting irrationally and the cause was identified as a 'wandering womb', which was thought to arise because they had not reproduced. Turner (1984: 102–3) suggests that hysteria was in fact the result of contradictory pressures on women at that time to get married, but to delay marriage in order to slow population growth. Meanwhile, agoraphobia (an intense fear of public spaces) in women is produced by the constant focus on the (sexual) dangers arising from new urbanized life. In addition, Turner uses Goffman to understand how efforts to control women also manifest as anorexia nervosa, a disease which sees prosperous women starve themselves – sometimes to death. This becomes more understandable within a society in which self and public appearance become merged. Turner develops these connections more than Foucault and also specifically engages with feminist explanations for women's subordination. Feminists have tended to suggest that capitalism reinforces patriarchy. He argues that capitalism actually undermines patriarchy in so far as it encourages an individualism incompatible with patriarchy. However, in the chapters Turner devotes to this discussion, women's bodily experiences fade into the background. Feminist work has arguably been somewhat more successful in using Foucault to talk about having a woman's body.

Feminist work that has appropriated Foucault's ideas about medicine have perhaps been most successful in maintaining a focus on how bodies are experienced and disciplined as gendered bodies (for example, Seymour, 1998; Howson, 2005). A focused example is Alexandra Howson's (1999) work on cervical screening as compliance and moral obligation. Although cervical screening programmes may have good intentions, her point is that they encourage women to be active in the policing of their own health. Women are expected to participate in smear tests and most feel obliged to do so. Such tests will evaluate them in relation to medical models of a 'normal' cervix, and are just one example of an array of ways in which people have come to be considered responsible for monitoring their own health in ways that reinforce particular notions of gendered embodiment. There is also literature on the disciplinary nature of other practices that reproduce feminine bodies such as those around beauty, cosmetic surgery, and other 'body work' (see, for example, Black, 2004; Davis, 1995; Gimlin, 2001). Much of this work discusses gender as an effect of social regulation.

Susan Bordo is an American feminist philosopher who also uses Foucault in very sociological ways to understand women's embodiment as highly regulated and docile. She also draws on his ideas about how power/knowledge shapes women's bodies via the classification of gender specific bodily disorders such as anorexia nervosa, agoraphobia and hysteria. Bordo, unlike Foucault or Turner, sees these as more than signs of women's subordination; they all are extreme versions of current cultural expectations about femininity. Women are encouraged to be quiet, to stay home, to not take up too much space. Hysterics, agoraphobics and anorexics are conforming in an exaggerated way to expectations about femininity, but they are at the same time resisting them. By being hysterical, Victorian women were resisting the idea that they should be angels in the house, there to care for others. Agoraphobics cannot perform many of the duties associated with traditional feminine roles, such as doing the shopping or running the children to activities. Anorexics are unconsciously protesting against cultural ideals that encourage women to go hungry, feel ashamed of their appetites and prescribe constant body work to conform to ideals of feminine appearance. Bordo is very clear that these protests are not conscious and that they are extremely self-destructive. Such disorders illustrate the ridiculousness of norms about femininity by showing how dysfunctional conformity to them could be. However, even in extreme conformity there is resistance, although that very resistance may actually help reproduce women's oppression rather than challenge it (Bordo, 1989). Medicine and the mass media – and the discourses and practices surrounding them – all contribute to disciplining bodies. Women are encouraged to actively work on their bodies to, 'normalize' them, but there are narrow ideas about what is 'normal'; currently in the West these include, amongst other things, being slender and white (Bordo, 1993). Such feminist appropriations of Foucault usefully go beyond thinking about bodies either as passively oppressed or as active sites of (individual) resistance, but they are not without problems.

The Foucauldian emphasis on the discursive production of bodies under-appreciates the messiness and unpredictability of human bodies. Sometimes bodies defy the frameworks which supposedly construct them (Blaikie et al., 2003). For example, there are limits to understanding ageing bodies as socially constructed. Discourses do tend to produce old bodies as abnormal, disgusting, frail, out of control, and these are often inaccurate stereotypes. Nevertheless there are bodily processes that have particular effects as we age and these cannot be entirely ignored. No matter how much we might try to discipline aged bodies to conform to discourses which regard youth, beauty and control as normal, older bodies will at some point most likely be frail, weak, painful, incontinent, wrinkled, dead (Elias, 1985; Hepworth, 1995). Bodies have limits and the subjective experience of human bodies, both in pleasure and pain, may not be simply an illusion of social making. Bodies are not as docile in the taking on of social norms as much of Focault's early work seems to suggest. Considerations of bodies as something actively used in constructing the self become more evident in his later thinking about 'technologies of the self' (Foucault, 1988). Other feminist appropriations of his work have centrally addressed the issue of agency.

A Foucauldian approach to agency is noticeable in Judith Butler's (1993) ideas (see Chapter 3) about bodies as socially produced ('made') by discourse, but always in gendered terms. She argues that the classificatory relationship between sex and gender produces our bodies. Therefore bodies cannot be understood unless marked by sex/gender. Gender makes human beings culturally intelligible. What she means is that we always make sense of people in terms of gender. If you come across a person whose gender is unclear, you do not know how to interact. This is a useful idea, but Butler and Foucault have been accused of leaving us with a sense of humans as helpless victims of discourse. Her attempts to recognize agency are problematic because of her emphasis on discourse and there being 'no doer behind the deed'. Certainly sociologists might be sympathetic to her distrust of 'voluntarism', by which she means assumptions that human beings can do whatever they choose. Clearly sociology is often an exercise in destroying illusions of individual choice by revealing the determining power of social structures on people's lives. But it is very difficult to eschew voluntarism while trying to promote some vision of agency. Butler sometimes presents a view of sex/gendered bodies as docile bodies, produced by the social, regulated by discourse. There are alternative ways to consider how bodies play a part in producing the social, without returning to essentialism. Much of the feminist sociology cited so far does this, yet it has often been ignored in favour of more abstract theorizing on gendered embodiment arising from other disciplines (Howson, 2005). Corporeal feminism is one approach that has been seized on.

Corporeal Feminism

Australian feminist philosophers Elizabeth Grosz and Moira Gatens have endeavoured to develop a corporeal feminism which rethinks sexual difference without resort to essentialism. Grosz is perhaps the more influential of the two, so I shall discuss her ideas. Corporeal feminism relies largely on Jaques Lacan's interpretation of Freud. Women are seen as the representation of difference, but there is no content, or essence, to this. They are simply 'not masculine'. To overcome this dualism Grosz (1994) suggests that there is a need to go beyond Euclidean notions of space, to adopt more cyclical or rhythmical instead of linear appreciations of time, to rethink ideas about power, to reformulate the ways in which women are represented, and to redesign knowledges about the body. This is a highly ambitious project (Howson, 2005: 118). A Euclidean model of space must be superseded because its hierarchical relating of bodies within a point-by-point system of coordinates (think X, Y and Z axes) is the basis of patriarchal representations of the body. Adopting different understandings of bodies in relation to space will at least show that there are other possibilities. Similarly, to use alternative conceptions of time which are more cyclical might better represent the processes located in women's bodies. At least it will challenge the goal-oriented, progress-obsessed usual models and yet allow a consideration of the generation of difference through repetition. Power also needs to be rethought so that bodies are seen as both instruments of power and objects of resistance. This means seeing power as producing and not simply inhibiting embodied people and their actions. In addition, ways of representing women require changing. New languages and types of knowledge are needed which acknowledge the particular interests and limitations of all perspectives instead of pretending to be disinterested. For example, biology could be rethought so that women are understood as active instead of as passively related to men. Finally, in order to achieve a re-presentation of women as actively embodied subjects, knowledge about bodies must be redesigned. Disciplinary and other boundaries need crossing in order to better appreciate bodies as both biological entities, which we experience, and as products of social meanings and structures which we use in living our bodies. In constructing this alternative approach to thinking about bodies there needs to be particular attention to the specificity of women's bodies, without falling back into the idea that women's behaviour is determined by their biology. Grosz gives the example of menstruation. She argues that women's experiences of menstruation need to be understood as them responding to biological hormonal processes, but also to social meanings. In patriarchal culture menstruation has negative meanings and this makes it highly likely that women will experience it as unpleasant. Grosz's point is that if we recognize the way women experience their bodies as producing social meanings, but also being produced by them, then we can consider how those meanings might be changed for the better and how their embodied experiences could be very different from what they are at present.

Grosz (1994) sees embodiment as not entirely reducible to the social. It is through bodies that the social can come to exist. The bodies she invokes are sexually differing bodies. She says (and see Gatens, 1991) that there is not one neutral body but at least two types. However, she is refer-ring to these bodies as imagined, rather than as real bodies with essential properties. This is one way in which she draws on Lacan. However, he is criticized for his failure to support adequately his suppositions about sub-jectivity with reference to clinical cases from his psychoanalytic practice. He is taken to task for thinking too much in universals. These problems transfer to corporeal feminism, which struggles to deal adequately with the particularities of gender as a historical production (Howson, 2005: 137–8). However, Grosz does somewhat rework his ideas in ways that challenge gender hierarchies and their privileging of the masculine as the norm (Beasley, 2005: 67–70). She argues that women represent difference and that making present the embodied experiences of women challenges visions of the social based on a masculine disembodied norm as superior. While this has possibilities, the psychoanalytic aspect of her ideas means they remain immersed in the inevitability of a gender hierarchy with which we have to engage in order to gain selfhood. And her focus on sex-ual difference neglects other forms of social categorization of bodies which impose hierarchies; for example 'race' and class (Beasley, 2005: 70).

Grosz's concerns have been thought overall to be over-philosophized and over-theorized in ways that disconnect her work from the everyday experiences of women (Howson, 2005: 121). Grosz makes some efforts to deal with embodied experience via phenomenology, but other scholars have more fully engaged with that perspective to explore gender.

Phenomenology and Habitus: experiencing the body

Within the sociology of the body phenomenological approaches focus on how we experience our bodies. Phenomenology is the study of experiences, usually done via description. Maurice Merleau-Ponty's (2003/1945) work is central. He understands subjectivity as located in the body. He is going against Cartesian models which say that subjectivity is located in the mind (I think therefore I am). One way of putting his approach is to say that we know about ourselves as in the world through our bodies. Mauss is one sociologist who pursued this phenomenological approach, for instance describing the different 'techniques of the body' such as ways of walking in different cultures. Most of these techniques are gendered, in that men and women learn to use their bodies differently. As he remarks: 'Nor can I understand how women can walk in high heels' (Mauss, 1973: 83). However, more specific phenomenological consideration of gendered embodiment is famously found in a piece by feminist philosopher Iris Young.

Young's (1990) essay 'Throwing like a girl' is a well-known use of a phenomenological approach to understand how women come to experience their bodily capabilities as limited within patriarchy. She is careful to note that not all women adopt the restricted ways of using their body that she outlines. To use the throwing example on which she focuses, clearly some women such as champion netballers, softballers, javelin throwers and so on can throw very well. Some men are not so good at throwing. However, these are individual exceptions to overall general patterns of bodily movement that are heavily gendered. In relation to throwing, Young presents observations of girls as not putting their whole bodies into the motion in the way that boys do. Girls are more likely to throw from the hand and wrist, instead of from the shoulder. This failure to use their bodies really effectively is true generally of women's embodiment, they remain much more 'closed'. She suggests that women do not think they are capable of throwing or heavy lifting and when they try they do not poise themselves in ways that make full use of their muscles, balance and bearing. Women also do not feel entitled to take up 'too much' space. Young thus characterizes feminine embodiment as showing an ambiguous transcendence, an inhibited intentionality and a discontinuous unity with its surroundings.

When Young says that feminine embodiment is characterized by ambiguous transcendence, she is using a combination of ideas from Merleau-Ponty and Simone de Beauvoir about to what extent we can transcend or 'go beyond' our mundane bodily existence. For Merleau-Ponty transcendence is not about escaping bodily constraints in the way others such as de Beauvoir deem problematic for women as bodies; he argues that transcendence is about opening out the body in fluid actions on the world. But Young says that women do not trust their bodily capacities and therefore keep their bodies 'closed' to the world. A woman 'often lives her body as a burden, which must be dragged and prodded along and at the same time protected' (Young, 1990: 148). Thus women, you might say, lack a sense of confidence in the ability of their bodies to fulfil their intentions.

Intentionality means believing that you can use your body to appropriate your surroundings to fulfil your intentions. It is about believing that you can do something. Women typically lack a complete sense ofm 'I can' when it comes to using their bodies; they therefore have inhibited intentionality. When preparing to throw, for example, they freeze up or hesitate and the throw fails to succeed as it should (Young, 1990). This is aggravated, Young says, by the way in which women experience their bodies in relation to their surroundings.

Young (1990) argues that femininity involves a discontinuous unity of the body with itself and its surroundings. Merleau-Ponty (2003/1945) claims that by having an aim and moving towards it, the body unites itself and its surroundings. Young suggests that women do not have this sense of continuity between body-subject and environment. For example, women use only their wrist and forearm in throwing, instead of using their whole body; the rest of their body remains fairly immobile, as though it is not connected. This lack of connection means that the woman's intentions are not effectively translated into her surroundings.

All these problematic aspects of feminine bodily existence can be traced to the way in which women are objectified within society and tend to experience their bodies as objects, rather than as instruments. Women cannot go beyond their bodies because they are always referring back to them as the object instead of the originator of motions, as not entirely under their own control, and as things to be looked at. Women experience their bodies as fragile things that are slightly foreign and more of a hindrance than a help in engaging in 'the world's possibilities' (Young, 1990: 150). Thus Young is very clear that women's experiences of their bodies are not a product of some biological essence of femininity but are socially conditioned, produced by the constrained situation of women within a sexist society. She argues that '[w]omen in sexist society are physically handicapped. Insofar as we learn to live out our existence in accordance with the definition that patriarchal culture assigns to us, we are physically inhibited, confined, positioned, and objectified' (Young, 1990: 153). Young argues that girls are socialized into a bodily timidity and learn to restrict their movements more and more as they grow up, but socialization is only part of it. They also become used to the idea that their bodies are there to be looked at. In addition, women learn to fear bodily invasion in the form of rape, or of lesser unwanted physical contact which women must often endure. They are often touched by men in situations where it would not be deemed appropriate for them to touch others. Thus women contain their bodies and struggle with them.

Young's work on 'throwing like a girl' may illustrate that women take part in 'making' their own bodies by conforming to social constraints, but also demonstrates that how women learn to experience their bodies 'makes' them powerless. Young is focusing on bodily experiences oriented towards tasks 'that involve the whole body in gross movement' and she wonders herself whether what she says would apply equally well to other forms of bodily experience or even other tasks (Young, 1990: 155, 156). Much of the essay allows us to think about the particularity of women's bodies and how we learn to inhabit and use those bodies. However, in the end she returns to a structuralist argument that insists that women's bodies are determined by the social constraints of a male dominated society. This recalls de Beauvoir's assertion that the body is a problem for women. Young is using phenomenology to make sense of women's embodiment, but in saying that feminine bodies remain objects she is departing from the fundamental point of Merleau-Ponty's theory, which is that people must be understood as body-subjects. Women act, but in their very actions they reproduce a restricted femininity which constrains their ability to act. Bourdieu has faced similar problems in his attempts to use **habitus** to escape structural determinism and incorporate phenomenology into sociology (Howson and Inglis, 2001), but there are useful insights emerging from feminists who have drawn on the ideas of Pierre Bourdieu to make sense of women's embodiment.

One well-known feminist use of Bourdieu, elaborated on in Chapter 7, is Bev Skeggs's (1997) argument that working class women's **habitus** – their ways of thinking and doing things – is organized around notions of respectability. Her work draws on rich ethnographic study of English working class women to illustrate how they negotiate their sense of themselves principally in relation to ideas about what is respectable. Working class women are always aware that they are being judged in relation to such ideas and that the judgements are usually not based on knowledge of them as rounded individuals, but made on the basis of their appearance. One of Skegg's (1997: 88) participants who sends her child to private daycare in a wealthy suburb succinctly describes the problem:

> With the mums at school I couldn't compete clothes wise with all their designer labels and that, I don't even recognize. I do make some effort because I want to be accepted so I get changed when I go to pick him up. I wouldn't go in my slobby jogging suit that I live in. I do want to make an effort. … I don't want them to look at you and say they're the poor ones and it'll reflect on the kids and they won't be invited round to play so it'll be bad for them. You want to be accepted.

As this suggests, working class women are having to deal with stereotypes of women of their class as polluting and unworthy of respect. Bodies carry the markers of class and 'are the physical sites where the relations of class, gender, race, sexuality, and age come together and are em-bodied and practised' (Skeggs, 1997: 82). Those working class women trying to be judged respectable invest in their bodies as a form of **cultural capital**. Cultural capital can be thought of as wealth in the form of knowledge and ideas. Bourdieu notes that cultural capital has an objectified and an institutionalized state as well as an embodied state. The objectified state refers to knowing about valued things within society such as the 'right' books, the institutionalized state refers to qualifications which legitimate the type of knowledge you have as socially valuable. The embodied state refers to how we think and act, for example speaking with a 'refined' accent, having 'elegant' manners, or wearing 'classy' clothes.

Although use of Bourdieu does allow some reflection on the ways in which women experience their bodies, it makes sense of those experiences in terms of habitus as ingrained. Bourdieu's framework is one in which social structures, such as class, determine people's habitus. The ways people walk, talk, eat, speak, and dress are learnt by people as members of particular class groups. They become automatic and taken for granted and are very difficult to overcome. In fact Skeggs allows the women in her study a little more agency than Bourdieu does in his work. She conveys a sense, to paraphrase Marx, of the women she describes as making history but not in circumstances of their own choosing. They struggle to occupy femininity, because it is a virtually impossible ideal, from which their working class position bars them. They struggle to display their bodies and themselves as 'feminine' because they see some benefits in doing so, although there is also the risk of loss. The women had taken their supposedly 'natural' feminine knowledge and done courses on caring at local colleges in the hope that they might convert those educational qualifications into economic capital. They also invested a great deal in their appearance. If they could get the 'right' clothes and the 'right' look, they could feel they had some sense of control over their lives. If they could manage to achieve a glamorous femininity on nights out they might receive the cultural validation of being desired by men, and possibly the economic and cultural capital they might be able to accrue through alliance with a male partner. But doing femininity was hard work for the women in the study. As Skeggs (1997: 116) puts it, femininity was seen as 'a structural inconvenience which was difficult to avoid'. Working class women quite literally could not afford to ignore femininity, not necessarily because it would bring gains but because they could draw on femininity to stop their situation getting any worse. And that is the extent to which agency is thought possible, even from a phenomenological perspective. Phenomenology may offer an appreciation of gendered bodies as they are experienced, but it is difficult to maintain this focus from within sociology, which always brings us back to structures which construct and constrain those experiences (Howson and Inglis, 2001).

Conclusion

It has been a crucial aim of the sociology of gender to establish that inequalities can be challenged because they are the result of social processes, not 'natural' bodily differences. Feminists and social science scholars in the late twentieth century tended to see bodies as natural biological entities upon which cultural (gender) meanings were inscribed. Later, especially under the influence of Foucault, an appreciation developed of how cultural meanings and practices actually produce bodies in particular ways. Little was said about how people experience their bodies. For the feminist movement women's experience of their bodies was crucial, but 1970s' feminist attempts to understand that experience often became coagulated by essentialism and dualism. More recent work utilizing phenomenology thinks through women's active involvement in disciplining their bodies both around and in resistance to social norms.

It is difficult for sociologists not to slip back to insisting on material social conditions as finally determining of bodies/subjects. However, if bodies can be constructed as material entities as well as imagined and symbolic objects, and perhaps in other ways such as interactive, space producing, fluid instruments, then it may be more possible to think of people as constantly remaking (see Seymour, 1998) their bodies – if not always in positive ways and not in conditions of their own choosing.

Key Readings

Brook, B. (1999) *Feminist Perspectives on the Body*. London: Longman.

Howson, A. (2005) *Embodying Gender*. London: Sage.

Morgan, D. (1993) 'You too can have a body like mine: reflections on the male body and masculinities', in S. Scott and D. Morgan (eds), *Body Matters: Essays on the Sociology of the Body*. London: Falmer Press.

6

What are the politics of gender?

Feminist politics is an attempt to represent women's interests in order to overcome the gender inequalities which disadvantage women. Although women's struggles to improve their position have a long history, there have been two periods of particularly noticeable mass activity, which are referred to as the first wave and the **second wave** of feminism. The first wave in the nineteenth century is not discussed here. It was principally a liberal call for women's inclusion within public life – a demand for the vote and for entry to university and the professions (Rendall, 1985). The second wave from the 1960s until the early 1980s arguably had a more revolutionary agenda and contained the more recent debates about representing gendered interests relevant to this chapter. There have been a lot of jokes about feminism, and it and feminists have been much misrepresented. For instance, feminists are usually stereotyped as short-haired, man-hating, dungaree-wearing lesbians. There are homophobic undertones to such stereotypes, so that it is assumed that being a lesbian is a bad thing. Overall it is a negative image. Lesbian women have been an extremely important part of feminist movement, but the image is not an accurate one and feminist politics is much more diverse than the misrepresentations suggest. There were a broad range of issues attended to and the content of feminist events was often eclectic. For example, a day-long feminist seminar, run in New Zealand in 1981 (Broadsheet Collective, 1981: 21), included a wealth of topics from fixing your car, to getting out of marriage, to complaining about advertisements, to non-violent political activism. The breadth was impressive. But explaining how it was that 'masturbation' could find itself next to 'getting involved in your union' as part of feminist politics requires some discussion that situates the feminist movement within traditional politics.

Western politics has, during the modern period, focused on the individual's relationship with the state; distinguishing between their 'public' duties and a 'private' life supposedly free from political interference. This separation of public and private spheres has been crucial to the way political life has been conducted and especially to the way it has been gendered (Young, 1991). Politics has been defined in terms of activities related to decision making within formalized 'public' institutions such as parliament, local councils, and – more recently – union meetings and other activities such as demonstrations. Issues have been designated 'political' if they are matters of 'public' interest. In the transition to modernity, family relationships, friendships, love and sex became considered areas of personal decision making and women were not regarded as citizens (Benhabib, 1987: 83). Women's associations with 'personal' and 'private' matters, and most of all their feminine bodies, were said to make them incapable of the reason required for politics and therefore unfit to be citizens (Pateman, 1988). Into this arena came early liberal feminists (see Chapter 4), who sought reform within the traditional political system. They wished that system to be opened to women. However around half a century after the gaining of the vote by most Western women, it became clear that participation in the formal political sphere had not brought women full equality. Gradually, the small amounts of feminist activity that had continued from the Victorian period into the mid twentieth century swelled into what became known as second-wave feminism.

Understanding feminism, mainly as advanced within the second wave, is crucial to determining what the politics of gender are. The first five chapters have shed doubt on whether there are any 'natural' intrinsic things that make women different from men. We have also established that women and men are treated differently. Feminist politics has looked at that different treatment as disadvantaging women as a group, in relation to men as a group. Yet in the second wave they went beyond previous definitions of women's disadvantage as mainly consisting in their exclusion from the public world of education, work and politics. They redefined what political activity was about. However the story of second-wave feminism has been told as a story of a unified sisterhood that fell apart into ineffective fragments. I examine whether there might be better ways to understand the diversity of the feminist movement and also include a discussion of varieties of masculinity politics that resulted from men's reactions to feminism. I conclude by considering whether feminism still has any political relevance.

Second-wave feminism and a redefinition of 'the political'

Second wave feminism began to emerge in about 1968 as masses of women began struggling for 'liberation' from patriarchal dominance. It was part of a general upsurge in political activity as the baby boomers reached their teenage years and were keen to use their numbers to change the world. The year 1968 had seen some confrontations between the state and groups pushing for social revolution. In May of that year there were revolts on the streets of Paris, with groups of students, artists, intellectuals and workers demonstrating against what they saw as a rigidly bureaucratized and conservative society under tight state control and becoming increasingly enslaved to capitalist consumption. From this time a series of New Social Movements (NSMs) took shape in most democratic nations around issues such as the environment, peace, the rights of ethnic groups, and women's liberation. All of these movements challenged traditional democratic ideas about what issues were appropriate fodder for political decision making. They all brought onto the political agenda new issues relating to selfhood, knowledge production, sexuality and bodies (Seidman, 1994). Feminists made this clear in the early shaping of the demands that they wanted met.

There were a variety of demands made by feminist groups with different ideas and priorities, but there was considerable common ground. From America, to Britain, to Australasia (see for example, Dann, 1985: 6, 10; Tanner, 1970: 109–32; Wandor, 1990: 242–3), what second-wave feminists in the Western world declared they wanted could be summarized as follows: equal pay; equal education and opportunity; twenty-four hour childcare; free access to contraception and abortion. These aims were formulated as a challenge to liberal democratic conceptions of the political which were current around 1970. Some issues such as equal pay and opportunity fitted fairly comfortably within existing liberal attempts to reform society, rather than overthrowing it. Liberals argued that women needed to be treated as individuals who had a right to the same education, job opportunities and payment as men. However, the other demands, as I have summarized them, brought politics into areas which many argue should be matters of private decision making. Of course the state, for all its occasional rhetoric about the sanctity of the family as a haven from public and political life, has had a long history of intervening in how people organize their intimate lives. States formalise marriages, and through the legal system make decisions about those who divorce and their children and property. Through welfare policy the state enforces its decisions about what constitutes a family and what entitlements to state assistance people have. The state provides, does not provide, licences, regulates, subsidizes, or encourages a private market in childcare. The state allows or outlaws contraception and abortion to suit its purposes. Legislation discouraging contraception and abortion would often be tightened when there were concerns about the survival and fitness of the population, and especially when soldiers were wanted (Jamieson, 1998: 44). What this illustrates is that the supposed line between the public and private worlds is one which is often crossed. What then is **the public/private division** about?

Public/private

The division between 'public' and 'private' is artificial; the terms only make sense through opposition to each other. The public is that which is not private and vice versa (Pateman, 1988). For feminists 'the private' usually referred to the domestic sphere, but there are other usages of the term which refer to civil society, for example 'private enterprise' (Pateman, 1989: 133–4). Focusing on understanding the private as the domestic emerged from seeing it as opposite to a 'public sphere' thought to consist of things to do with the state, the economy and arenas of public discourse (Fraser, 1997: 70). The public, in other words, was the non-domestic. However, feminists mostly used these as useful working definitions rather than intransigent descriptions of truth. They clearly recognized that they needed to challenge the way in which most discussions of politics assumed that there really was a separation between public and private (Pateman, 1989: 131).

The slogan '**the personal is political**' was iconic in expressing this challenging of how public and private were distinguished. There were different interpretations of what the slogan 'the personal is political' actually meant. Some feminists took it as an insistence on the need to see women's everyday experiences put on the political agenda. Others began to promote it as an encouragement to women to change themselves as a political act (Whelehan, 1995: 13). Both interpretations emerged from the consciousness-raising groups which were crucial to the burgeoning of second-wave feminism and to the development of its political and intellectual distinction from earlier forms of feminist political activity. Consciousness-raising groups consisted of small groups of women who met regularly to share their experiences of living as a woman within a male-dominated society. So, for example, a group of women might meet to discuss menstruation. They were likely to discuss the shame they had been made to feel when menstruating and might see this as related to general negative social attitudes to women's bodies which help constrain women. The aim was to appreciate the similarities between women and thus achieve an understanding of their oppression within patriarchal society which would foster collective political action. However they did not always agree on which 'personal' issues were in need of political attention, or on what form that attention should take. Feminists were not simply revealing the reality of experiences previously thought 'personal', they were constructing new stories about the political significance of those experiences (Barrie, 1987). Feminists challenged the point at which, to paraphrase C. Wright Mills (1959), personal troubles became public issues. By seeing everyday aspects of women's lives as being political, feminists were challenging representations of 'the personal' in patriarchal society.

Not 'personal troubles' but public issues: childcare

One challenge of patriarchal society's representation of a 'personal trouble' came through feminist insistence on the need for access to twenty-four hour, free childcare. Women have borne most of the responsibility for childcare (see Brown et al., 2001; Oakley, 1972; 1980). There is no reason why, having given birth to the children, women should have to do most of the work of raising them. Even where women wish to breastfeed they do so only for a small portion of a child's life. With education, access to reasonable facilities, and tolerance of public breastfeeding, mothers can continue working and still breastfeed if they wish (Rea et al., 1997). However, children do continue to require attention and although many men are now more involved with childcare, the ultimate responsibility for children usually remains with the mother. If children are sick it is nearly always mothers who must reorganize arrangements for their care or take time off themselves. Women also continue to face attitudes within the workforce about them not being serious about their jobs either because they will soon have children or already have children, who are assumed to be their main priority. These attitudes affect women whether or not they actually do or will have children. They also affect a woman no matter how involved her partner (be they male or female) is in childcare and no matter how well a woman has made childcare arrangements (Adkins, 1995; Hochschild, 2003). Meanwhile, men can be fathers without that being thought to reflect on their job performance. Indeed it is possible in many cases that having a family can enhance a man's career prospects, especially in the professions. A politician, for example, can make considerable use of his wife and children to promote an image of himself as respectable, strongly heterosexual and effectively paternal. For women, even though caring for children may bring much joy, family-unfriendly workplaces can make combining work and care very difficult. For instance, mothers frequently end up with little to no leisure time that is not devoted to family activities (Brown et al., 2001).

For all the above reasons feminists saw childcare provision as essential in the fight for equality. Those feminists who were less radical may have thought that twenty-four hour, free availability was an unrealistic demand but nevertheless agreed that if gender equality was to be achieved then women needed access to decent care for their children. The less timid insisted that care needed to be freely and constantly available if women were to be able to participate in work and other aspects of public life to the same degree and with the same success as men. They also were not convinced that the nuclear family of Mum, Dad and the kids was the best way to raise children free from 'gender stereotyping'. Many felt that well-run childcare centres for all would help to raise a generation of children with more egalitarian attitudes. The 'private' approach to childrearing was thought outdated and conservative, tending to reproduce old-fashioned gender roles. It was time, many feminists felt, for the important work of childrearing to be shared by the community as a whole. Also important in working towards raising children free from old gender prejudices was that women be able to plan whether to have children and, if they did, how many and when. Thus contraception was a crucial feminist issue.

Body politics

For equality to be achieved it was argued that women must be able to control their reproductive capacities. The contraceptive pill had only become available in the 1960s. It did bring some improvement as it did not rely on the male partner's willingness to cooperate. However, it was not always 100 per cent effective and was not without side effects. Also access to the pill could be difficult for younger unmarried women. Given the lack of sex education in most Western nations, it was often the younger women who were most in need of contraception but most ignorant about it and often barred access to it by laws restricting access to older and often to married women (Goldin and Katz, 2002). Problems with the effectiveness and availability of contraception, the dangers of illegal abortions, along with the likelihood of women being coerced into sex, or raped, were key reasons why feminists argued that it was crucial for women to have access to legal abortion. Most importantly, however, feminists argued that women simply had a right to control their own bodies (for example, see Firestone, 1972; Greer, 1970; Millet, 1972/1970). Women could not really be liberated until they were free from the fear of unwanted pregnancies.

The fight for abortion was hugely controversial. Abortion was illegal in many countries, or only available in cases where the mother might be in danger of losing her life if the pregnancy continued. Conservative groups championed the rights of the unborn child, though they were often spectacularly unconcerned about what happened to unwanted children once they were born and had little to say about the rights of women. One of the crucial landmarks in feminist struggles for women's right to abortions was the United States' decriminalizing of abortion, which came about through a case famously known as *Roe versus Wade*. A single pregnant woman given the alias Jane Roe lodged a case against the state of Texas, where the Attorney General at the time was Henry Wade. Ms Roe challenged the Texas laws which made abortion a crime. The court eventually decided in her favour and declared that the Texas State laws, and by implication other similar laws in other states, were unconstitutional in depriving her of her right to personal liberty as established under the

Fourteenth Amendment (Supreme Court of the United States, 1973). This secured women's right to abortion in America, although that right has continued to be contested, and many states have recently returned to heavy restrictions against abortion (Wind, 2006). Elsewhere abortions remained illegal or exceedingly difficult to obtain in the 1970s. In New Zealand, for example, the process of getting a legal abortion was so difficult that feminists started Sisters Overseas Service to send women to Australia (Dann, 1985: 61–3). Fighting for abortion rights was therefore a crucial part of the feminist movement in most nations. However, for many black women and women of colour, obtaining abortions was not necessarily the issue. Racist attitudes and policies often meant that black women's fertility was heavily controlled. Black women in America and elsewhere have had to endure enforced sterilization, experimental contraceptive drugs and other efforts to prevent them having children (Roberts, 1997). Yet though the specific problems differed, feminists argued that they all illustrated the need for the control of women's fertility to be in women's own hands.

Demands for a woman's right to control her fertility were part of wider feminist concerns with a woman's right to control her body. This also encompassed issues of sexuality, sexual harassment, and physical violence against women. One area of feminist protest was around sexual objectification of women. One of the famous early feminist protests was against the Miss America beauty pageant. Feminists outside the pageant venue staged a symbolic protest whereby they put items of clothing that restrict women, such as brassieres, girdles, and high heels into metal drums. The plan was to set fire to the items, but the fire department would not let them. Nevertheless the media latched on to the protest and that is how feminists became labelled as 'bra-burners' even though the match was never lit (Echols, 1989: 94). Sexist advertising was also targeted, along with more serious pornography, as promoting images of women as always sexually accessible to men. This was an expression of and encouraged varying degrees of violence against women (Kelly, 1988). That force entered into relationships between women and men was one indication that power was operating.

Personal relationships, sexuality and power

Feminists were politicizing gender relations as power relations. This meant challenging their supposed naturalness (Pateman, 1989: 131; Mouffe, 1992: 372). Although this approach was intended to be an analysis of broad patterns of power which tended to favour men as a group over women as a group, feminists were often interpreted as critical of men as individuals. In other words they were accused of being man-haters (see, for example, Spender, 1985: 1–6). There were feminists who did believe individual men had responsibility for sexism, while others thought it more important to focus on patriarchy as a system in order to get away from the idea that women's liberation could be achieved if only individual men would change. While some feminist groups had included men in their early days, women had found that men tended to interrupt women and dominate the groups. Therefore most feminists argued that it was important for women to work together without men in order to develop their confidence and to ensure that women's needs were met. Men supportive of feminism were encouraged by some feminists to form their own groups to explore their complicity with patriarchal power and to consider how they might contribute to a more equal society (Holmes, 2000a). I return to masculinity politics later in the chapter, but it was an offshoot of feminism and there are other aspects of feminist politics which need to be covered first. These relate to other ways in which 'the personal' was politicized.

The politicization of sex, sexuality and sexual relationships included feminist debates about heterosexism. **Heterosexism** was a concept developed by lesbian feminists to describe the ways in which heterosexuality was taken to be 'natural', while homosexuals were the target of discrimination and, in some nations, of criminal punishment. Some lesbians were, it seemed, arguing that their sexuality was a fundamental part of who they were, not just a preference for a certain kind of sexual partner. This idea was present within consciousness raising and articulated within literature of the time (Klaich, 1974). Also lesbian experiences within a straight-dominated feminist movement played a part in making them aware of heterosexism. Heterosexual feminists seldom, if ever, saw their sexual orientation as a crucial part of their identity (see Kitzinger and Wilkinson, 1993). There was also much controversy around the position of some lesbian feminists who insisted that being a lesbian was a political statement. Many other feminists interpreted this as implying that only lesbians were 'proper' feminists. The notion of separatism was much misunderstood, often wrongly being equated with radicalism (Beasley, 1999: 53–8). Some lesbian feminists did argue that women should focus their sexual attention on women, and live their lives as separately from men as possible. This argument developed out of key feminist ideas about patriarchy as relying on demeaning sexualizations of women (see for example, Firestone, 1972; Greer, 1970). Most lesbians saw sexuality as far more complex than the sexual act, involving psychological, emotional and political factors as well as physical. For many this meant that separatism was not a viable political strategy, as they could not escape all these issues by avoiding men. However, there tended to be agreement among lesbian feminists, and many heterosexual ones, that the majority of a woman's energy should be channelled towards other women.

Seeing sexuality as a political choice marked an interesting shift towards seeing sexuality as socially constructed. This challenged common-sense ideas that sexuality was a natural attribute that could not be changed by will (see, for example, Jackson and Scott, 1996: 6–12, 17–20). However, there was also sometimes an assumption that women's true sexuality was repressed by patriarchy and lesbianism was that truth. The implication was that women could liberate themselves by 'choosing' to 'return' to this 'true' sexuality. Such an implication underestimated the complex operation of power in shaping bodies and sexuality. Although it was very important to politicize heterosexual relationships by revealing how power relations operated within them, there were problems with insisting that sexuality was fundamental to women's 'real' identity. Foucault has pointed out the problems of discourses which insist that the truth about ourselves lies in our sexuality. Western science has promoted such discourses since the nineteenth century and they have been used to control people who do not fit within scientifically sanctioned definitions of sexual normality, especially homosexual men and women (1990/1976: 69–70). However, it is important to note that not all lesbians were separatists (or even feminists) and that in some respects the insistence that sexuality was a political choice did suggest that it was not fixed by 'nature'. Also, lesbian feminists were not alone in encountering problems around issues of identity.

From unity to fragmentation?
Identity politics in feminism

In many respects the second-wave feminist movement, as with the first wave, was based on the idea that women shared a common, disadvantaged social position; that as women they had similar experiences of being treated as second-class citizens. Therefore their key **identity** was as a woman. Political unity between women was possible if they recognized this common identity and their shared oppression. Nancy Hartsock (1998) is well known for her intellectual rendering of this common early second-wave position, albeit she posits Marxist arguments for why women share common experiences, whereas within political activism feminists tended to refer rather more vaguely to women's shared oppression under patriarchy. She believes there is a **feminist standpoint** which emerges because women share a worldview based on their common material social position. In this extension of Marxian theory she proposes that women's reproductive activity, or close relation to that activity, makes them critical of patriarchy as partial and overly abstract, and relations within patriarchy as lacking connection. Because women are likely to be concerned with caring for others – be it children, husbands or elders – they are aware of the limitations of patriarchy's emphasis on individuals and competition. However, this does assume that all women are similarly involved in, or connected to, the reproductive activities of caring. Even if women do share similar experiences do they necessarily share the same ideas about how to address politically those experiences?

Ever since women have questioned their social position they have had varying ideas about what women want and need. This does not mean that women do not know what they want but that there are many different kinds of women, who have differing degrees and types of privilege or disadvantage according to their age, class, ethnicity, sexuality, ablebodiedness, region, religion and so on. The interests of young single women in a large city are different to the needs of elderly lesbian couples in rural areas, for example. A mass movement seemed to rely on unity, but there was also a need to have respect for differences among women.

The myth of sisterly unity

The notion of sisterly unity is in fact a feminist myth. Some accounts of second-wave feminism (for example, Mitchell and Oakley, 1997) have represented it as a united sisterhood torn apart by fragmentation because some women could not see their common cause with others. There was a great deal of excitement and fellow feeling, which emerged from women's struggles to fight their oppression. Yet from the very beginning there were women challenging some of the claims about women's interests made by the dominant white middle class heterosexual feminists. These challenges took place both within political activism and within scholarly debate – and the two were often closely connected in the 1970s and 1980s. In drawing on some of the excluded 'private' values associated with women, problems emerged because certain assumptions were made about which 'womanly' values were appropriate. Often the class and cultural location of these values were not considered. Those who did not fit easily within the class and culture or cultures to which those values referred, began to have difficulty in feeling that feminism represented their interests. Yet the attention given to process also allowed intense debate and demonstrated that unity did not pre-exist between women but had to be forged through acting together (see Laclau and Mouffe, 1985; Mouffe, 1992). To see feminism as only later acknowledging the importance of difference also ignores the fact that difference played a part not only in first-wave feminist arguments about what women would bring to politics, but also in second-wave attempts to further consider whether equality meant sameness. Although initially these arguments were ostensibly about women's difference from men they showed that, as Carol Bacchi has argued (1990), feminists have used both equality and difference arguments strategically in order to make material gains for women. At times feminists have suggested that women are different to men and could by this very difference enhance political life, bringing new perspectives and new skills. There are also cases, for example, pregnancy, where feminists have suggested that 'equality' can only be achieved if women are treated differently to men, because men do not get pregnant. In other situations such as arguing for educational equality, feminists have focused on similarities between women and men and therefore the rights of women to equal educational opportunities. All this proves that feminists did appreciate that there were differences among women as well as between women and men – and had ways of thinking about the political efficacy of drawing attention to differences. Many second-wave feminists argued that there were times when emphasizing similarities and building unity would bring the greatest rewards, but others suggested that this strategy usually excluded the needs of marginalized groups of women.

Women of colour from the USA to the Middle East, to former European colonies, mounted criticisms of white dominated feminist assumptions about women's interests and experiences, especially in relation to the family. Within the United States Afro-American women were at the forefront of challenges to white feminist versions of women's situation which failed to appreciate the importance of ethnic differences and racial inequalities. In the 1970s dominant feminist ideas about women's oppression, drawing explicitly or implicitly on Marxist debates, targeted the family as the key site through which women were subject to men's control (Barrett, 1980; Barrett and McIntosh, 1991). However, for most black women their families provided huge amounts of support and shelter in the face of a racist society (Martin and Martin, 1978). For black women to define men as 'the main enemy' (Delphy, 1984) was problematic given the common cause with their men in the fight against racism (Carby, 1982; hooks, 1981). Thus black women developed their own analyses of their oppression within a sexist and racist society, and encouraged white feminists to attend to their often racist treatment of non-white women within and beyond the movement (see for example, Davis, 1983; hooks, 1981; Hull et al., 1982). Such criticisms were not only made in an American context.

Indigenous women were also tackling issues of difference in former colonies such as Australia, New Zealand and Canada. They were arguing for their interests as women of colour; these often involving land rights claims, concerns about feminist and wider racism, and concerns about the physical and mental health of women who were still suffering from the consequences of colonial oppressions even after independence (see for example, Awatere, 1984; Kenny, 2002; Naples and Dobson, 2001; Pattel-Gray, 1999; Summers, 1975). Many of the ideas emerging from these criticisms are discussed in Chapter 8. Within feminist politics the debates centred on whether it was possible to act together to bring change for women.

Political alliances were still necessary and possible if it was recognized that unity did not 'naturally' exist because of identity but was created strategically in acting politically (see Laclau and Mouffe, 1985). There is a subtle but important distinction to be made here between this view of feminism as always being a debate (see Bacchi, 1990; Schor, 1992: 46) and the idea that feminists shifted from a concern with sisterhood to an emphasis on difference (see Evans, 1995; Oakley, 1997; Whelehan, 1995). The latter reproduces dominant strands of feminism (usually white and middle class) as central and 'other' feminisms as added later, rather than being parallel and equally important – even if often struggling to be heard.

Trying to construct unity and respect differences were things that were juggled simultaneously by feminists as they acted together. The emphasis on either unity or difference by particular feminists depended on their political and social location at the time and the aims they had in mind. It also depended on whether particular feminists or groups of feminists felt themselves represented by the movement. Those who believed strongly in unity often felt that they were clearly fighting for what women wanted – for equality for all. However, there was not always agreement on what constituted equality, which women were in need of it, or how it could be achieved. These problems were largely a product of feminist difficulties in analysing power.

Problems of power and identity

The emphasis on embodied identity/experience as the 'proper' basis for feminist knowledge and action was at times a radicalizing position, but sometimes produced an individualized approach to power and oppression caught up with how feminists oppressed each other within political action (Grant, 1987). In general, there was some doubt as to where the personal and political should be connected in representing yourself as a feminist. This resulted in a struggle over the place of the personal, some advocating the need for unity, others trying to think about how conflicts and differences between women could be dealt with more effectively. Feminists did not necessarily share the same 'personal' experiences, nor interpret them in the same way. Therefore, representing themselves in relation to 'the personal' highlighted differences. This made political action difficult if it was thought a unity of identity was necessary. However the process of struggling over how to represent the differing needs and interests of women was a crucial part of political action. A belief that women could or should avoid power in their relations with each other meant that identifying some as more powerful than others could be an accusation of personal and political failure. This was very painful for many of the women involved. It was a symptom of the general tendency within second-wave feminism to see power as something men have and women do not (see Curthoys, 1997; Yeatman, 1994). Understanding power is central to the feminist movement and Yeatman (1994) argues that its vision for change depends on the adequacy of its conceptions of power. Yet there are considerable problems with feminist understandings of women as subject to patriarchal 'power over' them. One is the way it contributed to an unhelpful categorization of hierarchies of oppression.

In trying to recognize difference some feminists represented themselves and others in terms of rigid sets of identities organized into hierarchies of oppression. White middle class women were closest to the top of the hierarchy and black working class lesbian women towards the bottom. And power relations were personalized. Lesbians attacked heterosexual women for dominating the movement, working class women denounced their oppression by middle class sisters. Power relations were defined in personalized and moralistic terms; 'racism, 'classism', heterosexism were [seen as] forms of personal oppression which certain women 'did' to others by dint of their membership of a more privileged group' (Jones and Guy, 1992: 8). The problem with the identity politics at the base of hierarchies of oppression was the cardboard cut-out notions of identity they enshrined. Overlapping, fluid and changing identities were difficult to deal with in that model (Adams, 1989). How might a middle class black lesbian understand her experiences via hierarchies of oppression? And where do you stop? What is significant – disability, religion, age, height? Hierarchies of oppression stifle debate and individualize problems.

Of course there are feminist scholars who have argued that all identity categories exclude – including the category 'woman'. In the shift from an emphasis on things to an emphasis on words, feminist intellectuals took issue with the way in which feminism had been based on a politics of identity which assumed a commonality of experience between women. Judith Butler, for example, explains her discomfort with the response of many feminists to postmodern interrogations of subjectivity and identity. That response insisted on the necessity of seeing a stable subject ('woman') as the foundation of feminist politics. However Butler proposes that this argument prevents political opposition and a questioning of the constitution of the subject. She particularly takes issue with the way in which subjects have been gendered in material ways by imposing ideas about the 'naturalness' of sexed bodies as the foundation for stable subjectivity. Therefore she suggests that:

> '[if] there is a fear that, by no longer being able to take for granted the subject, its gender, its sex, or its materiality, feminism will founder, it might be wise to consider the political consequences of keeping in their place the very premises that have tried to secure our subordination from the start. (Butler, 1992: 19)

To not challenge constructions of subjectivity was to ignore that 'the constituted character of the subject is the very precondition of its agency' (Butler, 1992: 12). In other words, feminism's reliance on a stable notion of 'woman' tended to assume that women were determined by their oppression, it tended to conceive of women as victims of patriarchy. Yet I would argue that Butler herself universalizes feminism too much. It is true that as a response to postmodernism many feminists may have promoted the advantages of a politics based on a subjectivity shared as women. However, the feminist movement fundamentally challenged liberal democratic conceptions of the political and this involved questioning dominant notions of subjectivity. Admittedly the focus was on the way in which women had been rendered non-subjects and therefore needed to claim a political voice. Nevertheless, this questioning existed and was arguably present in the attention to differences among women which I have suggested were always a part of the movement, even if initially given scant attention.

The problem with giving only scant attention to difference was that feminist politics often became based on notions of authenticity. Both Butler (1992) and Denise Riley (1988) discuss the ways in which feminist reliance on an identity as a 'woman' often produced squabbles over who was a 'real' woman. The same is true of more fragmented versions of identity politics; so, for example, in the USA there were debates about who might properly represent black women's interests which often fell into notions of who were the 'real' black women (hooks, 1981: 150). As already suggested there were debates about whether feminists should be lesbians and who were the 'authentic' lesbians. Even at the time, feminists saw the political limitations of such rigid definitions of identity and – contrary to stereotypes of them as humourless – they displayed a sense of humour about trying to account for the actual complexities of their 'personal' lives in such terms. In one feminist magazine in New Zealand a cartoon of two lesbians in bed read:

> I feel you should know that although I'm a downwardly mobile upper middle class non-monogomous socialist feminist lesbian separatist killer dyke … the little boy sleeping in the next room is not the neighbours'.
> (Anonymous, 1980: 6)

The resort to such hierarchies of oppression was brief; they prevented coalitions and indeed most meaningful debate. In addition they cast already disempowered groups of women as voiceless victims of oppression. Although the intention was to allow such marginalized women to speak, the ranking of oppressions assumed in advance that it would be extremely unlikely that those voices would be heard. This was not an empowering position for those women wishing to articulate different needs than those usually claimed as what women wanted by dominant feminists. Instead, therefore, feminists from more marginalized groups began to develop a politics of difference (Young, 1991) which emphasized the way in which identities were multiple, fluid and changing and yet were relational. This meant no longer viewing identity in terms of distinct boxes such as 'woman', 'white', 'middle class' and 'heterosexual'. In a politics of difference what was more crucial was the ways in which various key aspects of identity were constructed in relation to each other. Feminists – usually labelled postmodern – interested in the symbolic construction of gender, such as Riley and Butler, had already proposed that women's identity had to be understood as constructed in relation to what it meant to be a man. Marginalized women made this point in relation to class and sexuality, but perhaps most strikingly in relation to 'race'.

The black feminists discussed above and in Chapter 8 cannot perhaps be easily placed on one side of a 'turn' from emphasizing material inequalities to foregrounding symbolic constructions. It is true that some such as Davis (for example, 1983; 1998) had more to say about things, and others such as bell hooks (for example, 1981; 1992) wrote more of meanings and representations. But for black women a crucial factor in their oppression was their construction as non-white, and therefore as non-women. They were simultaneously invisible as 'blacks' because that term usually meant black men (see Hull et al., 1982). Their lack of access to material rewards within the societies they lived in needed to be understood in such terms. Even within nations where whites remained the minority the ramifications of colonialism meant that indigenous women in all their diversity of colour and culture were defined in relation to white European women and their descendants. Third World women were often represented by feminists in the West as all the same and as victims, always on the verge of starvation, enslaved to 'traditional' notions of women's inferiority within their culture. Such portraits, as Mohanty (1991) argues, lack an appreciation of the complexity and diversity of 'third world women' and their circumstances and serve largely to make Western feminists feel better about themselves and how relatively 'liberated' they are. Postcolonial feminism, as discussed in Chapter 8, has been one intellectual home of such new efforts to understand differences between women. This is a rather different project from understanding perceived differences between men and women as key. However, 'sexual difference' has continued to be addressed by feminists (see Beasley, 2005), and was also taken up by men within different types of masculinity politics.

Masculinity politics

Masculinity politics was only in some cases sympathetic to feminism, as men took up feminist challenges of masculine privilege in different ways. Small numbers of men supported and were involved in second-wave feminism. This made sense within discourses about the need for women and men to work together to achieve more equitable gender relations. Ideas about individual liberation from traditional constraints were voiced by a variety of new social movements in the 1960s and 1970s, including feminism (Laclau and Mouffe, 1985; Seidman, 1994). These ideas could imply that men also needed to be liberated from repressive roles. There was little evidence of men's repression within feminist political groups and meetings in which they were involved and they tended to dominate meetings. In most cases feminists found that women-only groups, whilst not without conflict, were preferable for achieving feminist goals, including equipping women with confidence and greater autonomy instead of relying on men (see Holmes, 2000a). For most men, however, feminism was challenging and demanded more thought be given to what it meant to be masculine and what privileges or costs that may involve. Responses varied as the politics of masculinity emerged from the realm of the taken for granted.

For powerful men, the benefits of masculine privilege have not been much thought about. Connell (1995) notes importantly that the defence of hegemonic (or dominant forms of) masculinity is political. Indeed it can be argued that powerful men closed ranks in response to feminism and that a 'backlash' emerged in the 1980s which saw women controlled in new ways (Faludi, 1991). I will talk about pro-feminist men's politics shortly, but other men's movements differ from feminist politics because they do not recognize men's institutional privileges; instead they focus on the costs of masculinity, and some are actively anti-feminist.

Therapeutic approaches to masculinity are one example of masculinity politics that have not been sympathetic to feminism. As Messner (1997) argues, such approaches move away from an agenda of socio-political transformation The mytho-poetic movement founded by Robert Bly, for example, implied that the problem was that men had become emasculated (and it was suggested that feminism had played a role in this) and needed to reconnect to their 'inner' masculinity. Groups of men, mainly in America in the 1980s, started going off into the forest to beat drums and find 'the warrior within' (Messner, 1997). The focus of such movements is on changing the self, not changing the world. While feminists have tended to be extremely sceptical about the value of therapeutic movements, Connell (2000: 201–2) argues that at least such movements show men giving some attention to what it means to be masculine and how that has changed. Even if their solutions might be considered reactionary or conservative, they are at least thinking about masculinity as something open to change, not as fixed and immutable. However, those men interested in masculinity therapies had a very limited vision of masculinity as a historical construct. Bly, for example, advocates a view of masculinity which supposedly encourages men to eschew macho aggressiveness, but he recommends a style of masculinity which essentializes certain types of emotional and physical strength as desirable for men – and as attainable if they can rediscover their connection with nature. He argues that '[e]very modern male has, lying at the bottom of his psyche, a large, primitive being covered with hair down to his feet. Making contact with this Wild Man is the step the Eighties male or the Nineties male has yet to take' (Bly, 1990: 6). His thinking reinforces the idea that women and men are naturally different, and that we should accept that and work with those differences rather than challenging them. The conservatism that such ideas embody has been subject to considerable criticism from feminists and sociologists (see Messner, 1997; Seidler, 1991) who wish to question the way things are and to examine the ways in which ideas about gendered behaviour being 'natural' usually reinforce inequalities.

Men pursuing masculinity therapy were not pursuing equality; they were only interested in changing themselves in ways that made them feel better. The focus on the self was perhaps partly a result of the shift to celebrating difference that was also apparent within feminism. It is interesting that the masculinity therapies movement apparently remained unified despite this shift, whereas many scholars believe that such a shift caused the fragmentation of feminist politics. Fragmentation was avoided arguably because all the men in such therapeutic movements were from similar, usually white middle class, backgrounds. They were not having to deal with much diversity within their groups and, as long as they were focused on changing the self and not on the world, a sense of communitas could be maintained. They were not trying to understand power relations as they existed in the world and their relationship to them. Their sense of solidarity with each other in 'rediscovering' the male power they thought lost was based on avoiding an analysis of patriarchy and denying they had privilege and power within patriarchy. As Connell (2000: 204) puts it: masculinity therapy 'offers personal comfort as a substitute for social change'.

Gay politics has been more oriented towards change and offered a questioning of masculinity more sympathetic to feminism; however, Connell (1995) argues that gay men do not inevitably resist complicity in the institutional privileges masculinity brings. Whilst some gay men adopt more feminine styles, for example as drag queens, there are others who take on a more rough and tough leather look which is very 'masculine'. And beyond their personal style some gay men might adopt a radical questioning of the current gender order, but others may conform to it. Similarly, straight men are not inevitably anti-feminist.

There are straight men who continue to seek to address gender inequalities in pro-feminist ways. If such men are involved in actively resisting hegemonic masculinity as part of their protest against gender inequalities then they are partaking in what Connell (1995) calls exit politics. This is a politics that is about exiting from the position and privilege associated with hegemonic masculinity. It is about refusing to be a man (Stoltenberg, 2000a/1989) in the socially sanctioned form of masculinity. So dressing in drag, expressing feelings, challenging homophobic ideas, protesting against male violence against women, respecting and supporting women in their struggles against sexism are all ways in which men might do exit politics. In places this exit politics has become connected to a queer politics which has emerged largely from lesbian and gay thinking.

Queer politics (see Chapter 4) questions the traditional reliance on identity as the basis for political activity. It promotes a fragmenting or 'troubling' (Butler, 1990) of identity categories such as those based on gender and sexuality. For queer politics the point is to break down ideas about femininity and masculinity as tied to your sex and for people to think about behaving in ways that do not fit into those categories or cross over boundaries so that masculine and feminine are not opposed any more. Gender and desire become fluid; they are ideas to be played with, not aspects of our identity internally determining who we are. But queer politics is thought to have limitations in bringing widespread social changes to address gender inequalities and differs from earlier ways in which feminists sought to politically address the way in which sexuality and gender are entwined. One question is whether such feminist politics still has any relevance.

Conclusion: Is feminism still relevant?

The politics of gender based around a shared identity as women (or men) has seemingly been subsumed by the advance of issues-based politics with a distinctly global character. Post-colonial struggle, environmental politics, peace, and indeed the anti-globalization movement itself have attracted not only members of the political left previously involved in feminism and other 'new' social movements prominent in the 1960s, but also a younger generation for whom amorphous 'enemies' such as the global corporation are the new threats. This is not quite the politics of difference which Iris Young (1991) spoke of at the end of the twentieth century. Such a politics, which recognizes the needs and interests of marginalized groups, has been rendered almost impossible by a post September 11 climate in which fear of the 'other' is rampant. Yet the new 'global' politics operates within such a climate and at times resists it, which it can do because it considers the impact of global processes on unique localities and cultures.

The potential to resist will vary considerably from one place to another, depending on whether it is a place which is of any material or ideological interest to powerful nations. Where there is oil controlled by 'friendly' regimes such as Saudi Arabia, there is likely to be little interference with that regime's tight restrictions on women within its borders. Where there was an 'unfriendly' regime in a poor but strategically important place such as Afghanistan, there was suddenly a surprising amount of concern about the rights of women. The actualities of women's lives in the two places are very different and in both many women continue to struggle for greater liberty. The problem is that their struggle is rendered unpredictable, subject to the vicissitudes of political and ideological conflicts stretching far beyond their borders. To what extent this is new is debatable. The newness perhaps lies in the level of complexity, of global interdependence, and of uncertainty. It may be that, as it might seem in Afghanistan, those conflicts bring greater freedoms. This I would argue is not the inevitable result of such actions, and indeed it remains to be seen whether extremist reactions to Western imperialism might again make life very circumscribed for women in Afghanistan and/or neighbouring regions.

While declaring its fight to be about 'freedom' the current American regime, as I have noted, has seen considerable curbs to women's freedom in the form of their ability to choose whether or not to have abortions within America's own borders. It is thus by no means certain what the gendered and other effects will be of the complex and often chaotic processes referred to as American imperialism or Indonesian or Israeli militarism or global corporate capitalism or environmental degradation. What is important from a feminist point of view is that there continues to be consideration of what those gendered effects might be and some struggle to try and ensure that women's lives, in all their diversity, are not made worse but enhanced and improved. Chapters 7 and 8 explore debates about class and ethnic differences to show how important diversity is in understanding gender. It may be difficult to agree on what constitutes 'improvement' in relation to gender inequalities and how to achieve it politically. What is crucial is that women are able to participate in making decisions affecting their own lives and those of other women.

Key readings

Echols, A. (1989) *Daring to Be Bad: Radical Feminism in America, 1967–1975.* Minneapolis: University of Minnesota Press.

Evans, J. (1995) *Feminist Theory Today: An Introduction to Second-Wave Feminism.* Edinburgh: Edinburgh University Press.

hooks, b. (1981) *Ain't I a Woman? Black Women and Feminism.* London: Pluto.

Messner, M.A. (1997) *The Politics of Masculinities: Men in Movements.* Thousand Oaks: Sage.

Young, I.M. (1991) *Justice and the Politics of Difference.* New Jersey: Princeton University Press.

7

How is gender intertwined with class?

Imagine two women, the same age, from the same city. They both work in the same office building. One has a comfortable office, starts work at different times each day depending on what needs doing, and lives by herself in a nice house in a quiet area of town. The other starts work at five in the morning, keeps her handbag in the cleaning cupboard, and lives with her two kids in a rented flat in a block with a lot of problems. The first woman is a lawyer, and earns at least four times as much as the second woman who is a cleaner. You can imagine that these women lead fairly different lives and that the lawyer is likely to have many advantages that the cleaner does not have. But if we remain at this individual level it is difficult to analyze why those differences might occur. At the individual level it is tempting to suggest that the lawyer got where she is because of her own hard work, which is probably true to some extent. But of course this implies that the cleaner has not worked hard, which is not the case. We could delve into the individual biographies of each of these women to find out how one became a single lawyer and the other a cleaner with two children. However, those biographies will tell us a lot more about women's lives generally, if we place them within their historical and social context. A sociological imagination (Mills, 1959) can help make sense of how the 'troubles' people experience result from disadvantages suffered by certain groups such as women, the working class, and ethnic minorities. We can imagine these women not as simply free-floating individuals but people living at certain times and in particular places, who are part of a number of social groups. The lawyer is a professional, a single woman. The cleaner is a low-paid worker, a mother. The different constraints and opportunities operating in these women's lives are better understood by appreciating not only economic structures but cultural discourses (ways of thinking and talking).

This chapter therefore directly discusses the shift from material to cultural explanations of gender. Here we see a transition from a focus on the economic and occupational categorization of class, through to analyses arising from Marxist ideas, and on to feminist critical responses to these ideas which embrace culture. I argue that these are the three major sociological approaches to considering how class and gender relate (see Skeggs, 2004). Within debates about the interconnections between gender and class we clearly see the attempts to understand gender as fundamentally a product of material, meaning economic, conditions – and we encounter the limitations of that approach. From this, new consider-ations emerge which add analysis of cultural factors in order better to understand class and gender. Those feminists taking this approach engage with Pierre Bourdieu's work, but also develop it in ways that offer some highly promising insights into the complexity of the relationship between gender and class as forms of inequality.

Chapter 6 discussed feminist efforts to broaden their thinking to consider inequalities amongst women, including those of class, and here we see how those ideas developed. Different forms of inequality have often been separated out because it is extremely difficult to try to think through how inequality may be simultaneously gendered, racial, and classed. This chapter begins with those who remain tied in some respects to identity politics (see Chapter 6), seeing it as important to continue to recognize that 'women' are a category of persons who continue to share material disadvantages as a group. A shared social identity as 'women' is argued to continue to play a large part in understanding inequalities, but not all women are equally disadvantaged. In explaining class disadvan-tages, the chapter focuses first on the material aspects of inequalities in relation to class. The term 'material' originally referred to relations of production and here we deal mainly with how gender was understood to connect to those relations. I therefore first discuss the analysis of gender and class which deals with relations of production and then consider attempts to examine class and gender in more cultural terms.

Class analysis

Class has always been of major interest to sociologists, but understand-ings and classifications of class have been based on men's life experi-ences. If we want to understand some of the key differences between the life of women lawyers and of women cleaners class is a useful concept because it can help us to think about how the different occupations they do affects the way they live, not only because one pays much better, but also because being a lawyer is considered more prestigious and involves having more control over your work. Class, for sociologists, can mean different things but, as my example suggests, it usually refers to some-one's position within a social hierarchy (or stratification system) based around the job you do, the money that it earns, the access it provides to other resources, the amount of control you have over your work, and how much respect is attached to that position within the hierarchy. However, women's class positions have not been accurately measured by traditional methods (Acker, 1998/1973; Delphy, 1984; Reay, 1998). As Joan Acker (1998/1973: 22) argues, classic class analysis has made several invalid assumptions when categorizing women.

Classic class analysis used the family as the unit for classifying people's class, which ignored class differences between women and men that might occur within families. For example, a builder may marry a business executive. How then can the class of the resulting family be accurately determined? In most cases the husband's class was thought to determine the class of the unit (Acker, 1998/1973). This was related to a second problematic assumption made when analysing class.

A second assumption early analyses of class made was that the woman's status is equal to her man's (Acker, 1998/1973). In other words, the idea is that the father's or husband's social status determines the status of the wives and/or daughters under his care. This assumption is based on a male breadwinner/female housewife model of the family that has always been largely restricted to middle class families able to survive on a single wage. That model does not apply to working class families where women have always engaged in paid work, or to more financially comfortable families where women have wished to work. In some cases where women work, their status may be higher than their husband's or partner's (McRae, 1986). This assumption also neglects evidence that the paid work women do is profoundly affected by gender inequalities.

Acker's third criticism of traditional class analysis (1998/1973) challenges the assumption that gender inequalities are irrelevant to how stratification systems are organized. Most models of class failed to note that the occupational opportunities open to women are delimited and devalued by those gender inequalities. Jobs defined as women's work continue to be of lower status and the average amount of pay they receive less than the average for men (see Armstrong et al., 2003; Charles and Grusky, 2004). Take the example of nursing (traditionally 'women's work') and policing (traditionally 'men's work'). Although there are male nurses and women police officers, the majority of nurses are women and the majority of police are men. Arguably the two jobs are in many respects very similar. They require of those who do them similar levels of education, specialized training and skills in dealing with people in crisis situations. The work involves unsociable hours and similar levels of stress and danger – nurses are exposed to disease and frequently subject to violent attacks from patients or their families and friends (Waters, 2005: 10). Yet even after the Equal Pay Acts passed in the 1970s, the predominantly male police force were paid more than the largely female nursing profession (see for example, *American Journal of Nursing*, 1984), prompting calls for equal pay for work of equal value (see for example, Armstrong et al., 2003; Gunderson, 1994).

Occupationally based class categorization originally ignored such differences between what was labelled 'men's work' and 'women's work'. It also ignored evidence showing that when women and men did work in the same jobs, gender discrimination often prevented women from reaching the highest levels (see Catalyst, 2006; Hymowitz and Schellhardt, 1986). Assessments of class that failed to appreciate such gender factors were liable to misrepresent women's social position. So if the assumptions behind the categorization of class were invalid when applied to women, then feminists needed to rethink how to explain women's class position.

Materialist feminism: Marxist feminism

Marxist feminists were among the first to try systematically to determine the nature of women's class position (see for example, Benston, 1969). The way in which women combined Marxism and feminism varied. Apart from Marxist feminism, sometimes it was called socialist feminism or materialist feminism. Although these were largely different labels for the same kind of approach, there were slight distinctions. Materialist feminism can operate as an umbrella term for these types of feminism, however it signalled the adaptation of Marx's methods rather than simple adoption of Marx's ideas as in Marxist feminism (Hennessy and Ingraham, 1997). Socialist feminism was perhaps also an adaptation, but especially described the more politically active aspects of materialist feminism rather than the theoretical approach (Beasley, 1999; Jackson, 1998b).

All the types of materialist feminism emerged out of engagement with Marx's historical materialism, but of particular importance to feminists was his claim that the point was not only to understand the world but to change it (Hennessy and Ingraham, 1997: 4). Historical materialism looks at how people produce what they need to survive; how they meet their material needs. It is particularly interested in how systems of production change, so for example Marx was looking at how a feudal system of production was being replaced by a capitalist one by the nineteenth century. **Capitalism**, according to historical materialism, is an economic system governed by those who control or own the means of production (the machinery, premises and so on used in making things). Different groups of people participate in making what we need, but the profits are not shared equally. Workers do not get their full share of the wealth that comes from selling what they have worked to produce. The argument is that without the labour of workers nothing could be made, no services provided, but the owners/employers (capitalists) accumulate fortunes for themselves by keeping most of the profit. Marx argues that profit is made from exploiting (mainly underpaying) the labour power of workers. The capitalists have achieved their wealth only because of that exploitation. This argument goes against some of the dominant ideas still heard – stories about business tycoons who have succeeded through their own hard work. Historical materialism suggests that such arguments are part of the dominant ideologies (justifying sets of ideas) that legitimate capitalism. Materialist feminists sought to adopt or adapt these ideas about historical materialism to explain and overcome 'women's oppression'.

Noting the gender-blindness of Marxist concepts, feminists also drew on postmodernism and psychoanalysis – especially the visions of meaning and subjectivity these knowledges offered (Hennessy and Ingraham, 1997: 7) – in order to forge new approaches to class. Although a little simplistic, it might help to categorize three different ways in which materialist feminists saw the intersection between capitalism and patriarchy:

1   Women's oppression is a side-effect of capitalism and would disappear in a socialist revolution.
2   Capitalism and patriarchy are dual-systems that reinforce one another.
3   The inequalities to which women are subject are best understood as the effects of capitalist patriarchy as one unified system. (Adapted from Hennessey and Ingraham, 1997.)

From this emerged what are known sometimes as the domestic labour debates (for an excellent account see Christine Delphy and Diana Leonard 1992: 51–7), which became increasingly difficult arguments disputing whether women's unpaid labour benefited capitalism or patriarchy.

The domestic labour debates

Most materialist feminists follow at least the key argument made in Margaret Benston's (1969) early article, that capitalist accumulation relies not just on paid labour but on women's unpaid labour in the household. I focus on her work as one of the most influential, earliest, and clearest contributions to the domestic labour debate. However, there have been many disagreements around aspects of her and similar approaches. In using Marxist concepts to understand women's oppression, she argues that a structural definition of 'women' within capitalist conditions is required. That definition involves making a classic Marxist distinction between use-value and exchange-value. Every 'product' supposedly has a use-value, which means that people can make use of it to fulfil some of their needs. Within capitalism, most but not all 'products' (or commodities) have an exchange-value – they are worth money on the market. Even in capitalist systems where the market is central, there are some commodities that remain outside the market and have only a use-value. In particular, it is suggested that things produced within the home remain outside the market. The meals that housewives make, the clothes they sew or mend and so on, are used by the family without being exchanged on the market (sold). This work within the home is seen as women's work. 'Women', Benston argues, are therefore the people seen as responsible for the production of use-value within the home. This is viewed as their primary task and any paid labour that they perform is seen as secondary, and therefore trivial. Meanwhile men's primary task is producing products with exchange-value. Because women's housework is unpaid it is not valued within capitalist society, where money determines value. Of course what Benston does not really explain is why housework is seen as women's work. This is a point taken up by Christine Delphy (see below), but first there is more to be said about how Benston argues that women's unpaid work at home is central to women's oppression.

Even if women do paid work, women's wages are typically lower than men's so the male wage remains crucial for the economic survival of most women. Within the nuclear family under capitalism, the man's wage is supposed to 'pay' for the woman's work and support children (even if a couple divorce – hence the child maintenance payments expected of husbands). If the male wage is assumed to 'pay' for most of the household work done by women then it 'pays' very badly. This is most clearly seen if you look at how much the work done by women at home fetches if it is done through the market. Look at the rates paid for babysitting, professional childcare, cleaning and so on. Low as the market rates for these might be compared to other jobs, wives and mothers typically perform them in return for their 'keep'. And though women may feel that they do this out of love and do not require payment, nevertheless the fact that their work at home is not actually paid – and therefore not valued – is key in making sense of gender inequalities.

Within the family women produce clean houses and cared for husbands and children and, because this is regarded as their main task, they can also be used as a reserve army of labour when other labour is scarce. When they are no longer needed in the labour market, they are expected to return to home and family. Thus the benefits that capitalists receive from women remaining primarily tied to their role in the home mean that capitalists will continue to encourage women to perform that role. So even when they are working, women are still expected to care for everything at home. Trying to do two jobs obviously affects the ability of women to perform in the labour market, and Benston (1969) argues that true equality of opportunity will require women's freedom from housework. She argues that capitalist attempts to free women by providing services on the market, such as childcare, are of dubious benefit as the services remain expensive and therefore not available to all. Indeed feminists following in the materialist tradition have recently pointed out how such solutions can merely shift oppression from privileged to less privileged women. For example, professional women in North America hire immigrant women to do their housework and childcare, and many of those women have to leave their own children in their home country to be cared for by often-overburdened female relatives (Ehrenreich and Hochschild, 2003). This supports Benston's argument that although the nuclear family may not be the best way to meet humans' practical and emotional needs, feminists must ensure that any alternatives will end women's oppression. She understands that oppression as fundamentally economic, but other materialist feminists introduce cultural aspects.

French radical materialist feminism

A less strictly economic analysis of the relation between gender and class is evident in French forms of materialist feminism, which were developing alongside – but largely independently from – the Anglo-American versions. Hennessy and Ingraham's (1997) collection, for example, includes only Delphy's work. In fact there were five French women who were key figures in this version of materialist feminism. They were Monique Wittig, Christine Delphy, Nicole-Claude Mathieu, Colette Guilliamin and Monique Plaza. These women produced the ground-breaking journal *Questionnes Féministes* with Simone de Beauvoir in the 1970s. Also closely involved was an Italian feminist called Paola Tabet. These feminists were principally concerned with how gender, sex and sexuality were constructed in relation to each other (Leonard and Adkins, 1996). Christine Delphy's work has been perhaps most renowned and of most utility to sociologists. Much that is key to her approach is initially outlined in her essay on 'The Main Enemy' first published in 1970, but also elaborated in that and other pieces in the collection *Close to Home* (1984) and in the later work with Diana Leonard (1992) on *Familiar Exploitation*.

In 'The Main Enemy', Delphy argues that an analysis of women's unpaid housework is central to understanding women's oppression, as all women are judged and their social positions determined in terms of the housewife role. In this, and other of her work, she looks at how patriarchal ideologies support male domination, so this is not entirely an economistic approach. Critical reflection on the women's movement is also formative in producing her theoretical framework. This framework is Marxist influenced, but unlike other Marxist feminists she wishes to draw on his methods without trying to bend concepts that were designed to explain capitalist class relations too far. These concepts she thinks are not well suited to the task of exploring women's oppression. In fact she argues that those terms have worked in ways that hide women's oppression. So, for example, she thinks many Marxist feminists became stuck because they saw exchange value and use-value as opposites. Delphy, on the other hand strove to see the fact that housework was without market value not as a problem but as key to understanding it. She characterizes her position as having three threads, which I have simplified somewhat:

1 Housework is unpaid because it is excluded from the market – it is not excluded because it is unpaid.
2 This is an exclusion not just of certain types of work but of certain social groups (women within patriarchal social relations).
3 Housework cannot be seen simply as a particular set of tasks – it is part of the domestic mode of production

Delphy's early work is also critical of ahistorical and universalized conceptions of patriarchy. For her, patriarchy is a system 'peculiar to contemporary industrial societies' (1984: 17). It is a system that subordinates women primarily through its economic bases in the domestic mode of production.

For Delphy, **the domestic mode of production** is key to explaining women's class position. Like other modes of production (forms of social organization through which things are made), she notes that it is also 'a mode of consumption and circulation' (Delphy, 1984: 18). Those exploited by this mode are maintained and not paid, and this means that their consumption is not self-selected. Within this system women do not really have the freedom to purchase what they want and when they wish. Also circulation occurs via the handing on of male property – usually from father to oldest son, which creates possessors and non-possessors (women and younger sons) within families. However sociologists have tended to ignore these inequalities within families and to focus on how systems of inheritance produce capitalist relations through passing on differences between families. For women these patterns of inheritance, which do not favour them, are not alleviated by recourse to the labour market. Women's lower wages within that labour market – and remember Delphy is writing initially in the 1970s and 1980s – push most women into marriage as the only real way to ensure their material survival.

Although this work is highly useful in understanding the relationship between class and gender inequalities, Delphy does not claim that it is a total account of women's subordination. She notes that her model of the domestic mode of production fails to account for all of the ways in which women experience oppression, even within the family. In particular she recognizes that she has not considered violence and sexuality.

However, she argues that in trying to explain everything, feminist theories often lose the ability to locate women's oppression in relation to other things and other inequalities. She is adamant that any explanations must see women and men as social groups, related to each other via hierarchies that are socially – not naturally – constructed. She argues that gender as a concept should recognize this, but has unfortunately remained tied to biological sex. Gender thus needs to be taken more seriously as a social construction – not just mapped onto, but constituting, sexual division. It is because of some of these problems with the term 'gender' that Delphy uses the term 'class' to look at the divisions between women and men. The term class keeps the explanation social. It sees women and men as groups that are related via domination. In short: women are a class, exploited as unpaid housewives by men (both individual husbands and male capitalists) through the domestic mode of production. Other aspects of the gender system, she notes, are waiting to be elaborated and in *Familiar Exploitation* (written with Diana Leonard) Delphy restates, clarifies, and in some cases updates these ideas.

Delphy's fundamental premise is that '[w]ithin the family in our society, women are dominated in order that their work may be exploited and because their work is exploited' (1992: 18). Just because much of the work might be done with/for love does not mean it is not exploited. Love actually disguises that exploitation; an exploitation best understood by analysing women's relations with the men in their families as being like the relations between employee and employer. It is also noted that the Marxist definition of work must be extended beyond its usual reference to the paid labour of producing things and the paid services associated with that. By 1992 there had been some recognition among Marxists that the non-paid work of physical care must be added. The authors further proposed that emotional, cultural (for display), sexual, and reproductive work must be counted. They were adamant that just because work might be chosen and enjoyed does not mean it is not work. Yet they also clarified that housework should refer to all domestic work, done by any person, though most of it is done by women. From this perspective it is easier to argue that housework is unpaid because it is done within a relation where those doing the work (usually women) do not own the products of their labour. It is not the work itself but doing it within this particular type of relation that means it lacks exchange value. The family is not a unit, but a hierarchy. Within the domestic mode of production constituted by such relations, gender and class inequalities are reproduced because: individuals learn different skills, some own what they produce and some do not, some have restricted access to the labour market – and varying inheritances, education, and training are given to different individuals within and between families. But this does not mean that Delphy regards women as victims. Echoing Marx again, she suggests that women 'certainly contribute to the making of their own worlds. But they do so not in conditions of their own choosing' (Delphy and Leonard, 1992: 261). Neither does she regard men as individually horrible, but suggests that as a group they benefit, whether they like it or not, from the way the system operates. This all restates or clarifies Delphy's earlier position, but there is also some updating in that some of the criticisms made by black feminists are also briefly addressed. Delphy and Leonard acknowledge that black women's oppression does differ and that racism may weigh heavily for black women, unifying black families to some extent. However they argue that family plays 'much the same role in black women's oppression as women as it does in white women's' (Delphy and Leonard, 1992: 19). This does not deal adequately with the ways in which 'race' is intertwined with gender and class, and we turn in the Chapter 8 to black feminists for a fuller analysis. That analysis of 'race' and gender began to gain attention as the kinds of class analysis usually contained within materialist feminism waned.

Structural, political and intellectual problems emerged by the late 1980s which shifted many feminists away from a preoccupation with class. Hennessy and Ingraham (1997) argue that class analysis declined as feminist intellectuals became disconnected from oppression and absorbed into the professional classes. A move away from class politics can be attributed to structural changes such as a centralization of government and provision of welfare – the type of structural change that makes unions less necessary, undermines class identities, and instead promotes group adherence around cultural values (Hechter, 2004). However, Hennessy and Ingraham assume that one has to suffer oppression to know about or discuss oppression, and they ignore the political problems dogging second-wave discussions of class and other identities. These included fierce debates about whether feminism was a project intrinsically based on understating or even ignoring differences between women – an issue dealt with in Chapter 6. Intellectual problems with materialist efforts to link class and gender were also key in encouraging a turn to culture. The domestic labour debates became very turgid by the close of the 1970s. These debates fizzled out because they became stuck on intricate, and not very interesting, details concerning what exactly 'value' meant within Marxism (Delphy and Leonard, 1992: 51–7; Jackson, 1998b: 16). Instead of acknowledging such problems Hennessy and Ingraham (1997) are critical of the transfer of attention to matters of sex or 'race', arguing that if considered at all, class simply was added to these other issues as though one of a series of oppressions. They suggest that to see class in such a way was profoundly non-materialist, losing sight of 'proper' comprehensions of class based on a structural view of the world. There are difficulties that emerged in moving away from structurally based understandings of inequalities towards more identity based ones, but it is grossly simplistic to imply that all interrogations of gender in relation to race lacked analysis of structure. Chapter 8 will elaborate on how approaches to race attended to structure as well as identity. In relation to class it was not only materialist feminists who debated the connection between capitalism and patriarchy.

Stevi Jackson (1998b) has proposed that rather than seeing Marxist feminism as opposed to radical feminism, with the first interested only in capitalism and the second only in patriarchy, it is more useful to think of these approaches as part of a continuum. The key concepts for all, according to Jackson, were production, reproduction, culture and ideology. Feminists more towards the materialist end of the continuum tend to emphasize production and reproduction, while those towards the radical end might talk more about culture and/or ideology. These are just some of the debates within feminism around how to understand inequalities and there was considerable criticism within and beyond feminism of the continued tendencies to gloss over differences between women. The utility of strictly economic definitions of 'the material' in overcoming such problems is doubtful. This may be one reason why what 'material' means has changed. Different ways of defining it do not necessarily make its meaning 'vague' (Hennessy and Ingraham, 1997: 10), but may allow greater attention to the nature of difference. According to Rahman and Witz (2003), the concept of 'material' has wandered within feminist thought from its initial reference to relations of production, to a broader and less economic definition that could be used to understand the construction of gender and sexuality. In particular, it was thought that a notion of the material could help to deal with thinking about the physicality of the body (see Chapter 5). Some feminists have found 'the material' in need of problematizing.

Rethinking class: a cultural take on the material?

More recent criticisms of materialist based approaches to class have drawn on elements associated with the cultural turn. Discursive approaches have been used to try to go beyond the limitations of Marxism and attend to how class is thought of and talked about. Materialism and discursivity are not inevitably opposed, indeed the ideological aspects of class formation have always been considered. Within feminist attempts to think about women's class position, material conditions tell only part of the story. The concept of ideology was previously used to complete the picture, but this often meant using psychoanalytic approaches that did not sit well with the anti-essentialist approaches feminists favoured toward gender (Rahman and Witz, 2003). A post-structuralist focus on discourse promised a perhaps more social and yet less deterministic way to consider gender and its relationship to class.

However, Barrett (1992) has suggested that to introduce a notion of discourse is to challenge materialism. She claims that the concept of discursivity involves a critique of materialism in its assumption that things are produced by discourse. However, this does not preclude a discussion of the materiality of the things thus discursively constructed (see Rahman and Witz, 2003). Materiality, as compared to 'the material', may be 'stretched' as a concept in order to understand some socially constructed objects such as bodies as involving a kind of non-linguistic substance. However, I would argue that a more traditional usage of the term 'material' can be applied in understanding other social phenomena. Class, for example, can be seen as a product of both material conditions and discursive formations.

The discursive construction of class and gender

Many feminists (see for example, Adkins and Skeggs, 2004; Duggins and Pudsey, 2006) wishing to move beyond economistic or structuralist theories of class have turned to the thinking of Pierre Bourdieu, who is highly critical of crude materialist distinctions between the real and the symbolic. He has extended the Marxist understanding of class (for example, in Bourdieu, 1987) to look at the importance of not just economic but also cultural and social forms of capital. He turns the notion of capital into a metaphor and identifies three main forms: economic, cultural and social capital. **Economic capital** can simply be described as monetary wealth or assets. **Cultural capital** is something more abstract but can be thought of as like wealth in the form of ways of thinking and being. Bourdieu argues that middle class ways of thinking and being are privileged. If you know about classical music, fine wines, and how to wear classy clothes, and hold your knife and fork 'properly' for example, you are likely to be recognized as having cultural capital. These and less privileged tastes are learnt within people's class backgrounds and are used by the middle classes to create distinctions between themselves and 'lower' classes. **Social capital** refers to the connections and networks with others to which people belong; for example, an old boys' network or a group of trade union activists. Hierarchies of class are organized around how much these different capitals are thought to be 'worth'.

Class is not just about material situation but is a discourse about what and whom is valuable and respectable in society. The forms and types of capital valued differ in different fields. A **field** is a set of structured relations between people, for example the political field or the intellectual field. Within say the cultural field, including the art world, 'good' aesthetic taste is valued (Bourdieu, 1987). However, fields are always a battleground on which struggles over capital are played out. According to Bourdieu, habitus is crucial to the success of privileged groups of people within these battles. **Habitus** is the set of learned and embodied ways of doing and thinking (see Chapter 8). For example, a middle class habitus is likely to involve learning ways of speaking and thinking that prepare children well for the field of education, where school systems value analytical and generalized views of the world. Therefore middle class children are more likely to do well at school because they have a habitus that 'fits' with the field; they already have the cultural capital that is valued in the field of education (Bourdieu, 1974). Class therefore reproduces itself because dominant classes are advantaged in the struggles over capital. In this respect Bourdieu refers to a fourth form of capital: symbolic capital.

Symbolic capital is about the legitimacy that certain forms of capital take on, and how all the varying types of cultural capital and social capital are weighted in relation to each other and how this shifts. This is about power. Remember that Bourdieu is using capital as a metaphor. Symbolic capital acts as a kind of umbrella term which captures the processes of legitimation that Bourdieu is trying to describe. Those processes 'misrecognize' socially constructed hierarchies of worth for 'real' worth. In other words, if something has symbolic capital it means it is thought to have 'innate' value (see Duggins and Pudsey, 2006: 113). An example might be that a Picasso painting is thought to be unquestionably 'good' art. It has symbolic capital because its value is thought to come from some innate artistic merit, but Bourdieu would argue that its value is actually created by the dominance of middle-class forms of cultural capital, which means their view of what is 'good' art is seen as the 'correct' view. Symbolic capital legitimates, allowing or restricting the ability of different types of economic, cultural and social capital to be converted into other forms. You can convert your knowledge of Picasso (cultural capital) into economic capital by, say, writing art criticism or working for fine art galleries or auction houses, more easily than you could convert a knowledge of graffiti art. Yet how might gender be part of these legitimation processes?

Diane Reay (for example, 1997; 1998; 2005) has argued that in order to understand how class and class inequalities are lived in gendered ways, sociologists need to move beyond an economistic (structuralist) focus to include discourses. She claims that middle class discourses on class are dominant. For example, the discourse of classlessness that has emerged within everyday life in most Western nations (she focuses on Britain) suggests that class is a thing of the past and that people can now succeed through hard work if they wish. Reay notes that this discourse blames the working class for not succeeding and that the working class are seen as 'other'. The psychic effects of this class creation are further explored in her later work (Reay, 2005), but all her work asserts that working class people continue to have limited opportunities partly because of the way ideas about class and gender influence their ability to take advantage of any opportunities available for themselves, or their children. In one of her articles she discusses the example of education, based on her research with working class mothers. She finds that the way mothers consume education is shaped by class. One mother talks about her son's education:

> For me it's all rather confusing because I didn't get that far ... I feel incapable. A bit of me thinks why shouldn't he go to Oxford or Cambridge. But there are certain courses you should take and people like me just don't know. (Quoted in Reay, 1998: 270)

Here a mother expresses her lack of cultural capital. She does not have the 'right' kind of knowledge to help her son get to Oxbridge and thereby get qualifications which would allow him to convert that into social capital (meeting the 'right' kind of people) and economic capital (getting a 'good', well-paid job). However, Reay fails to develop the idea of how gender is important. Quite what this mother might mean by 'people like me' is open to interpretation. Does her femininity make her even less likely to be able to pass on not only the right kind of knowledge, but the right kind of connections (she is unlikely to belong to 'old boy' networks) – or even to provide much economic support? Reay seems to lose an account of gender in the details of the data. I return to the promise of her later work shortly. Meanwhile, more precise considerations of how class and gender intertwine can be drawn from the work of Beverley Skeggs.

Beverley Skeggs's (1997) work *Formations of Class and Gender* develops Bourdieu's analysis in order to consider the importance of class in the symbolic construction of gender. She argues that the forms of capital outlined become organized and valued within the social relations of gender and class (and indeed 'race' (see Hunter, 2002)). For working class women the notion of respectability is key to their struggle with constructions of class and gender. In her ethnographic study Skeggs follows a group of young women who were enrolled on caring courses at a further education college. By taking such courses the women hope to convert their limited feminine cultural capital into economic capital. Women are thought to have cultural capital in the form of knowledge of how to care for others, which they hope to legitimate by getting qualifications. Yet those qualifications do not necessarily provide the chance for the women to convert their cultural into economic capital. Even if they do get caring-related jobs they are often insecure and poorly paid, and do not guarantee respectability. Skeggs provides some telling illustrations of how notions of respectability reinforce class distinctions within everyday life. Working class women are constantly reminded that they are thought lesser beings, not entitled to privileged treatment, sexualized and given little respect. One woman, for example, talks about her experience of working for a middle-class family:

> When I first went to work as a nanny I couldn't stand it. They [the middle class people] really think they are something else. They treat you like shit. What I've noticed is they never look at you. Well they do at first they look you all over and make you feel like a door rag, but then they just tell you what to do. One of them asked me if I had any other clothes. Some of them want you to know that you are shit in comparison to them. (Quoted in Skeggs, 1997: 92)

Skeggs's highly evocative analysis of the realities of class domination for working class women indicates the myriad ways in which they are made to feel worthless. Their femininity is always implicated in these distinctions. They may scorn the snobbishness and pretensions of middle-class women, but are acutely aware that if they can approximate to the taste of that middle-class feminine style, there will be social rewards attached. They might be able to get 'better' jobs, 'better' men, and 'better' lives. However, it is not easy – especially when compared to masculinity – to convert femininity into 'good' jobs.

Lisa Adkins (1995) has explored the labour market as one in which continued prejudices about gender and sexuality as markers of particular types of capabilities help create 'women's jobs' and 'men's jobs'. For example, masculinity is thought to be a marker of physical strength and femininity a marker of pretty pleasantness. This is illustrated in one of the workplaces that Adkins studied: 'Funland', a leisure park in a declining British seaside resort. The managers almost exclusively chose men to operate the rides (90 per cent of operatives were men). They claimed that the fast rides, especially, required operators with physical strength and assumed that only (young) men had this. In fact operating the rides only required the pressing of a switch, but managers were adamant. Meanwhile women were almost exclusively employed in the catering jobs at the fair. They were selected for having the 'right' kind of appearance, which seemed to be a kind of feminine prettiness. Why this was necessary was unclear because 'you do not have to be pretty to make sandwiches' (Adkins, 1995: 107). However, the catering manager was insistent that customers would expect that kind of prettiness, therefore she must employ women with the 'right' look. By looking at this and other workplaces Adkins shows that not only is women's appearance key to judgements and regulation of them as workers, but that women's sexual labour is also exploited by customers and by their male co-workers. Women are subject to considerable sexual innuendo and general sexualization. Just one example is the women bar staff at

Funland being expected to wear gingham dresses and the bar manager frequently pulling the sleeves down so that the dresses were worn 'off the shoulder', as he insisted they should be. Women workers have to go along with this in order to keep their jobs and although sometimes they may find sexually charged repartee with co-workers enjoyable, if they do not go along with it they know it could turn nasty.

What Adkins deduced from this gendered sexualization of labour evident in Funland and other workplaces she studied is that capitalism is a profoundly gendered system. She argues therefore that women are not 'workers' in the same way as men. Her work offers an extremely important corrective to a class theory which has failed to understand why capitalism should care who does the different types of jobs available. Adkins could be used to understand managers as exercising a 'taste' for particular types of workers to do particular jobs. She allows us to appreciate the significance of gender and sexuality in producing men's labour market advantage and therefore their greater command of economic capital. What slips away in her otherwise careful considerations is a view of the relationship of class to the production of what are considered the 'right' kinds of feminine appearance and behaviour.

Adkins's (2004) argument is that gender is an ingrained habit remade and reinforced by reflexivity, rather than transformed by it; but the actual role that class might play remains unanalyzed. She attempts to develop an analysis of the 'feminine habitus' as it has altered in a shift from private (domestic) to public spheres. It seems clear empirically (see for example, Holmes, 2004; Jamieson, 1998; Skeggs, 1997) that there is no 'easy association' between supposed increased reflexivity and detraditionalization (a freeing from past rigid constraints) (Adkins, 2004: 191). Gender and gender inequalities are reproduced in relation to sexualized power hierarchies which continue to restrict women. Adkins notes in analysing an empirical study that one respondent commented 'it depends who I am going to be seeing. Sometimes I'll choose the 'executive bimbo look', at others … [a plain but very smart tailored blue dress] looks tremendously professional' (McDowell cited in Adkins, 2004: 203). Adkins fails to comment on the class implications here. What is an 'executive bimbo look'? Is the 'professional' woman distinguished by a middle class respectability from that sexualized image of a working class woman made good? The links between the economics of capitalism and the discourse of patriarchy remain unclear and there are other difficulties with discursive approaches to class.

Criticizing a discursive approach to class

Looking at discursive constructions of class is useful to clarify the interweaving of class with gender in valuing people. Such an approach helps recognize the hierarchical basis of conceptions of sex/gender/sexuality. To paraphrase George Orwell: some women are more equal than others. In some respects a discursive approach helps answer questions about why women do housework and other work regarded as 'women's work'. They do this work to display themselves as respectably feminine – as worthwhile. However, with working class women there always appears to be an awareness that others may not be convinced. Working class women have, if we follow Bourdieu, an ingrained habitus. These ways of thinking and doing cannot be entirely shaken off, nor do working class women always wish to negate their background and become 'snobby'. Yet they know that there are social rewards available if they can achieve some success in shaping themselves to the norms of 'respectable', meaning middle-class, versions of feminine behaviour (Skeggs, 1997).

Bourdieu's conception of class and his focus on its reproduction is not thought to account well for social mobility or social change (Skeggs, 2004). He does not make it clear how habitus can be reshaped if it is so ingrained. He recognizes that people do reform themselves, but usually implies that this is more of a superficial and highly conscious imitation of socially valued ways of doing things. Skeggs takes this on board and illustrates how tenuous working class women's performances of respectability can be. The problem is that Bourdieu is arguing that your class habitus fundamentally affects how you think and do things and how you are judged by others. How then are some individuals (and not others) able to succeed in overcoming, or remaking, their habitus successfully enough to gain social mobility? 'Successful' individuals can easily be demonized as having 'sold out' and taken on dominant middle-class values. Accruing a certain volume of capital might bring upward social mobility, but is not simply a matter of those who are successful being able to compensate for a lack of say cultural capital by having good social capital. The notion of symbolic capital is an attempt to explain why the struggles over capital that he acknowledges occur within different fields do not significantly alter existing class hierarchies. Those struggles in fact reinforce and reproduce such hierarchies, principally because of the symbolic violence which frames them. Symbolic violence is a violence which is 'imperceptible and invisible even to its victims, exerted for the most part through the purely symbolic channels of communication and cognition (more precisely misrecognition), recognition, or even feeling' (Bourdieu, 2001: 1–2). His attempts to use the notion of symbolic violence specifically to understand masculine domination (Bourdieu, 2001), do not substantially add to existing feminist arguments about the importance of representations as well as economics in the oppression of women. Although his formulation of the problem is useful in thinking about how power becomes sedimented into repeating patterns (Holmes, 2004), it is less useful for considering how some working class women are able to overcome cultural evaluations of themselves as disreputable and accrue some valued forms of capital.

Despite the perception of working class (and indeed all) femininity as a flawed form of cultural capital, a gendered habitus can be converted into other forms of capital if women can maintain the 'right' ways of looking and behaving. Adkins and Skeggs both have things to tell us about what constitutes those 'right' ways of doing femininity and how precarious the performance can be. The precariousness of gender performances can be very usefully considered by thinking more about the relations between gender, class, and emotions.

Gender, class and emotions

The devaluing of working class (women's) ways of thinking, doing and being includes a devaluing of their ways of feeling. The term 'emotional capital' was coined by Helga Nowotny in 1981 and Reay (2004: 60) explains that it is a variant of social capital 'generally confined within the bounds of affective relationships of family and friends and encompasses the emotional resources you hand on to those you care about'. She notes that it is women who are expected to deal in emotional capital, balancing and attending to the needs of family members in particular. However, she makes the point that not only 'positive' emotions profit families; for example, a mother's anger might spur children on to better educational achievement (Reay, 2004: 62–3). Yet emotional capital is not equally distributed. Despite no evidence of real class difference in emotional involvement with children, for instance (Reay, 2004: 65), the difficult conditions of working class women's lives may make it more difficult for them to 'supply' emotional capital. The 'costs' of supplying that capital in terms of time, energy and conflict management, may be ones they are unable to meet. Discourses are again seen as important, because middle class practices of trading emotional for cultural capital (such as deciding long stressful journeys are acceptable to send a child to a 'good' school) are represented as normal. Reay found working class parents tended to put the emotional well-being of the child first, which in comparison to the middle class norms can look naïve. Although Bourdieu recognizes that such misrecognition can constitute symbolic violence, and therefore do damage, he provides little discussion of the affective dimensions of class.

The reproduction of class in gendered ways, physically (see Hall, 2000; Hunter, 2002) and emotionally (see Skeggs, 1997), hurts. Although exploring the 'hidden injuries of class' (Sennett and Cobb, 1972) is not new, Skeggs offers an understanding of these injuries in gendered terms. Recently she has argued that the white working class woman is seen as lacking moral value, as repellent and repulsive, and sexually unrestrained. As a figure she is used to demarcate what lies beyond the moral limits of 'respectable' society, although the form of this figure has changed somewhat:

> Shifting the emphasis from the 1980s political rhetoric, which figured the single mother as the source of all national (British) evil, we now have the loud, white, excessive, drunk, fat, vulgar, disgusting, hen-partying woman who exists to embody all the moral obsessions historically associated with the working class now contained in one body, a body beyond governance. (Skeggs, 2005: 965)

Such representations cause substantial problems for working class women in terms of constructing and regulating a self. Skeggs's work keeps firmly in view the pain of being thought 'shit in comparison with them' (quoted in Skeggs, 1997: 92). Thus she provides a keen sense of the 'emotional politics of class' (Skeggs, 1997: 75) and the integral part gender plays in these politics. The perceived unworthiness of working class femininity is a crucial marker within the all important hierarchies of 'taste' or value that reproduce class. For Skeggs (1997: 10) femininity can be thought of as a form of cultural capital which can be used and resisted in different ways. Yet this cultural capital cannot readily become symbolic capital.

What remains unclear is how some women are able to overcome the hurt and embrace sufficiently valued ways of doing femininity, enough to shift up the hierarchy – and whether such individual 'successes' actually disrupt existing relations of power or merely reinforce them. It would seem that one working class woman's ability to 'pass' as respectable and gain the rewards attached merely underlines the notion of individual hard work as the key to 'success'. It also perpetuates middle class notions of what constitutes success. Questions remain about how one woman is able to overcome her class habitus, if she has a gendered habitus with low social value. That gendered habitus is detachable from class habitus seems unlikely from the detailed arguments of researchers such as Adkins, Reay and Skeggs; but we are left wondering about the extent to which they may be relatively autonomous from each other and whether this might make them less ingrained than Bourdieu allows. If gender and class habitus can be used as levers against each other to disrupt sedimented relations of power then symbolic violence might hold within itself seeds of resistance. A better understanding of the emotional aspects of class tastes and distinctions is certainly key in progressing towards an analysis of capitalism and patriarchy as connected via a hurtful lack of recognition of femininity as valuable.

Conclusion

This chapter has dealt with feminist attempts to understand diversity among women, and in particular the different degrees of privilege women experience due to class differences. Initially feminists endeavoured to see how class differences between women were difficult to demarcate using traditional class categories based around relationship to paid work. However, by considering gender as it emerged within both relations of production and of reproduction within the household, materialist feminists were able to make some headway in linking gender and class inequalities. However, why it should be women who undertook the caring and servicing of other workers could not be adequately explained within this framework. This led many feminists to turn away from Marxism towards other ideas which might better account for the differential access to material rewards and social recognition.

The general cultural turn and the insights of sociologists such as Bourdieu have brought rethinkings of class. I have only briefly touched on that rethinking here, illustrating that it can provide rich possibilities for the consideration of how class and gender are intertwined. Dealing with the limitations such an approach might have can be done only briefly within this chapter. The notion of gender and class as ingrained and intertwined into a habitus is useful for trying to understand how gender and class are lived by women. It allows us to understand processes through which class is reproduced, but it does not explain why that reproduction is not total. Emotions, and especially anger, can be crucial in moving relations with others away from hurtful devaluations and towards greater respect for diversity (Holmes, 2004). This diversity obviously extends beyond the intertwining of class and gender. The discussion of the intersections between 'race' and gender in Chapter 8 will further our considerations of the relative importance of material and cultural factors in the imperfect reproduction of inequalities affecting women.

Key readings

Acker, J. (1998/1973) 'Women and social stratification: a case of intellectual sexism', in K.A. Myers, C.D. Anderson and B.J. Risman (eds), *Feminist Foundations: Towards Transforming Sociology*. London: Sage.

Adkins, L. and Skeggs, B. (eds) (2004) *Feminism After Bourdieu*. Sociological Review Monograph Series. Oxford: Blackwell.

Delphy, C. and Leonard, D. (1992) *Familiar Exploitation: A New Analysis of Marriage in Contemporary Western Societies*. Cambridge: Polity Press.

Skeggs, B. (1997) *Formations of Class and Gender: Becoming Respectable*. London: Sage.

How is gender intertwined
with 'race'?

'Race' is not just something black people have; all of us are shaped and indeed gendered by it. 'Race' developed primarily as a term to try and explain differences between whiteness and blackness, and to account for the different ways of life of white and black peoples around the world. The majority of the world's population is not white. That majority is, strikingly, also not rich (for example, see UNICEF, 2006). Understanding the way in which such racial inequalities have emerged and to what extent they are connected to gender involves considering in particular why it is that black women and women of colour are among the world's poorest. Here I use the word 'black' in a broad sense of 'not white'. The term 'women of colour' is used by some writers to be more inclusive of Asian, Polynesian and other peoples aside from those of black African heritage, but I use the terms fairly interchangeably to indicate that most major racial divisions have occurred around the opposition white/non-white, where white has become synonymous with European (Bonnett, 2000). The term 'non-white', however, tends to reinforce the idea that white experience is the norm. Therefore I use these other terms to draw attention to the lives and experiences of women who are not of European origins. An appreciation of colonizing processes is necessary to understand how 'race', or ethnicity, and gender interrelate; but first, it is important to define some of the other highly loaded terms in this field, especially the concepts of ethnicity and of race.

Defining 'race' and ethnicity

'Race' is a highly problematic term. Categorizations of race are usually inflicted upon people in ways that carry judgements about their supposed inferiority. Sociologists recognize how ideas about race produce racial inequalities, even if those ideas are wildly inaccurate. **Racism** is a form of prejudice based on 'common sense' and inaccurate beliefs about the differences between 'races'. 'Race' was a concept used by Victorian scientists in their attempts to understand physical differences between peoples from different parts of the world. Skin colour was the most obvious observable difference and nineteenth century scientists were particularly obsessed with classifying black people as a 'race', separate from whites. These white European scientists measured skulls and discussed lip and eye shape and tried to prove that 'whites' were more civilized than and superior to blacks, Asiatic or other peoples. The 'science' used has now been discredited and it is accepted that there are no such things as distinct races; underneath superficial differences like eye shape or skin colour there is nothing biological that really distinguishes Asian from non-Asian people or black from white. A particular black African person may have more genetically in common with a white European than with another African. 'Race' is now recognized as a scientifically inaccurate and meaningless way of trying to make sense of superficial physical differences between peoples. Differences in skin colour or eye shape do not have any relationship to differences in intelligence, character, or behaviour. Nevertheless, the myth of 'race' remains influential in the commonsense ways people use to make sense of their relations to each other (Banton, 1998).

Sociologists usually prefer the term **ethnicity** to the term 'race', because it focuses on social and/or cultural differences between groups of human beings. Ethnicity is usually self-defined: a way of identifying yourself in terms of a group to which you feel you belong. An **ethnic group** is one that shares common ancestors, a set of cultural beliefs, traditions and ways of doing things. Usually this includes sharing a language (see Smith, 1981). So I might identify myself as Pakeha (a white New Zealander); many of my current students will refer to themselves as Australian, others as Indian; other people might identify as Finnish, Angolan, Iranian, Cantonese, or Samoan. Ethnicity is crucial for exploring the ways that such different groups of people live their lives and relate to each other. For example, comparisons between gender roles in different ethnic groups can help establish how gender is socially constructed not naturally given; however, care has to be taken in making such comparisons.

Looking at gender as it is done differently in a variety of cultural contexts helps us to undermine the idea that differences between women and men are 'natural', and to examine relationships between gender and ethnicity. If biology makes women behave differently from men, would we not expect women's behaviour to be the same across cultures? But 'feminine' and 'masculine' behaviour are different in different cultures, as shown by the examples from different cultures that have been discussed elsewhere (especially Chapter 2). There are similarities, but this is hardly surprising within an increasingly interconnected world where most ethnic groups are aware of and influenced by other ways of thinking and doing gender. Nevertheless, most cultures think their way of doing gender is best.

It is important to avoid ethnocentrism in looking at cultural variations in practices around gender. **Ethnocentrism** is the belief that your own cultural practices are the most 'normal' or 'natural' way of doing things. White Western women, in particular, are prone to thinking that 'other' women are less liberated than themselves (Mohanty, 1991). For example, much comment is made about the oppression of Moslem women; but this is a gross generalization. For example, Pakistan is an Islamic nation that has had women participating in most areas of society including politics. A woman, Benazir Bhutto, was prime minister of Pakistan in the late 1980s. Note that the USA has yet to have a woman President. When talking about 'Islamic nations' we need to separate out religion, and political and cultural practices. Just as Western nations have, within and between them, varying interpretations of Christianity and different relationships between religion and the state, so it is the case with nations based around Islam (see for example, Afshar, 1997; El Saadawi, 1982; Saliba et al., 2002). It is not Islam itself that necessarily oppresses women, but other cultural practices within some societies where Islamic people live. There is little evidence, for example, that the Moslem women of Pakistan have less autonomy than their Hindu neighbours in India and regional differences in culture rather than religion are what determine how much education, the degree of participation in paid work and how much control over decision making women have (Jejeebhoy and Sathar, 2001). In some 'Islamic' countries, such as Iran (see Afshar, 1997) and Saudi Arabia, women do not enjoy the same individual rights as men and may be severely restricted in terms of their opportunities and movements. These are politically imposed restrictions, often condemned by more liberal interpreters of Islamic religious teachings. In addition, looked at from a less ethnocentric point of view about what is important, women in such countries may enjoy a status and respect within their traditional roles that most Western wives and mothers do not have. Of course not all women in Iran and Saudi Arabia will feel content with the limited roles offered them and often protest (El Saadawi, 1982; see BBC News, 2003), but these limitations are not always part of Islam or of Islamic women's lives. It may be illuminating to consider what women from other cultures might make of women in the West. Just as Westerners are often critical of other gender practices, people in other cultures might find Western practices strange.

Awareness of different cultural understandings about gender is important but this can raise problems of relativism. **Relativism** means believing that you can only understand and judge a culture in terms of its own worldview. This tends to mean believing truth is relative to those cultural beliefs, rather than there being one truth or 'rightness' by which all cultures can be judged. A relativist stance can make it difficult to be critical of other cultures. For example, there have been heated feminist debates (see Moruzzi, 2005) over the practice of female circumcision in some African nations. This practice varies between tribal groups, but usually involves an older woman removing the clitoris of adolescent girls in order to ensure their fidelity to future husbands. Sometimes the vagina is also sewn up, leaving just a small opening for urination; on marriage, husbands literally cut open their brides. There are those feminists who see this in relativist terms. They may not agree with it, but look at the wider culture in which it takes place to understand why it happens and why it is women who do it to each other. Girls go through this painful procedure and older women inflict the pain because circumcision is seen as crucial in becoming a woman. Without being circumcized a girl cannot take her place as a 'normal' adult member of her society. The older women want to help and support her in doing this. If a girl remains uncircumcized she will be an outsider, looked on with some suspicion by other women, and men will be unlikely to marry her. Where it is difficult to survive as a single woman, this would be a serious problem.

Other feminists argue that harmful practices such as genital mutilation (as some call female circumcision) show that there are limits to a relativist approach. They believe that it is possible to have some cross-cultural or universal standards by which to judge cultural practices. Those practices judged as harmful to women should be campaigned against with the help of women in more privileged cultures. Relativists see this Western feminist view as interfering, patronizing and arrogant. However, while the relativist view helps explain why women may endure circumcision, it does not help us consider that many of the women involved would wish not to have to endure it. Relativists often end up in a trap of seeming to condone the way things are without being able to think about how they might change. This sometimes means taking a rather ahistorical view of non-western cultures, assuming that peoples living in 'traditional' cultures have gender relations that have not changed over time. Ethnicity is a concept that can help us avoid such static views of other cultures and to understand them in terms of that culture's worldview. However, that worldview is likely to have been shaped in relation to other cultures and to notions of 'race'. 'Race' therefore still warrants attention as it is a myth upon which people continue to act. Ideas about 'race' produce racism.

The idea that 'racial' groups exist and that some are superior has been used in gaining power, and these ideas and practices are what constitute **racism**. In particular, ideas about white superiority were conveniently appearing just as European powers were becoming firmly established as colonial powers, with huge amounts of control over the non-white populations of the world.

Colonization and slavery

If we are to really understand inequalities of 'race' and how they relate to gender then it is crucial to know about **colonization**, which is a process by which an invading people impose their economic and political structures and their cultural beliefs upon the indigenous people. The material changes consequent from economic colonization have been vast. There is not a precise date for the beginning of the European expansionist trading and settling activities that eventually constituted colonialism. Nor is it certain whether racial hierarchies followed from, or caused, the establishment of slavery at an international level. However, a key moment was in the late sixteenth century when Portuguese and Dutch companies set up sugar plantations in Brazil before production shifted to the West Indies from the 1660s. The importation of African labour to work as slaves made the plantations especially profitable. That encouraged later colonists to follow this precedent when in need of labour to work the vast areas of land they were opening up to cultivation. Slavery in the south of the former British colony of America arguably emerged under such circumstances (Thomas, 1997).

Feminist writers such as Angela Davis (1971) and bell hooks (for example, 1981) have noted the importance of understanding the experiences of women slaves in order to analyze current inequities around 'race' and gender. Hooks (1981:15–49) argues that though women slaves were valued as breeders of more slaves this does not mean they were treated better than their men. A crucial difference between men and women's experiences of slavery was that, for women, their sexuality was exploited as well as their labour. A variety of practices constituted this exploitation, including rape. Rape was used by white masters to degrade and humiliate black women and sometimes these women were also vulnerable to rape and abuse from black male slaves. Sexist views of women as temptresses and racist beliefs that black women were promiscuous made contemporaries likely to blame black women. Black women themselves began to challenge white ideals of delicate womanhood that excluded their experience as strong survivors who were certainly not chivalrously protected by (white) men. Such histories, as both hooks (1981: 51–86) and Davis (1971) point out, are not over and done with but still inform the ongoing devaluation of black women. The slave past may have effects not only for those whose forebears were slaves, but also for other women of colour.

Slavery has had particularly pernicious effects, but other forms of unfree labour have also been important in gendering particular ethnic groups. Among poor white Europeans indentured labour was common, where a worker's passage to the New World was paid, but they were bonded to their employer until they repaid the debt – with interest (Fogleman, 1998). Indian and Caribbean men were also taken to Australia under such systems, which given that male labourers were favoured, left gender imbalanced settler populations (Duffield and Bradley, 1997; Woollacott, 2006; Summers, 1975). Convict labour was also crucial, especially in Australia, but distinctions were made between white women convicts, still thought feminine, and black women slaves expected to labour like men (Woollacott, 2006). However, not all colonization involved slavery or other unfree labour. While the exploitation of slave and other bonded labour allowed raw materials to be profitably produced and extracted in much of the new world, changing conditions in the old world prompted further colonial expansion, to new territories and taking new forms.

The various European empires that developed were diverse and shifting, but each did have a certain cohesion in terms of the highly 'raced' and gendered solutions they appeared to offer to some of the old world's social as well as economic problems (Woollacott, 2006). As Britain and then other European nations industrialized from the eighteenth century onwards, a whole range of new needs and problems began to emerge within those rapidly changing societies. Urban overcrowding and the need for raw materials and land, combined with ideas about the superiority of the white European 'race', were key factors in promoting territorial expansion. Britain, having a slight head start in the Industrial Revolution, became foremost in acquiring and settling territories across the world and making use of their resources. Indian cotton, tea and spices flowed into Britain, as did South African diamonds and other mineral treasures (Wilson, 2003). In addition to the resources and markets new territories could provide, they also promised a way of relieving social unrest at 'home', thought to arise largely from overcrowding and the resulting poor conditions. Britain was perhaps most 'creative' in this respect, using Australia as a prison where not only criminals but the poor, desperate and undesirable could be sent – often for the commission of small offences (Duffield and Bradley, 1997; Summers, 1975). Yet the British government also began to encourage and assist non-criminal emigration to the outposts of its empire and women were encouraged to go to 'civilize' the initial overwhelmingly male settler populations (see for example, MacDonald, 1990; Summers, 1975). In the nineteenth century large numbers of English, Scots and Irish left in the hope of finding a better life in Canada, Australia, British Africa and New Zealand. Each wave of immigration had an impact upon indigenous populations and in some cases (Canada, Australia and New Zealand) the white population rapidly began to outnumber the original inhabitants. In other regions, especially Africa, white settlers from various European nations achieved dominance despite being in the minority.

White women were complicit in colonial domination, but also removed from colonial power (for example, Ware, 1992). Although some tried to resist some of the more violent aspects of colonization, it is difficult to write about their experiences without making indigenous women even more invisible (Haggis, 2001; 1990). An analysis of white identities as 'racial' is important (Bonnett, 2000; Lewis and Mills, 2003: 7), but this needs to be undertaken within a framework which takes whiteness to be a global phenomenon which was intrinsic to colonization and the onset of modernity (Bonnett, 2000). White women's often ambiguous position in relation to colonization is clearer if colonial power relations are not over-simplified. Some writers have controversially argued that colonies were often seen as costly responsibilities, rather than as simply treasure chests waiting to be exploited (Ferguson, 2004). Certainly in some cases Britain was somewhat reluctant to accept the responsibilities and difficulties of governing far off populations (see, for example, King, 2003), having had bad experiences with America and in the 'scramble for Africa' (Pakenham, 1990). Given that Europeans were often exploiting distant territories without the expense of governing them, it is possible to see why they may have been reluctant officially to adopt new lands. It is also possible to see that formal colonization could bring some stability and benefits, compared to the unrestrained exploitation and lawlessness that characterized many early European pre-colonial settlements (Ferguson, 2004). However, colonization fundamentally initiated a process that – in both intended and unintended ways – robbed indigenous peoples of full control over themselves and their affairs. And colonization not only made the colonies, it also made the imperial nations (Woollacott, 2006). Current 'race' and gender relations have to be understood with these colonial histories in mind.

Mona Etienne and Eleanor Leacock (1980) argue that colonization did not always clearly bring patterns of gender relations more egalitarian than those existing in the indigenous population. Colonization, and its effects on the 'racing' of gender, need to be seen as an ongoing process with usually rather blurred beginnings and complex effects. Western ideas and practices often began to have an impact on indigenous people's gender relations before colonization became firmly established, and most anthropologists have looked at those gender relations within a colonial context. In other words some of the ways indigenous men and women related may have already changed under colonial influence, and indeed were not 'pure' and unchanging before white settlers arrived. Colonization also created new 'raced' and gendered relations between nations, not just within them. Colonies were connected, and people and ideas circulated within particular empires (Lester, 2002) – with administrators and the military shifting, for example, from Africa to Australia to New Zealand; from New Caledonia to Quebec. Current inequalities of gender and race, wherever they may be, therefore need to be understood in relation to the historical legacy of colonialism. I begin by focusing on economics-based explanations of the linkages between race and gender inequalities, then shift to those which place more emphasis on culture.

The economics of colonization, decolonization and development

The most prominent explanation of inequalities between developed and underdeveloped nations in the 1950s maintained that what was needed was for poorer nations to modernize via the same route as 'successful' Western nations. W.W. Rostow's (2000/1960) **modernization theory** argued it was tradition that was holding developing nations back. According to this view, aid and internal agents educated in and committed to Western ways of working were needed to break free from tradition and 'catch-up' with the USA and Western Europe. Rostow set out the exact stages of economic growth that he thought wealthy nations had followed and that developing nations needed to go through. In doing so he assumed that developing nations were starting from the same kind of situation that Western nations had been in a hundred years or more previously. This ignored the far-from-even economic playing field left by the ravages of colonization. His theory also ethnocentrically assumes that West is best, and that it is to competitive capitalism and its associated emphasis on individual success that all right-thinking people must aspire. In other cultures, such as China – where the interests of the community, rather than individuals, are privileged – very different paths towards economic success have been apparent (Stockman, 2000). Rostow's model of economic success is one especially likely to ignore not only cultural differences in values but also in the ways in which women contribute to the economy.

Within feminist economics, writers such as Lourdes Benería (for example, 1995) and Marilyn Waring (1999/1986) challenged the assumptions of mainstream economics that lie behind Rostow's theory and indeed inform The United Nations System of National Accounting (UNSNA) which determines public policy in most parts of the globe. Waring (1999/1986) notes that this system of accounting neglects the environment and has tended to view women as non-producers. It is a system which justifies war and only 'counts' cash-generating activities. The UNSNA is used, in particular, to control cash generation in countries that owe money to governments of wealthier nations and multinational banks and agencies. It is a powerful system in which women literally – as her book title suggests – count for nothing. Benería (1995) argues that progress has been made in incorporating women's work within national accounting and feminist economics has provided alternative macroeconomic models to encourage gender development. However, empirical work continues to show that women bear the brunt of many economic policies and their unpaid work is still underestimated. To illustrate: one study outlines how black women in Zimbabwe continue to be found at the lowest socio-economic level, despite post-independence efforts to improve their status. These women undertake a range of informal work such as cross-border trading and foreign currency exchange, in addition to the copious amounts of domestic work required given that they lack plumbing and other amenities (Moyo and Kawewe, 2002). Like Benería and Waring, these authors are critical of the current dominance of patriarchal views about what is valuable. But unlike Benería and Waring, Moyo and Kawewe (2002) indicate how these views became dominant because of historical colonialism's role in establishing the neo-colonial power of Western-controlled banks, companies and agencies. This is the kind of argument promoted by dependency theorists.

Dependency theory attributes the relatively strong economic and political position that America, Britain and other 'advanced' nations have in the world today to how they benefited from colonial and slave pasts (for example, Frank, 1972). Colonial powers fuelled the Industrial Revolution that made them wealthy by exploiting land, resources and people elsewhere. Trees were felled to clear land for farming and to provide timber, minerals were mined, new crops were planted. Much of the spoils were exported back to the homeland or remained in the hands of the white settlers. Local populations worked in new industries, but often as poorly paid labour. Then over the course of the first half of the twentieth century, due to the expense of running vast empires, the cost of the two World Wars, and political pressure or revolt from native populations, colonies gained independence. Yet by the time European nations withdrew they had denuded much of Africa, India and the Americas, destroyed most traditional systems of governance, and left many peoples largely impoverished and economically dependent on their former colonial masters (Frank, 1972). It seems clear that the economic consequences of colonization were to concentrate the world's wealth in the hands of a minority of its population: white European men. However, initially at least, colonization required some degree of economic cooperation. White folk often were not very good at finding their feet in new climes and many would have starved were it not for the assistance of the locals. Such acts of kindness are most famously celebrated in the American feast of Thanksgiving, but occurred in other colonies (for example, see King, 2003). However, as colonizers gained economic and political control via varying combinations of persuasion and coercion, indigenous populations found themselves subject to new forms of constraint within structures not of their own making.

Andre Gunder Frank (1972) claimed that the plundering and reshaping of colonies made them economically dependent on the West. His dependency theory argues that through trading and colonizing, capitalism became a global system within which the wealthy nations maintained their privilege by keeping the underdeveloped nations poor. If Western capitalists were to continue to enjoy increasing profits, they needed to keep wages down. Having a source of cheap (usually non-white) labour in the Third World, remains to this day advantageous for First World nations. For example, large companies like Nike and Gap increase their profits by making use of women who, despite codes of conduct, live and work in poor conditions within supply companies located in the developing world – in Cambodia for example (Klein, 2002/2000). Immanuel Wallerstein (1974) has developed an arguably more complex version of these ideas in his **world systems theory**. He locates capitalist economic dominance as a primarily Western but more shifting exploitation of peripheries by the global centres (for example, 'metropoles' such as New York and London). Both Frank and Wallerstein say little about the gendered effects of capitalism as a system of global exploitation, but there have been feminist contributions based on and related to these influential Marxian based models.

Catherine Scott (1995) has engaged with both modernization and dependency theory in order to show how women are associated with the tradition deemed to be holding back development. The theorists see modernization as crucial if men are to free themselves from the maternal household and gain their identity. Women and the household are thereby supposed to be part of a past that must be escaped. States which fail to become masculinized in this way are seen as 'soft', as unsuccessful. Such a view of Western ways as superior is not entirely avoided by dependency theorists such as Frank. These theories, though critical of capitalism, still represent it as dynamic and technologically superior. Within these theories women tend to be regarded as doubly oppressed – which assumes that oppressions can be added onto each other rather than seeing them as entangled in complex ways. Revolution by people within dependent nations is encouraged by dependency theorists, in order to establish 'self-reliant, autonomous development' (Scott, 1995: 103), but women are not seen as revolutionaries. They are seen as victims within male dominated households, as stagnant products of colonial exploitation, or contradictorily viewed as 'naturally' male dominated. This is despite efforts within dependency theory to portray the household in a more complex light than in modernization theory. One of the most celebrated efforts in this respect is Maria Mies's research on lace making in Narasapur in India (see Mies, 1982). There the women make lace at home, their labour exploited within a patriarchal system of purdah that restricts their movements. Their lace is exported and sold to wealthy women in Western nations. This capitalist process is fuelled by the male domination of women in that locale. Attempts such as Mies's have not succeeded, according to Scott, in seeing the household as a place of conflict and change. Dependency theory inherits a Marxist focus on production at the expense of reproduction and this leads to a view of practices at home as 'backward'. Opposition movements can then play on male anxieties about changing these 'backward' practices. What work such as Scott's suggests is that, in order to break free of colonizing influences, reform is required not only of economics, but also of the related ideologies. We can begin to see that it is difficult to maintain a distinction between those feminists who analyze the economic and those interested primarily in symbolic practices. In trying to understand the continuance of inequalities between ethnic groups, a notion of post-colonialism in which economics is present but less central becomes relevant.

Post-colonialism: Changing economics and ideas?

An emphasis on economics

It can be argued that much of the debate about relationships between gender, 'race', and ethnicity began to shift from the late 1980s into the field of feminist post-colonial theory where the cultural or discursive aspects of colonial processes and their ongoing aftermath were the central issues. However, from the 1970s black feminists thinking through issues of gender and 'race' have referred to both material conditions and to ideas. Those who have foregrounded the continued relevance of material, in the sense of economic, issues include Angela Davis and Hazel Carby.

Angela Davis has argued that colonization lingers on for black women in the conditions they face. For her the notion of post-coloniality perhaps suggests too much that all that is finished, although Stuart Hall (1996) argues that the term '**post-colonial**' does not necessarily suggest that colonialism is over. Davis's work certainly relies on considering the ongoing legacy of slavery and imperialist expansion. Davis comprehensively sets out her ideas in *Women, Race and Class* (1983), which traces the historical entanglement of sexism, racism and classism within the USA and the struggle feminists had to overcome their prejudices and see these connections. She argues that there has been some success in this struggle and that 'the most effective versions of feminism acknowledge the ways that gender, class, race, and sexual orientation inform each other' (Davis and Martinez, 1998: 304). Yet the conjunction of inequalities of race and gender (and class) have continued to shift, especially as a result of deindustrialization and the way that capital has moved globally. The civil rights movement helped to establish a black middle class in America, but the global restructuring of capitalism has seen many poor black women in the US reduced to welfare dependency and their black sisters in the Third World exploited for their cheap labour (Davis, 1998: 308). This illustrates that Davis's work is very much located within a Marxist tradition. In her analysis, it is racist ideas about white superiority that shore up a global economic system in which non-white women in poorer nations labour for a pittance to provide the West with consumer goods for all to buy. Her critique of capitalism is specifically anti-racist and therefore explicitly deals with ideologies around race as central to capitalist economic exploitation.

British scholar Hazel Carby (1982) also shows that to try and separate material and cultural analyses is not always straightforward in her analysis of how 'triple oppression' determines the lives of black women. Her most influential work came out of that offspring of British sociology, the Centre for Contemporary Cultural Studies at Birmingham in 1982. 'White Woman Listen' is highly materialist in many aspects, but also considers at length the way in which dominant discourses about sex and gender impact on black women's lives. Initially this is a response to white feminism's failure to represent the experiences of black women. Carby (1982) gives the example of arguments which suggest that the family is the source of women's oppression. For Carby this fails to account for the ways in which, for black women, families may be crucial in resisting racist oppression. Carby also notes that white feminist discourses tend to follow imperialist lines in assuming that introducing First World ways to Third World women brings them emancipation. In fact, Carby argues rather that colonization has often instituted new forms of subordination for Third World women, for example using them to meet labour needs in ways that allows white women's role at home to be maintained. Here she is implying that white women are relatively privileged in being able to labour for their own families rather than other people's, as black women often have to do (see Ehrenrich and Hochschild, 2003). Colonialism as an economic as well as a cultural project has been crucial in establishing such flows of labour and it benefits all white women, not just colonials. Meanwhile all Third World women are lumped together. Carby is suspicious of the term patriarchy for the part it plays in universalizing women's oppression and contributing to views of Third

World women as backward. She prefers instead Gayle Rubin's (1975) conceptualization of sex/gender systems.

According to Carby (1982) to think about sex/gender systems is useful because it refers not just to the mode of production but to how other culturally specific social formations organize life and are subject to historical change (for example colonial oppression) in specific ways. These sex/gender systems can be judged in their own terms, avoiding ethnocentric assumptions such as those suggesting that whites historically brought more liberal sex/gender systems to black societies. In fact, women often had important roles in those societies, which were not recognized by colonials (for example, see Smith, 1999: 46). Thus it is important to look at societies through the eyes of the women who live within them, not through western eyes. Often Western eyes fail to recognize the issues that indigenous women themselves see as most crucial (Mohanty, 1991). Where researchers are interested in female circumcision, the local women may be more concerned with access to clean water, and so on.

Carby's (1982) approach, despite such nods to culture, continually returns to material inequalities; and indeed the language of metropoles and peripheries she uses shows an engagement with dependency and/or world-systems theory. She is directly critical of Wallerstein's dismissal, within his world-systems theory, of the possibility of the simultaneous existence of feudal and capitalist social forms. If imperialist colonization has produced a world market, as he argues, why would non-wage related social forms exist? Carby says that 'feudal' relations organized around land and the agricultural division of labour are in fact still prominent for many women. Indeed many of women's rebellions have focused around land seizure and related issues, rather than just wage-related exploitation (see for example, Smith, 1999). Black women support each other in these and other struggles. Feminism must be transformed to account for such experiences and thus address black women. To some extent the rise of feminist post-colonial theory has seen greater attention paid to black women's experiences, and indeed to relations between black and non-black women.

More recent post-colonial feminist writers such as Anne McClintock (1995) have used a materialist based analysis as part of their approach to understanding how white colonial women's role within the home was crucial in helping reproduce colonial power. White women in the colonies were expected to keep, usually via their management of servants, a spotlessly clean household. This was supposed to assist in illustrating the superiority of Western 'civilization'. I have already mentioned Maria Mies's (1982) work on lace making. Similarly Chaudhuri (1992) has talked about the role white women played in the economics of imperialism in her article 'Shawls, jewelry, curry and rice in Victorian

Britain'. In this she argues that women as consumers of colonial products helped produce the imperialist worldview of Victorians. By taking Indian things such as shawls to England they helped make them popular there. While in 'the colonies' the role of white women was to uphold Britishness, back in Britain their enthusiasm for exotic commodities could be indulged, showing that the culture they appeared to reject had in fact influenced them – and indeed Victorians more widely. While this illustrates that there were economic factors implicated in the relational construction of 'race' and gender, some writers began to highlight the importance of meanings.

An emphasis on (cultural) meanings

The cultural turn shifted focus from how colonization and slavery produced material inequalities between the mainly white West and the non-white 'rest' to attempts to understand the gendered production of colonized or racialized subjects. Stuart Hall (1997) has provided a useful framework for considering this production, drawing on new approaches to colonization. One of the most influential works to break with materialist explanations was Frantz Fanon's (1967) account of the psychological damage inflicted on colonized non-white peoples. In *The Wretched of the Earth* he makes a grim assessment of the psychological effects of colonization on the colonized. He argues that colonization destroyed indigenous peoples not simply through physical violence and/or material deprivation, but because they learnt to believe that white was better. Colonized peoples internalized the hatred and fear of blackness that the dominant white settlers promulgated. Despite the political independence many former colonies had achieved by the twentieth century, he argues that this legacy of psychological damage has meant continued tribal warfare and political instability in many former colonies – in Africa especially. However, Fanon does not specifically talk about the effects of colonization on gender relations. Hall's framework can be used to help correct this lack of attention to gender. I will deal with this framework in reverse order: from primitivism, to exoticization, to sexualization, because the latter then leads into debates about how colonization discursively produced gender.

Hall (1997) argues that one of the major pillars of colonial discourse is a belief in **primitivism**, which entailed seeing gender relations amongst non-white peoples as backward. White colonizers justified their actions by labelling indigenous peoples as primitive: meaning uncivilized and lacking in culture. Blackness was reduced to a natural and therefore unchanging essence. Such ideas allowed white people to see themselves as civilizers, bringing progress to 'backward' peoples. But primitivism failed to recognize the often complex sociocultural and political systems that operated amongst non-white peoples. In terms of gender, an important part of the colonial mission was to instil, especially in the women, what were regarded as the 'proper' or even 'natural' gender roles. Victorian notions of passive, obedient womanhood were imposed on indigenous women and they were cajoled and sometimes compelled to accept new standards of domestic arrangements, dress and behaviour (Woollacott, 2006: 97). The established gender roles and expectations of non-white cultures were usually remade within the colonial context. Colonial powers imposed their own ideas about appropriate 'feminine' behaviour and about gendered divisions of labour. This was not always an improvement and assumptions that white women were more liberated were not always justified (Etienne and Leacock, 1980). For example, there has been considerable debate about whether pre-colonial African societies would be better described as matriarchal 'in the sense of female rule, female transmission of property and descent, and man being the mobile element in marriage and sexual union' (Amadiune, 2005: 85). However it is perhaps not as simple as matriarchal rather than patriarchal. A focus on motherhood existed alongside patriarchal ideologies about descent and another more matriarchal ideology related to the original ownership of land and to natural fertility (Amadiune, 2005). Yet judgements about the status of women in non-white cultures were made based on, often misplaced, European assessments of what was important in a society (Smith, 1999).

A second key to understanding colonial discourse and its effects on gender is to examine the processes of **exoticization** involved in marking difference. In elaborating on these processes Stuart Hall (1997) relies largely on the well-known arguments of Edward Said (1978). Said focuses on the exoticization fundamental to orientalism. Orientalism is the construction of the 'Orient' through processes of power/knowledge. Said argues that the West creates the Orient and those within it as 'other' to itself in order to maintain a sense of superiority. The West is portrayed as rational, the Orient as irrational; and so on. The Oriental is presented as utterly different, as exotic. Said's work on orientalism is certainly one of the earliest and most influential statements of this kind of position, his book *Orientalism* being first published in 1978 and aspects of these ideas having appeared in article form earlier in the Seventies. However, as already noted feminist analysis of colonialism was also underway in the early 1970s.

Feminist work noted that exoticization of 'other' women and men has not inevitably equated 'exotic' with beautiful, and thus colonization and slavery have raised particular problems for how to be 'feminine' and black (hooks, 1981). The problem is that images of proper femininity have been based mostly on white, middle class Western women. For many non-white women there is a constant battle to maintain self-worth within a world that judges them in relation to white notions of beauty and femininity. Much of Afro-American Toni Morrison's fiction deals with this as tragedy, especially her book *The Bluest Eye* (1999/1970). One of the central black women characters in this book believes that if only she was beautiful in white blue-eyed terms then she would be treated well and her sufferings would end:

> Each night without fail, she prayed for blue eyes. Fervently, for a year she had prayed. Although somewhat discouraged, she was not without hope. To have something as wonderful as that happen would take a long, long time. Thrown in this way, into the blinding conviction that only a miracle could relieve her, she would never know her beauty. She would only see what there was to see: the eyes of other people. (p. 35)

Blue eyes are symbolic of whiteness and the value placed on it that marks black women out within racial hierarchies. Yet paradoxically their difference, while it might be experienced as lack of beauty, is maintained through the exploitative titillation associated with blackness as otherness (Hall, 1997; hooks, 1992).

Non-white subjects have been racialized through reference to their primitive and exotic difference, a difference that has often been **sexualized** in controlling ways. This is not the case everywhere; for example, the story of white treatment of indigenous Australians is perhaps more one of dehumanization than sexualization. Meanwhile, men of African origin have tended to be stereotyped as super masculine and African women as 'primitive' and promiscuous; thus non-white peoples have been sexually objectified via white fantasies (Hall, 1997; see, hooks, 1992). What this can mean for black people's loss of independence and ability to self-define is often represented through the tale of Sartjie Baartman, known to her Victorian contemporaries as the Hottentot Venus. Taken from her homeland and displayed in Europe because she was an example of her people's tendency to have enlarged buttocks and genitalia, this woman's story epitomizes a prurient racism which makes black women into objects of white sexual curiosity and exploitation. Hall (1997) himself uses this story and I do not wish to repeat it in detail here. Similar stories can be told of the sexual objectification of many non-European women. Jaqui Sutton Beets (1997) for example describes the ways in which Maori women have been represented as exotic and sexually available in postcards since the nineteenth century. They are portrayed as dusky maidens, but those chosen conform most closely to western standards of beauty. The 'native' settings in which they are placed are aimed to convey a 'natural', unrestrained sexuality – displayed for the enjoyment of the European male. Beets argues that such images transfer the guilt of the white male viewer onto the indigenous woman, equate colonial possession of land with sexual possession of its women, and serve as a kind of reminder that Maori – and other indigenous men – are not in a position aggressively to protect their women. Those women are shown as being trophies for the 'victors' in the colonial struggle: white men. These women are 'other', represented in ways calculated to sell to white men, and they illustrate the ways of thinking that are crucial in structuring gender relations in contexts of racism.

If the Orient (which specifically refers to Asia and the Middle East) is broadly conceived as anything 'other' to white Western societies, then there are variations in the meanings attached to black women and men. They have been portrayed as exotic and promiscuous. However there is an ambivalence (see Bhabha, 1994) in the way non-white subjects are gendered. Said (1978) maintains that Orientalism feminizes Arab men; however Hall (1997) notes that men of African descent tend to be seen as hyper-masculine. African, Afro-American and Afro-Caribbean women tend to be seen – as Baartman was – as sexually aggressive; while 'Oriental' women are represented as passively erotic. These stereotypes tell us more about white Western attitudes to sex/gender and sexuality than they do about the peoples they supposedly describe. Black and brown people have not merely been passive victims of these processes, but have struggled and resisted (Lewis, 1996). Nevertheless colonial encounters reshaped the ways in which gender operated, and colonization was a highly gendered process.

Colonists were typically portrayed as heroic male adventurers heading off to tame 'savages' who were rendered as effeminate in comparison (Mills, 1998; Sinha, 1995; Woollacott, 2006). This may seem a little contradictory, but colonial discourses did not make a lot of sense; they were highly contradictory. Sara Mills (1998) points out that the notion of an exotic sexuality was important in the domination of new peoples and new lands. Typically colonies were seen as sexual playgrounds for men, who exploited women and young boys, sometimes violently. This was mirrored in contemporary representations of colonial invasion as a raping of virgin land (McLintock, 1995). There was also sexual danger thought to arise from being in close contact with 'natives'. Guarding the purity of white (colonial) women was used as a justification for colonialism generally and for some of the violent repressions of local rebellion (McLintock, 1995; Woollacott, 2006). The white woman stands for racial and sexual purity. Fear of racial degeneration is part of the obsessive nineteenth century categorization of race. Such racial categorizations linger, and it has been an ongoing challenge for non-white peoples to remake positive conceptions of self within a world still saturated with racism. This is partly why post-colonial scholars are interested in issues of subjectivity and agency.

Many feminist post-colonial theorists are concerned with notions of subjectivity, and in particular with rethinking indigenous women's agency in terms of how they negotiate the subject positions available to them. Woollacott (2006: 104–21) notes that women were important in resisting and overthrowing colonization through anti-colonial and nationalist struggles. There were also more 'everyday' and individualized instances of resistance. For example, it is possible to try to understand sati, the historical Hindu practice of burning widows on their husband's funeral pyre, without condoning it. Women might have 'chosen' or felt forced to die. These decisions were made within a context where there were limited options available to widows for maintaining themselves and the shame of not dying with their husband would make family assistance unlikely. Nevertheless some women did choose to live, and this is often neglected (Mills, 1998: 104). The gendered practices of non-white peoples need to be understood within the context of their own views and understandings of the world, and of the social and material conditions in which they live. The failure of most scholars, including white feminists, to produce such understandings of non-white women has been criticized.

Writers such as Chandra Mohanty (1991) argue that feminists have made women who are not white or from the First World invisible. She suggests that this has been done through a process of othering. She proposes that Third World women are understood through the following series of oppositions:

Western	Third World
Privileged	Marginalized
Colonizers	Colonized
Central	Peripheral
In control	Victims

Mohanty suggests that assumptions that there is a group called women who are all oppressed is based on seeing Western women's experiences as the norm and universal. This makes Third World women's specific oppression invisible or represents it as homogeneous. It is therefore important to explicitly address that diversity. The situation of women in the Sudan is different from that of women in Egypt, or in Mexico. And in Mexico there will be vast differences between the life chances and experiences of rural peasant women and wealthy urban women. Mohanty's point is that such differences have largely been ignored. Watch the television news, for example, and you are likely to get the impression that all Third

World women are starving and usually traumatized by some recent natural disaster or war. While it is important to recognize the inequalities which produce hunger, wars, and make natural disasters so difficult to deal with in the developing world, such pictures represent Third World women as eternal victims. It is important to remember that there are many women living comfortably in peaceful villages, towns and cities throughout Africa, Asia, Central and South America. It is also important to consider processes of decolonization in assessing current formations of 'race'/ethnicity and gender.

Decolonization

Wendy Brown (1995) deals with the difficulties of overcoming histories of colonization and slavery as central to understanding the intertwining of inequalities of gender and of race. She re-reads Nietzsche's ideas about resentment being a major part of a dominant modern morality emerging within more democratic societies. He sees that modern morality as a result of a slave morality based on revenge for past wrongs. It is a morality, he argues, that sees enemies as wholly different, and as intrinsically 'evil' rather than temporarily 'bad'. Brown uses her take on these ideas critically to interrogate identity politics as a politics based on resentment, which relies on and reinscribes its exclusionary relation to dominance. In other words, rather than moving beyond notions of regarding people like ourselves as good and those who are different as evil, identity politics reproduces these ideas. A marginalized identity thereby 'resubjugates itself through its investment in its own pain' (Brown, 1995: 74). Memory of the past is crucial in this process, but peoples who have been marginalized cannot be simply told to forget, because that fails to recognize the importance of remembering for them. These people have often been made historically invisible or deprived of much of their past through genocide and cultural cleansing which tried to erase indigenous stories, beliefs and practices. In order to alleviate the pain and overcome cycles of resentment, Brown argues that marginalized peoples have to be 'heard into a certain release', to allow a self-overcoming which will allow for losing itself (1995: 74–5). This then is not about slipping into individualized therapy, but about constructing political discourses based on shifting, possibly collective, desires – claims of 'I/we want' rather than 'I am'.

   Though unlikely that she would identify herself as a post-colonial theorist, bell hooks is similarly interested in how to overcome the effects of colonization, especially as a psychic state which still holds sway over women. In later work, hooks (1992: 1) sets out the process of decolonization she thinks is needed for black women to be properly valued and to come to understand their femininity in positive ways. **Decolonization** is a term she uses to describe a process of reclaiming subjectivity, rescuing the power to define blackness from white hands. To decolonize is to re-present colonized identities and interests as independent. This process will involve both colonized and colonizer, and must recognize diversity between and within colonized groups (hooks, 1992: 1). Knowledge is therefore crucial.

Many feminists working within post-colonialism have highlighted the importance of knowledge in overcoming racist oppression and its gendered implications, Audre Lorde's (1984) famous claim that 'The Master's Tools Will Never Dismantle the Master's House' being a classic statement of this. Although old ideas about race have long been scientifically disproven, people's belief in the significance of superficial physical differences supposed to distinguish separate 'races' remains powerful and is enacted in racist ways (Banton, 1998). Much Western knowledge has been explicitly or implicitly racist, and through colonization that knowledge has become hegemonic. In that light, Linda Tuhiwai Smith (1999) outlines one of the key tasks within 'post-colonial' societies as being to reclaim indigenous ways of knowing. These can then be used to more carefully research and understand non-white peoples in former colonies. In particular, this approach can provide better understandings of indigenous women.

Smith argues that decolonization will lead to self-determination only if there are also processes of transformation, political mobilization, and healing at work – and these are therefore key to a successful indigenous research agenda. Some researchers, such as Patricia Hill Collins (1990), say outsiders cannot understand or analyze what it means to be oppressed as a black woman; Smith suggests that Maori views of research are similar. This reclamation of control over knowledge about themselves is a crucial part of decolonization. This will be a process that aims towards self-determination and includes also political control, social agency, spiritual and psychological strength. However, Smith (1999) notes that challenging the way in which gender and race are intertwined is difficult. She cites the example of some Maori women who have recently gone before the Waitangi Tribunal, established in New Zealand to deal with land claims and grievances arising from non-compliance by the Crown with the Treaty of Waitangi signed with the Maori in 1840. They claim 'that the Crown has ignored the rangatiratanga, or chiefly and sovereign status, of Maori women' (Smith, 1999: 46). Rangatiratanga is usually seen as chieftainship, which in colonial terms was thought to be male. Proving otherwise is very hard for women to do in such situations because it involves questioning ideas about what constitutes 'proper' knowledge. In Western-dominated environments, written knowledge is privileged over oral and Western frameworks determine what are seen as 'objective' or 'scientific' facts and who is expert. Therefore a simple statement of claim is not simple at all and involves a process of decolonization, challenging current power relations and how they structure what and how we know about people. As indigenous people have regained some strength they have been able to look at how colonial practices have marginalized women, elders and other groups and have been able to recentre these people (Smith, 1999: 111).

In order to rethink gender in such new terms, the kind of oppositions based on white Western constructions of what is feminine and masculine need to be challenged. Gayatri Spivak (1990) has suggested that this means white Westerners unlearning privilege as loss. Their privileged positions are usually based on excluding difference. We represent ourselves via a 'certain production', which means that there is a history and context framing what we say. In order for change to result, those who are dominant must rethink what is 'normal' about themselves. Those aspects of whiteness usually regarded as positive need to be reassessed and considered perhaps problematic. Those who have power and privilege should consider the historical processes which have made that possible, and the actual and moral poverty resultant from over-celebrating whiteness. White guilt and other forms of intellectual self-flagellation are not useful. What might be useful are appreciations of the production of whiteness in relation to blackness. Some of these appreciations have been presented in this chapter and I would like to briefly summarize and synthesize what I take to be the chief insights of this work as a set of positive prescriptions for thinking through the interconnections between 'race'/ethnicity and gender.

Conclusion

First, it is necessary to appreciate that racist sexism has gained much of its weight in the service of economic gain through capitalist expansion via colonization. Secondly, we must consider that affirming non-white identities is not about rediscovering a lost purity but about re-knowing what different ethnicities might mean for women if they are able to exist within conditions which are more of their own choosing. Thirdly, it must be insisted that such re-knowing struggles against dominant knowledges which privilege white European thought and frameworks. Fourthly and finally, acknowledgement is required of the agency exercized by non-white women in their ongoing struggles against racism and sexism. The cleaner we imagined in Chapter 7 might be a black woman who goes back to further education and maybe becomes a lawyer. She may, in conjunction with other black women of different classes and cultures, continue to work against systems of domination in which femininity and blackness are hindrances instead of celebrations of diversity. We have seen here the part that combinations of economic and cultural analyses of 'race'/ethnicity and gender can play in efforts to address inequalities.

Key readings

Brown, W. (1995) *States of Injury: Power and Freedom in Later Modernity*. Princeton, NJ: Princeton University Press.

Davis, A.Y. (1983) *Women, Race and Class*. New York: Vintage Books.

Scott, C. (1995) *Gender and Development: Rethinking Modernization and Dependency Theory*. Boulder, CO: Lynne Rienner Publishers.

Woollacott, A. (2006) *Gender and Empire*. Basingstoke: Palgrave.

9

Conclusion:
So what is gender?

Having read the whole of this book, you are no doubt hoping that I have written a conclusion which will provide a nice neat answer to the question: what is gender? I can promise no such tidy tying up of final loose ends into a pretty bow. Gender is a complex phenomenon. The first task in establishing the complexity of gender was to challenge the biological determinism common in everyday thinking about differences between women and men. Once it was established that those differences are more social than 'natural', a much more sociologically useful map of theories of gender could be outlined. This set out the major thesis of the book: that there has been a traceable shift in approaches to gender, from a focus on the material to one on meaning. That cultural turn has seen explanations of gender as an effect of material, meaning economic conditions give way to analyses of gender as a product of symbolic processes. What the book illustrates is that this shift has not meant wholesale rejection of the importance of the material in the social construction of gender. However, the notion of materiality now tends to include more than economic processes; most importantly it has been a way of reassessing the significance of bodies in thinking about gender. Nevertheless, a concern with inequalities has continued to be central in the politics of gender, while there have been attempts to think in more detail about how gender relates to other inequalities around class and ethnicity. I provide a brief summary of the key points made in relation to these issues and suggest possible future directions.

Differences

When the sociology of gender emerged as a specific field in the 1970s the concern was to show any differences that do exist between the sexes to be exaggerated or indeed socially constructed. The claim that men and women are simply 'naturally' different was called into question by examining how understandings of those differences vary across cultures and change throughout history. Indeed the interpretation of biology is something that is subject to social and historical change, as evidenced by the shift within Western science from a one- to a two-sex model of ifference (Laqueur, 1990). However, there are bodies that cannot be definitively classified as either 'male' or 'female' and these intersex people throw light on the social aspects of sexual classifications (Fausto-Sterling, 2002a; 2002b; Hird, 2004; Kessler and McKenna, 1978). Any perceived differences in ways of using bodies and minds are heavily shaped by the way people live. A Chinese peasant woman used to carrying heavy loads, for example, is likely to be physically stronger than a young American man who spends all day in front of the television and his computer. And how social meanings attached to sexual difference contribute to the formation of gender identities has been usefully explored by psychoanalysis. However, the way psychoanalysis characterizes feminine identity as precarious and subordinate, and based on understanding female biology as lack, is not always helpful in trying to imagine a more egalitarian gender order.

The problem with many of the attempts of social scientists and humanities scholars to examine 'scientific' claims about 'sex' is that most have a limited understanding of biological and related sciences. Scientists are often criticized by social scientists for ignoring factors that are not measurable within their discipline. For example, geneticists, look at the potentials certain genes contain, but cannot measure the effects of social factors on whether or not these potentials develop. Of course, good social scientists are not suggesting that genetics or biology definitely have no importance, they are merely illustrating that social environment plays a major part in determining our actions. The ways in which physical bodies and their (social) environment are entwined are extremely complex. Nevertheless attempts to engage with natural science understandings of differences between women and men are crucial because of the way in which commonsense ideas are usually based on misinterpretations of that science. For sociologists it is crucial to clarify what kind of scientific information actually exists about how men and women differ, and to analyze the social factors affecting how that information is interpreted. Once we establish that men and women are not simply born, we can begin to examine how they are socially made and what part individuals play in that making.

Doing gender and having it done to us

To appreciate agency as a factor required a shift from looking at how we become gendered to how we do gender. To say that gender is something we 'do' can mean that we perform it like a role in a play (for example, Goffman, 1979), or it is accomplished through the ongoing work we do in interaction with others (see West and Zimmerman, 1987). How people do gender and how it is done to them emerges within particular social situations in which judgements are always being made about what is 'properly' feminine and masculine in those situations (see Garfinkel, 1967). There is considerable effort, or work, involved in this ongoing management of our actions in relation to gender. The trick is to try and make it look effortless, to make it look 'natural' (Goffman, 1979; Tyler and Abbott, 1998; West and Zimmerman, 1987).

Judith Butler's work (for example, 1990) also emphasizes the way in which gender is a masquerade – the point of which is to make it look natural. Butler, however, is trying to argue that gender is not something we do, but rather that gender produces us. It is almost impossible to make sense of anyone without thinking of them as gendered – even if we decide that a man is rather 'feminine'. So doing gender is not optional, but gender does us; and therefore understanding gender is crucial to understanding how the world works and how societies could be organized differently. Gender theorists take up these challenges.

Mapping gender theories

A post-structuralist attention to meanings had challenged structuralism's search for underlying frameworks which might explain gender oppression. Post-structuralism questions binary systems of classification which insist gender must be fixed as either feminine or masculine. In contrast to structuralism it proposes that gender has no 'real' basis as part of individuals and their bodies, but that gender differences are created by language. However, these themes have emerged, albeit in slightly different guise, within second-wave feminism where both material inequalities and the production of meanings around difference were of concern. Debates about equality or difference were used strategically to fulfil particular goals (Bacchi, 1990). The difficulties involved in these debates were partly responsible for prompting an intellectual and political shift away from the complexities of materially based gender inequalities towards an interest in discourse and 'texts'. The cultural turn saw language, meaning and representation become the core concerns in examining gender.

The cultural turn offers new appreciations of the agency or choices we are able to exercize in regard to gendering processes. However, it leaves us with questions about to what extent social structures continue to impose constraints on how we are gendered and how we do gender. Problems remain in using more language based analyses to understand such issues as gendered power relations (Roseneil, 1995) and gendered embodiment (Howson, 2005).

Back to (gendered) bodies

Reintroducing the body has been important for understanding the relationship between sex and gender and sexuality. They fall into two categories: those who theorize the body as a social object and those who attempt to embody social theory. The latter are typically feminist sociologists whose work does not feature as centrally within the sociology of the body as it perhaps should (Howson, 2005). The key tension in sociologically oriented work on the body centres around the problem of to what extent (gendered) bodies are natural entities with some sort of fundamental essence and to what extent they are endlessly malleable products of social life and of discourse. The point of the sociology of gender initially was to highlight social construction in order to challenge arguments that gender inequalities were the inevitable result of 'natural' differences between the sexes. The result of this was a bracketing off of the body, despite the influence of second-wave feminism, which paid considerable attention to how women experienced their bodies within patriarchy. In setting aside the importance of bodies within social life, much thinking about gender fell foul of the very dualistic principles that relegated women to the status of unreasonable prisoners of nature because of their supposed inability to transcend their messy bodies (see Beauvoir, 1988/1949; Bordo, 1987). It also reinforced patriarchal power, which was premised on notions of men as exercising cognitive control free from bodily distractions.

The masculine privilege resultant from denying embodiment, however, has not been equally available to all men and there have been recent attempts to characterize hierarchies of masculine embodiment which privilege white middle class men's embodiment as under rational control (Connell, 1995; Donaldson, 1991; Hall, 1997; Morgan, 1993). However, following Foucault, many feminists have reiterated that new forms of power/knowledge have subjected women to greater surveillance and regulation, with consequences for their autonomy (see Howson, 2005). Yet, corporeal feminism in particular has striven to see embodiment as not entirely reducible to the social (see Grosz, 1994). The strong influence of psychoanalysis within this approach causes an inability to see beyond the development of non-dysfunctional embodied selfhood as a struggle with inevitable gender hierarchies. Phenomenology has more fruitfully explored how bodies are experienced and how the social becomes ingrained or habituated within bodies. The limitations of a feminine gendered habitus can be convincingly set out via explorations of the specific techniques of the body (for example, Young, 1990) as they are organized around related formations such as class (Skeggs, 1997). Yet for sociologists actual bodies often disappear into abstractions as they revert to their disciplinary reflex of trying to situate those embodied experiences within structural analyses (Howson and Inglis, 2001). The politics of gender has remained central in teasing out connections between the individual and social structure.

Gender as politics

Second-wave feminism continued the fight against material inequalities but offered a much more radical challenge to the entire liberal democratic political system and to ideas about womanhood. Second-wave feminists questioned divisions between private and public spheres, highlighted the political nature of relations between women and men, experimented with new political processes and re-wrote political agendas to attend to issues they thought central to women (Holmes, 1999). All types of relationships with men were subject to analysis, but there was considerable attention to sexuality and the ways in which heterosexism contributed to the reproduction of conservative gender roles thought to constrain women. And although there were debates and disagreements among different groups of feminists such as lesbians and heterosexuals, this does not mean that the movement fell apart due to in-fighting. The movement was an amazing collection of women of different classes, ethnic groups, ages, sexualities and so on. White middle class educated women tended to be the most dominant voice in that movement but black working class, lesbian and other groups were always there asking questions about whose interests were being forwarded (Holmes, 2004).

The question of whether women, in all their diversity, can share political interests seems largely – but not entirely – to have been answered in the negative. Women, very broadly speaking, do still share a disadvantaged social position relative to men (see Chapter 1) and are still subject to violence which is directed against them specifically as women (Dobash and Dobash, 1992; Kelly, 1988). However, there are huge differences between women; between women in the First and Third Worlds, or between poor black women in America or Britain in relation to their white middle class peers. As a political movement, feminism has continued to struggle with identity politics and some of the problems it involves were highlighted when certain groups of men began to insist that there were costs associated with being masculine. Searching for the 'real' man within became a popular project for middle class men in the 1980s, partly as an individualistic response to the perceived threat to their privilege that feminism posed (Connell, 1995; Messner, 1997). More pro-feminist versions of masculinity politics tended to stress the need for both women and men to be liberated from repressive traditional gender roles, or the need to refuse to be a man within the hegemonic terms proscribed (Connell, 1995; Stoltenberg, 2000a/1989). From this and feminist questionings of the gender order emerged queer politics (see Chapter 4; Jagose, 1996; Seidman, 1996), which argued the need radically to reconfigure the gender order via freeing individual desires and making gender a matter of fluid choice rather than fixed ascription. Yet this is unlikely to alter significantly the realities of most of the population. Questions arose about the continued relevance of feminist politics in a world where identities are supposedly no longer thought stable and yet divisions around religion and culture are becoming the source of major global conflicts. It is uncertain whether these conflicts are economically (i.e. resource seeking) rather than culturally or religiously motivated, and what their effects will be on local and global gender relations. Yet feminists maintain alliances, sometimes across difficult real and imagined borders, and they and pro-feminist men continue to attempt to bring greater control over their lives to more of the world's women. At the same time differences are not ignored and the intricate tangle of gender with other forms of inequality is the subject of continued political and intellectual scrutiny. The engagement of class with gender has been particularly important within feminist sociology.

Classing gender

Within feminist sociology there are three major approaches to understanding the links between class and gender; one criticizes standard classifications of class (Acker, 1998/1973), another extends materialist visions to encompass gender (for example, Delphy and Leonard, 1992), and the third turns to discourse and culture (for example, Skeggs, 1997). French Materialist feminists, most especially Christine Delphy, offer a partial turn to culture in the way they develop Marx's ideas (Jackson, 1998b). Delphy concentrates on explaining the domestic mode of production as a crucial concept in understanding women's subordination. This is a mode which excludes women and the household tasks they perform from the market and exclusion from the market means that housework is unpaid. The unpaid nature of household labour also means that women cannot consume when and as they choose. Women are additionally disadvantaged because the domestic mode of production is also a mode of circulation in which wealth is conventionally passed to oldest sons, reproducing women as non-possessors. This does not consider all areas in which women are constrained, neglecting violence and sexuality, for example, but Delphy (1984) has acknowledged this.

Without some understanding of the operation of ideology or discourse, it remains difficult to explain why it is women who are exploited within the domestic mode of production. And yet the notion of ideology was often rather underdeveloped within materialist and radical approaches to gender. Contemporary accounts of how gender inequalities are classed use Bourdieu in promising ways to elaborate how meanings make class distinctions in gendered ways that have real effects (see Adkins and Skeggs, 2004; Duggins and Pudsey, 2006). They employ his concepts of capital and habitus to examine class as specific sets of ingrained ways of thinking and being, played out in gendered ways within particular social worlds or fields (for example, Reay, 1998; Skeggs, 1997; 2004; 2005). In addition Adkins can be used to consider how it is that a 'taste' for certain kinds of workers to do particular jobs helps explain why women's labour is exploited in specific ways within capitalist patriarchy. It is through constant battles to be deemed respectable that class distinctions operate for working class women, who strive for some of the markers of middle class femininity (such as caring skills or elegant clothes) in the hope that they might be able to convert any limited cultural capital they may gain into economic capital. Even though this may be unlikely, they however have to maintain the struggle in order to ensure their social position does not worsen. This struggle is one with considerable emotional costs (Reay, 2004; Skeggs, 1997; 2005).

What could be clearer is how it is that some individuals are able to overcome or relearn their habitus sufficiently to accrue various forms of capital sufficient to gain social mobility. This might be better understood if we appreciate that it is possible to 'move' the kinds of sedimented power relations that Bourdieu and feminist followers describe, and that emotions – especially anger – may play a part (Holmes, 2004). If such shifts towards respect for diversity are to be more than utopian fantasies they require an understanding of how gender intersects with other forms of inequality and, most importantly, how it intertwines with racial inequalities.

Racing gender

Racial inequalities, and the way in which they are gendered, are largely a product of a world history which saw the first industrialized nations go forth to appropriate the land and resources of people on other continents. Colonization was an economic process but was justified by ideas that represented whiteness and white ways of doing things as superior. White women may have been central in attempts to 'civilize the natives', attempts that assumed that native women would be better off if they turned away from traditional cultures. However 'traditional' cultures may have offered women more status and autonomy than the Western cultures they were being exhorted to accept (Etienne and Leacock, 1980). Whatever the state of gender relations pre-contact, it is certainly the case that colonization reshaped these relations on a global scale. Most of those theorizing the gendering of racial inequalities within a global framework have rejected modernization theory's 'West is best' model of economic development. Feminist economists have interrogated systems of national accounting and found them neglectful of women's contributions (Benería, see for example, 1995; Waring, 1999/1986). Other feminists (for example, Mies, 1982) have drawn on dependency and world systems theory to argue that capitalist patriarchy in the West is maintained by exploiting the labour of Third World women. However, it has been noted that dependency theory tends to see women as trapped within the domestic sphere and its 'traditional' practices, and therefore as victims within patriarchal households rather than as potential revolutionaries. More questions need to be asked about the complex role women and the household play within 'dependent' nations (Scott, 1995). This requires consideration of colonization as both an economic and a cultural process, concerned with both the distribution of resources and the flow of meanings.

Dominant meanings around colonialism remain influential in understanding how gender and race are intertwined. Views of non-white peoples as primitive, exotic, and/or highly sexual were used to justify the invasion of their lands, the devaluing of their existing ways of doing gender, and the conquest of indigenous women. Women have been central in resisting these views and indeed in asserting the rights of indigenous and previously enslaved peoples (see hooks, 1992; Smith, 1999; Wollacott, 2006). Such processes of decolonization are ongoing and need to include the problematizing of whiteness and all the privileges attached (Bonnett, 2000; hooks, 1992; Spivak, 1990). Further work is needed to see how class inequalities are interwoven with those around gender and 'race', but some brief suggestions can be made.

Women, race and class

It might now be possible, due to their greater presence in the paid workforce, to categorize most women's class on the basis of their occupation as individuals. However, to do this would be to ignore the effects that their gender has on the wages and status accorded to women's paid work. In addition such an approach to class does not consider the role played by women's unpaid work in reproducing gender and class inequalities. In this regard Delphy's (1984) insistence that class is a relation within the domestic mode of production is a useful one. This can help us to understand patriarchy as a system in which we are all caught up, but that privileges men more than women. The work women do without payment in loving and caring for others, much as it may have rewards of its own, is exploited in ways that have many implications for how women lead their lives – and what else they are able to achieve. However, to suggest that women are best thought of as a class, exploited by men, also has limitations. It means that class substitutes for gender as a term, because gender is thought to remain too closely tied to notions of a 'natural' division between the sexes. But within sociology the term gender was introduced to refer to *socially created* inequalities between 'women' and 'men'. Seeing women as a class in relation to men makes inequalities within genders difficult to deal with.

Most women, whatever their ethnicity or sexual orientation, share a similar position within the domestic mode of production, but that mode (as Delphy, 1984, acknowledges) does not account for all aspects of women's oppression. Also necessary is an appreciation of how a global capitalist mode of production emerged, and to what extent or in what ways that is related to the domestic mode. The racial and gendered inequalities arising from that global system, forged by past (and continuing) imperialist ventures have begun to be explored, but the relationship to the domestic has been less so (though see Ehrenrich and Hochschild, 2003; Mies, 1982). The following are tentative suggestions for ways forward in thinking about gender, and they chart a rather different path to the one proposed by most post-structuralist and/or meaning focused accounts of gender.

Beyond the linguistic turn

'Masculine' and 'feminine' are not clear and fixed opposing identities based on biological sex but shifting categories, defined in relationship to each other, that order social relations. To think thus is to contemplate the possibilities and promise of causing 'gender trouble' (Butler, 1990). Sex/gender may bring us into being as individuals of whom others can make sense, but if our very embodiment is fashioned around social fictions about what it means to be feminine or masculine, then those embodied ways of being are open to change. However, there are problems in considering how such change is possible especially because the sex/gender divide is powerfully regulated by the idea that heteronormativity is the 'natural' and necessary foundation of human societies. Butler (1993: x) does not wish to suggest that individuals can voluntarily select how they do their gender. In fact she does not want to think about people doing gender, but about how gender as a system of meanings constitutes us as feminine or masculine individuals. In order to not make this seem overly deterministic, she conceives of gender as a masquerade involving the citation of gender norms in line with heterosexual imperatives. It is possible to think of this as a collective and relational exercise (see Connell, 1995; 2002), rather than a matter of individuals doing or performing gender.

Any collective or relational situation is basically constituted by individuals presenting themselves to and judging others in gendered ways (for example, Goffman, 1979; West and Zimmerman, 1987). The question is: where does gender come from? Symbolic interactionists tend to see gender as a pre-existing role, or set of scripts, that we perform, with slight variations. They note, but do not challenge, social prescriptions that those thought to be of the female sex will behave in a feminine manner and that 'males' will do masculinity. What Butler proposes is that it is possible to much more radically detach femininity from femaleness and masculinity from maleness. Other queer theorists (see Jagose, 1996) agree that it is possible to create much more fluid gender identities that challenge the very heterosexual distinction between 'feminine' and 'masculine' and highlight that sex is constructed as a binary but does not always exist as either female or maleness. In theory this seems possible, but many examples of people who cause 'gender trouble', such as drag queens, transvestites, and some transsexuals, do not seem to radically call into question what it means to be feminine or masculine, instead reinforcing quite conservative ideas about how to do gender (Garfinkel, 1967; Kessler and McKenna, 1978; Jeffreys, 1996; Seidman, 1994). Perhaps theorists need to think of better examples, returning for instance to look further at intersex individuals (see Fausto-Sterling, 2002b; Hird, 2004) and to what extent it is possible for them to occupy a 'no-man's' (sic) land between the gender categories. But intellectual and political challenges remain.

As an intellectual exercise much current thinking on gender continues to worry away at the key questions dealt with in this book. What relationship, if any, is there between bodies and gender? To what extent are individuals gendered by the economic and social structures within which they live and with what results? What level of control, or choice, do people have about how they express gender? And crucially, why does being feminine continue to mean being likely to share less in the rewards and recognition society offers?

As a political exercise the challenge of some of the new thinking on gender is that it questions the very relevance of gender as a category for organizing social life. On the one hand this offers extremely radical opportunities to abolish binary distinctions between feminine and masculine, and to live out our lives in a freer expression of ourselves and our desires for other human beings. On the other hand, there are concerns that to disregard gender dichotomy will merely institute ways of being in which the feminine might disappear (Braidotti, 2001). The concern is that insisting on the artificiality of gender dichotomies is important, but can mean that attention strays from the material and embodied effects those dichotomies have on women's and men's lives (Howson, 2005).

Gender is a product of material conditions but is also a sometimes habituated, sometimes reflexive practice in which people engage in relation with each other. Symbolic interactionism provides a relational account of how embodiment is formed and 'done' in relation to others. Feminist appropriations of Bourdieu offer explanation of the importance of both material (as in economic) as well as symbolic processes in the social distinction of some kinds of bodies as more worthy of recognition. Bodies signify a range of tastes and tastes are exercized around different types of bodies. A taste for particular types of feminine or masculine bodies is exercized in different social fields, according to hierarchies of taste that usually privilege middle class forms of masculinity. However, there are questions about whether it is possible or desirable to talk about different 'tastes' without considering some to be 'better' than others. Although dismantling sexist, racist and classist valuations of embodiment may be liberating, declaring all tastes equally good may have its problems. Where does this leave us if, for example, we want to criticize an older man's 'taste' for young girls? Conceptualizing sex/gender/sexuality as a 'taste' might only be fruitful if we consider to what extent tastes for particular forms of embodiment are likely to challenge sedimented patterns of domination which reinforce patriarchy and make feminine embodiment fraught with difficulties.

Gendered bodies are not simply the object of others' 'tastes', but the instrument via which individuals experience and practice tastes. Gendered embodiment is the ingrained material and symbolic expression of tastes. Gender is an embodied practice done in relation to others, and done to us by others. We constantly shift our embodied doing of gender in accordance not only with structural demands, but with our imaginings of what 'others' expect. Structures regulate individuals according to gender, pushing them into manly sports or womanly careers, domestic caring or goal-oriented success in the public world. Yet not all men play rugby and not all women aspire to be domestic goddesses. Individuals engage with structures and with social expectations as they are represented via linguistic and non-linguistic communication with others (see Martin, 2003). Decisions are made about how to do gender within the constraints of a particular situation. There are limits on our freedom to 'do' gender in any way that takes our fancy, and the less privilege we have in terms of class and age and ethnic origin, the more constrained our choices are likely to be. When faced with severe limits and with constant reminders that others do not value them, those less privileged within hierarchies of gender (and class, ethnicity and more) may feel humiliated, but they may also feel angry. And it is this emotional reaction – both a response to, and located within, gendered embodiment – that offers the possibility of change. It does not have to be like this. There is no natural order that must be maintained. We have made gender and the inequalities that attend it and therefore it can be remade. There is not some utopian endpoint in which women and men will no longer be unequal or no longer even exist as categories. There is simply an ongoing struggle to relate to each other in more respectful ways. But this is a struggle worth getting up for in the mornings.

References

Acker, J. (1998/1973) 'Women and social stratification: a case of intellectual sexism', in K. A. Myers, C.D. Anderson and B.J. Risman (eds), *Feminist Foundations: Towards Transforming Sociology*. London: Sage.

Adams, M.L. (1989) 'There's no place like home: on the place of identity in feminist politics', *Feminist Review*, 31: 22–33.

Adkins, L. (1995) *Gendered work: Sexuality, Family and the Labour Market*. Buckingham: Open University Press.

Adkins, L. (2004) 'Reflexivity: freedom or habit of gender?', in L. Adkins and B. Skeggs (eds), *Feminism After Bourdieu*. Sociological Review Monograph Series. Oxford: Blackwell.

Adkins, L. and Skeggs, B. (eds) (2004) *Feminism After Bourdieu*. Sociological Review Monograph Series. Oxford: Blackwell.

African Development Bank Group (2002) 'Gender, Poverty and Environmental Indicators on African Countries – 2002–2003'. http://www.afdb.org/knowledge/statistics/statistics_indicators_gender/gender/indicators_gender.htm

Afshar, H. (1997) 'Women and work in Iran', *Political Studies*, 45 (4): 755–67.

Amadiune, I. (2005) 'Theorizing matriarchy in Africa: kinship ideologies and systems in Africa and Europe', in O. Oyěwùmí (ed.), *African Gender Studies: A Reader*. Basingstoke: Palgrave Macmillan.

American Journal of Nursing (1984) 'Comparable worth study: nurses really underpaid', *American Journal of Nursing*, 84 (2): 256–7.

Anonymous (1980) *Bitches, Witches, and Dykes*, August: 6.

Armstrong, M., Cummins, A., Hastings S. and Wood, W. (2003) *Job Evaluation: A Guide to Achieving Equal Pay*. London and Sterling, VA: Kogan Page.

Awatere, D. (1984) *Maori Sovereignty*. Auckland: Broadsheet.

Bacchi, C.L. (1990) *Same Difference: Feminism and Sexual Difference*. North Sydney: Allen and Unwin.

Banton, M. (1998) *Racial theories*. New York: Cambridge University Press.

Barker, D.K. (2005) 'Beyond women and economics: rereading "women's work"', *Signs: Journal of Women and Culture*, 30 (4): 2189–209.

Barrett, M. (1980) *Women's Oppression Today*. London: Verso Books.

Barrett, M. (1992) 'Words and things: materialism and method in contemporary feminist analysis', in M. Barrett and A. Phillips (eds),

Destabilizing Theory: Contemporary Feminist Debates. Cambridge: Polity Press.

Barrett, M. and McIntosh, M. (1991) *The Anti-Social Family.* London: Verso.

Barrie, L. (1987) 'The personal is a cultural construction', *Sites*, 15: 68–75.

Barthes, R. (1967) *Elements of Semiology.* London: Cape.

Baudrillard, J. (1983) *Simulations.* New York: Semiotext(e)

BBC News (2003) 'Saudi women join reform call' *BBC News UK*, Edition Tuesday, 30 September. http://news.bbc.co.uk/1/hi/world/middle_east/3152380.stm.

Beasley, C. (1999) *What is Feminism? Understanding Contemporary Feminist Thought.* London: Sage.

Beasley, C. (2005) *Gender and Sexuality: Critical Theories, Critical Thinkers.* London: Sage.

Beechey, V. (1978) 'Women and production: a critical analysis of some sociological theories of women's work', in A. Kuhn and A.M. Wolpe (eds), *Feminism and Materialism: Women and Modes of Production.* London: Routledge and Kegan Paul.

Beets, J.S. (1997) 'Images of Maori women in New Zealand postcards after 1900', *Women's Studies Journal (NZ)*, 13 (2): 7–24.

Benería, L. (1995) 'Toward a greater integration of gender in economics', *World Development*, 23 (11): 1839–50.

Benhabib, S. (1987) 'The generalized and the concrete other: The Kohlberg-Gilligan controversy and feminist theory', in S. Benhabib and D. Cornell (eds), *Feminism as Critique: On the Politics of Gender.* Minneapolis: University of Minnesota Press.

Benston, M. (1969) 'The political economy of women's liberation', *Monthly Review*, 21 (4): 13–27.

Berger, P.L. (1963) *Invitation to Sociology, A Humanistic Perspective.* New York: Anchor.

Bernard, J. (1981) *The Female World.* New York: Free Press.

Berrill, R. and Wallis, P. (1976) 'Sex roles in mathematics', *Mathematics in School*, 5 (2): 28.

Bhabha, H.K. (1994) 'Of mimicry and man: the ambivalence of colonial discourse', in H.K. Bhabha (ed.), *The Location of Culture.* London: Routledge.

Birke, L. (1999) *Feminism and the Biological Body.* Edinburgh: Edinburgh University Press.

Black, P. (2004) *The Beauty Industry: Gender, Culture, Pleasure.* London and New York: Routledge.

Blaikie, A., Hepworth, M., Holmes, M., Howson, A. and Inglis, D. (2003) 'The sociology of the body: genesis, development and futures', in A. Blaikie, M. Hepworth, M. Holmes, A. Howson, D. Inglis, and S. Sartain (eds), *The Body: Critical Concepts in Sociology.* London: Routledge.

Bly, R. (1990) *Iron John: A Book About Men*. Reading, MA: Addison-Wesley.

Bonnett, A. (2000) *White Identities: Historical and International Perspectives*. Harlow: Pearson/Prentice Hall.

Bordo, S. (1987) 'The Cartesian masculinization of thought', in S. Harding and J. O'Barr (eds), *Sex and Scientific Inquiry*. Chicago and London: University of Chicago Press.

Bordo, S. (1989) 'The body and the reproduction of femininity: a feminist appropriation of Foucault', in S. Bordo and A.S. Jagger (eds), *Gender/Body/Knowledge*. New Brunswick, NJ: Rutgers University Press.

Bordo, S. (1993) *Unbearable Weight: Feminism, Western Culture and the Body*. Berkeley: University of California Press.

Bossert, S.T. (1981) 'Understanding sex differences in children's classroom experiences', *The Elementary School Journal* 81 (5): 255–66.

Bourdieu, P. (1974) *Education, Opportunity and Social Inequality*. London: John Wiley.

Bourdieu, P. (1987) *Distinction: A Social Critique of the Judgement of Taste*. Cambridge, MA: Harvard University Press.

Bourdieu, P. (2001) *Masculine Domination*. Cambridge: Polity Press.

Braidotti, R. (2001) *Metamorphoses: Towards a Materialist Theory of Becoming*. Cambridge: Polity.

Bridges, S. and Disney, R. (2004) 'Use of credit and arrears on debt among low-income families in the United Kingdom', *Fiscal Studies* 25 (1): 1–25.

Broadsheet Collective (1981) 'Broadsheet Do it Yourself Seminar', *Broadsheet*, April: 21.

Brook, B. (1999) *Feminist Perspectives on the Body*. London: Longman.

Brown, B. and Adams, P. (1979) 'The feminine body and feminist politics', *m/f*, 3: 35–50.

Brown, P.R., Brown, W.J., Miller, Y.D., Hansen, V. (2001) 'Perceived constraints and social support for active leisure among mothers with young children', *Leisure Sciences* 23 (3): 131–44.

Brown, W. (1995) *States of Injury: Power and Freedom in Later Modernity*. Princeton, NJ: Princeton University Press.

Butler, J. (1988) 'Performative acts and gender constitution: An essay in phenomenology and feminist theory', *Theatre Journal* 40 (4): 519–31.

Butler, J. (1990) *Gender Trouble: Feminism and the Subversion of Identity*. London: Routledge.

Butler, J. (1992) 'Contingent foundations: feminism and the question of "postmodernism"', in J. Butler and J. Scott (eds), *Feminists Theorize the Political*. New York: Routledge.

Butler, J. (1993) *Bodies That Matter: On the Discursive Limits of 'Sex'*. London: Routledge.

Butler, J. (2004) *Undoing Gender*. New York: Routledge.

Carby, H.V. (1982) 'White woman listen: Black feminism and the boundaries of sisterhood', in Lawrence, E., Gilroy, P., Carby, H.V. and Parnas, P. (eds), *The Empire Strikes Back: Race and Racism in Britain*. Centre for Contemporary Cultural Studies, London: Hutchinson.

Catalyst (2006) '2006 Catalyst Census of Women Board Directors of the Fortune 1000'. http://www.catalystwomen.org/index.htm

Chaney, D. (1994) *The Cultural Turn: Scene-setting Essays on Contemporary Cultural History*. London: Routledge.

Charles, M. and Grusky, D.B. (2004) *Occupational Ghettos: The Worldwide Segregation of Women and Men*. Palo Alto, CA: Stanford University Press.

Chaudhuri, N. (1992) 'Shawls, jewelry, curry and rice in Victorian Britain', in N. Chaudhuri and M. Strobel (eds), *Western Women and Imperialism: Complicity and Resistance*. Bloomington: Indiana University Press.

Chodorow, N. (1978) *The Reproduction of Mothering*. Berkeley, CA: University of California Press.

Cooley, C.H. (1902) *Human Nature and the Social Order*. New York: C. Scribner and Sons.

Connell, R.W. (1995) *Masculinities*. Cambridge: Polity.

Connell, R.W. (2000) *The Men and the Boys*. Berkley, CA: University of California Press.

Connell, R.W. (2002) *Gender*. Cambridge: Polity.

Connell, R.W., Ashden, D., Kessler, S., Dowsett, G. (1982) *Making the Difference: Schools, Families and Social Divisions*. Sydney: Allen and Unwin.

Corea, G. (1985) *The Mother Machine*. London: Women's Press.

Cortis, N. and Newmarch, E. (2000) 'Boys in schools: what's happening?' Manning the next Millenium, Masculinities Conference, Queensland University of Technology, 1–2 December. http://www.dest.gov.au/sectors/school_education/publications_resources/profiles/boys_schools_whats_happening.htm

Coward, R. (1978) 'Re-reading Freud: the making of the feminine', *Spare Rib*, 70: 43–6.

Crompton, R. (2005) 'Attitudes, women's employment and the domestic division of labour a cross-national analysis in two waves', *Work, Employment & Society*, 19 (2): 213–33.

Crossley, N. (1995) 'Body techniques: agency and intercorporeality: On Goffman's *Relations in Public*', *Sociology*, 29 (1): 133–49.

Curthoys, J. (1997) *Feminist Amnesia: The Wake of Women's Liberation*. London: Routledge.

Dann, C. (1985) *Up From Under: Women and Liberation in New Zealand 1970–1985*. Wellington: Allen and Unwin.

Davies, B. (1993) *Shards of Glass: Children Reading and Writing Beyond Gendered Identities*. St Leonards, NSW: Allen & Unwin.

Davis, A.Y. (1971) 'Reflections on the black woman's role in the community of slaves', *Black Scholar*, 3 (4): 2–15.

Davis, A.Y. (1983) *Women, Race and Class*. New York: Vintage Books.

Davis, A.Y. (1998) 'Reflections on race, class and gender in the USA', in J. James (ed.), *The Angela Y. Davis Reader*. Malden, MA: Blackwell Publishers.

Davis, A.Y. and Martinez, E. (1998) 'Coalition building among people of color: A discussion with Angela Y. Davis and Elizabeth Martinez', in J. James (ed.), *The Angela Y. Davis Reader*. Malden, MA: Blackwell Publishers.

Davis, K. (1995) *Reshaping the Female Body: The Dilemma of Cosmetic Surgery*. New York: Routledge.

de Beauvoir, S. (1988/1949) *The Second Sex*. London: Pan.

Delamont, S. (1978) 'The domestic ideology and women's education', in S. Delamont and L. Duffin (eds), *The Nineteenth Century Woman*. London: Croom Helm. pp 134–87.

Delamont, S. (1990) *A Woman's Place in Education: Historical and Sociological Perspectives on Gender in Education*. Aldershot: Avebury.

Delphy, C. (1984) *Close to Home: A Materialist Analysis of Women's Oppression*. London: Hutchinson.

Delphy, C. and Leonard, D. (1992) *Familiar Exploitation: A New Analysis of Marriage in Contemporary Western Societies*. Cambridge: Polity Press.

Department of Education, Science and Training (2005) 'Higher education sector in Australia', in *The Higher Education Report 2004–05*. Canberra: Commonwealth of Australia. http://www.dest.gov.au/sectors/higher_education/publications_resources/profiles/highered_annual_report_2004_05.htm

Dobash, R.E. and Dobash, R.P. (1992) *Women, Violence and Social Change*. London: Routledge.

Donaldson, M. (1991) *Time of Our Lives: Labour and Love in the Working Class*. Sydney: Allen and Unwin.

Douglas, M. (1978) *Purity and Danger: An Analysis of Concepts of Pollution and Taboo*. London: Routledge Kegan Paul.

Doyal, L. (2002) 'Putting gender into health and globalisation debates: new perspectives and old challenges', *Third World Quarterly*, 23 (2): 233–50.

Duffield, I. and Bradley, J. (eds) (1997) *Representing Convicts: New Perspectives on Convict Forced Labour Migration*. London: Leicester University Press.

Duggins, S. and Pudsey, J. (2006) 'Care ethics, power, and feminist socio-analysis', in L. Burns (ed.), *Feminist Alliances*. Amsterdam and New York: Rodopi.

Dworkin, A. (1981) *Pornography: Men Possessing Women*. London: Women's Press.

Echols, A. (1989) *Daring to Be Bad: Radical Feminism in America, 1967–1975*. Minneapolis: University of Minnesota Press.

Ehrenreich, B. and Hochschild, A.R. (eds) (2003) *Global Woman: Nannies, Maids, and Sex Workers in the New Economy*. London: Granta.

Elias, N. (1985) *The Loneliness of the Dying*. Oxford: Basil Blackwell.

Elias, N. (2000/1939) *The Civilizing Process: Sociogenetic and Psychogenetic Investigations*. Oxford: Blackwell.

El Saadawi, N. (1982) 'Women and Islam', *Women's Studies International Forum*, 5 (2): 193–206.

Engels, F. (1985/1884) *The Origin of the Family, Private Property and the State*. Harmondsworth: Penguin.

Engender (2000) *Gender Audit 1999/2000: Putting Scottish Women in the Picture*. http://www.engender.org.uk/publications.htm

Equal Employment Opportunities Commission (2006) 'Facts About Women and Men in Great Britain'. http://www.eoc.org.uk/pdf/facts_about_GB_2006.pdf

Etienne, M. and Leacock, E. (1980) *Women and Colonization: Anthropological Perspectives*. Westport, CT.: Bergin & Garvey.

Evans, J. (1995) *Feminist Theory Today: An Introduction to Second-Wave Feminism*. Edinburgh: Edinburgh University Press.

Faludi, S. (1991) *Backlash: The Undeclared War Against Women*. London: Chatto and Windus.

Faludi, S. (1999) *Stiffed: The Betrayal of the Modern Man*. London: Chatto and Windus.

Fanon, F. (1967) *The Wretched of the Earth*. Harmondsworth: Penguin.

Fausto-Sterling, A. (2000) *Sexing the Body: Gender Politics and the Construction of Sexuality*. New York: Basic Books.

Fausto-Sterling, A. (2002a) 'The five sexes: why male and female are not enough', in C. Williams and A. Stein (eds), *Sexuality and Gender*. Malden: Blackwell.

Fausto-Sterling, A. (2002b) 'The five sexes, revisited', *Sciences*, 40: 18–23.

Fausto-Sterling, A. (2004) 'How to build a man', in M.S. Kimmel and M.A. Messner (eds), *Men's Lives*. London: Allyn and Bacon.

Figes, E. (1978/1970) *Patriarchal Attitudes*. London: Virago Press.

Ferguson, N. (2004) *Empire: How Britain Made the Modern World*. Harmondsworth: Penguin.

Finkelstein, J. (1991) *The Fashioned Self*. Cambridge: Polity.

Firestone, S. (1972) *The Dialectic of Sex: The Case for Feminist Revolution*. London: Granada.

Fiske, J. (1989) *Reading the Popular*. Boston: Unwin Hyman.

Fogleman, A.S. (1998), '"From slaves, convicts, and servants to free passengers: the transformation of immigration in the era of the American revolution". Deference or defiance in eighteenth-century America?: A round table'. *The Journal of American History*, 85 (1): 43–76.

Foucault, M. (1967/1961) *Madness and Civilization: A History of Insanity in the Age of Reason*. Transl. Richard Howard. London: Tavistock.

Foucault, M. (1973/1963) *The Birth of the Clinic: An Archeology of Medical Perception*. Transl. A.M. Sheridan. London: Tavistock.

Foucault, M. (1979/1975) *Discipline and Punish: The Birth of the Prison*. Transl. Alan Sheridan Smith. Harmondsworth: Penguin.

Foucault, M. (1990/1976) *The History of Sexuality: Vol. 1. An Introduction.* Transl. Robert Hurley. London: Penguin.

Foucault, M. (1988) 'Technologies of the self', in H. Gutmans and P. Hutton (eds), *Technologies of the Self: A Seminar with Michel Foucault.* London: Tavistock.

Francis, B. (1998) *Power Plays: Primary School Children's Constructions of Gender, Power and Adult Work.* Stoke-on-Trent: Trentham Books.

Frank, A.G. (1972) 'The development of underdevelopment', in J.D. Cockcroft, A.G. Frank and D.L. Johnson (eds), *Dependence and Underdevelopment: Latin America's political economy.* Garden City, NY: Anchor Books.

Fraser, N. (1997) *Justice Interruptus: Critical Reflections on the 'Postsocialist' Condition.* London: Routledge.

Freeman, C. (2004) *Trends in Educational Equity of Girls, 2004.* Washington: National Centre for Education Statistics, US Department of Education. http://nces.ed.gov/pubs2005/equity/

Freud, S. (1910) 'Fourth lecture', in *The Origin and Development of Psycho-Analysis. The American Journal of Psychology* 21: 181–218.

Freud, S. (1932) 'Femininity', in *New Introductory Lectures on Psycho-Analysis.* London and New York: The Hogarth Press/W.W. Norton. pp. 139–67.

Freund, P. and Maguire, M. (1999) *Health, Illness and the Social Body.* New Jersey and London: Prentice Hall.

Freidan, B. (1965) *The Feminine Mystique.* New York: Norton.

Fuss, D. (1989) *Essentially Speaking: Feminism, Nature and Difference.* New York: Routledge.

Gagnon, J. and Simon, W. (1973) *Sexual Conduct.* Chicago: Aldine Publishing Co.

Garfinkel, H. (1967) 'Passing and the managed achievement of sex status in an intersexed person' and 'Appendix', in *Studies in Ethnomethodology.* Englewood Cliffs, NJ: Prentice Hall.

Gatens, M. (1991) 'A critique of the sex/gender distinction', in S. Gunew (ed.), *A Reader in Feminist Knowledge.* London: Routledge.

Gauntlett, D. (2002) *Media, Gender, and Identity: An Introduction.* London and New York: Routledge.

Giddens, A. (1986) *Sociology: A Brief but Critical Introduction.* Basingstoke: MacMillan.

Gimlin, D. (2001) *Body Work: Beauty and Self-image in American Culture.* Berkeley, CA: University of California Press.

Goffman, E. (1987/1959). *The Presentation of Self in Everyday Life.* Harmondsworth: Penguin.

Goffman, E. (1968) *Stigma: Notes on the Management of Spoiled Identity.* Harmondsworth: Penguin.

Goffman, E. (1979) *Gender Advertisements.* Basingstoke: Macmillan.

Goldin, C. and Katz, L.F. (2002) 'The power of the pill: oral contraceptives and women's career and marriage decisions', *Journal of Political Economy,* 110 (4): 730–70.

Grant, J. (1987) 'I feel therefore I am: a critique of female experience as the basis for a feminist epistemology', *Women in Politics*, 7 (3): 99–114.

Greer, G. (1970) *The Female Eunuch*. London: MacGibbon and Kee.

Grosz, E. (1989) *Sexual Subversions: Three French Feminists*. Sydney: Allen and Unwin.

Grosz, E. (1994) *Volatile Bodies: Toward a Corporeal Feminism*. Bloomington, IN: Indiana University Press.

Gunderson, M. (1994) *Comparable Worth and Gender Discrimination: An International Perspective*. Geneva: International Labour Office.

Haggis, J. (1990) 'Gendering colonialism or colonising gender? Recent women's studies approaches to white women and the history of British colonialism', *Women's Studies International Forum*, 13 (1/2): 105–15.

Haggis, J. (2001) 'The social memory of a colonial frontier', *Australian Feminist Studies*, 16: 91–9.

Hall, J. (2000) 'It hurts to be a girl: growing up poor, white and female', *Gender and Society*, 14 (5): 630–43.

Hall, S. (1996) 'When was "the post-colonial?" Thinking at the limit', in I. Chambers and L. Curti (eds), *The Post-Colonial Question: Common Skies, Divided Horizons*. London and New York: Routledge.

Hall, S. (1997) 'The spectacle of the "other"', in S. Hall (ed.), *Representation: Cultural Representations and Signifying Practices*. London: Sage/OU.

Haraway, D.J. (1985) 'A manifesto for cyborgs: science, technology, and socialist feminism in the 1980s', *Socialist Review*, 80, March–April: 65–108.

Hartmann, H. (1981) 'The unhappy marriage of Marxism and feminism: towards a more progressive union', in L. Sargent (ed.), *Women and Revolution: The Unhappy Marriage of Marxism and Feminism*. London: Pluto Press.

Hartsock, N.C.M. (1998) *The Feminist Standpoint Revisited and other Essays*. Oxford: Westview Press.

Hasbro (2005) 'G.I. Joe: Sigma 6' http://www.hasbro.com/gijoe/default.cfm/page=toys

Hechter, M. (2004) 'From class to culture', *American Journal of Sociology*, 110 (2): 400–45.

Hennessy, R. and Ingraham, C. (1997) 'Introduction: reclaiming anticapitalist feminism', in R. Hennessy and C. Ingraham (eds), *Materialist Feminism: A Reader in Class Difference and Women's Lives*. New York and London: Routledge.

Hepworth, M. (1995) 'Positive ageing: what is the message?', in R. Brunton, S. Nettleton and R. Burrows (eds), *The Sociology of Health Promotion: Critical Analyses of Consumption, Lifestyle and Risk*. London: Routledge.

Herdt, G. (1994) *Third Sex, Third Gender: Beyond Sexual Dimorphism in Culture and History*. New York: Zone.

Hill, M. and Hoecker-Drysdale, S. (eds) (2001) *Harriet Martineau: Theoretical and Methodological Perspectives*. London: Routledge.

Hill Collins, P. (1990) *Black Feminist Thought: Knowledge, Consciousness, and the Politics of Empowerment*. Boston: Unwin Hyman.

Hird, M. (2004) *Sex, Gender, and Science*. New York: Palgrave.

Hochschild, A.R. (2003) *The Second Shift*. New York: Penguin.

Holmes, M. (1999) 'The Representation of Feminists as Political Actors'. Unpublished PhD Thesis, University of Auckland.

Holmes, M. (2000a) 'Second-wave feminism and the politics of relationships', *Women's Studies International Forum*, 23 (2): 235–46.

Holmes, M. (2000b) 'When is the personal political? The president's penis and other stories', *Sociology* 34 (2): 305–21.

Holmes, M. (2004) 'Feeling beyond rules: politicising the sociology of emotion and anger in feminist politics', *European Journal of Social Theory*, 7 (2): 209–27.

hooks, b. (1981) *Ain't I a Woman? Black Women and Feminism*. London: Pluto.

hooks, b. (1992) *Black Looks: Race and Representation*. London: Turnaround Ltd.

Hood-Williams, J. and Harrison, C. (1998) 'Trouble with gender', *The Sociological Review*, 46 (1): 73–94.

Howson, A. (1999) 'Cervical screening, compliance and moral obligation', *Sociology of Health & Illness*, 21 (4): 401–25.

Howson, A. (2004) *The Body in Society: An Introduction*. Cambridge: Polity.

Howson, A. (2005) *Embodying Gender*. London: Sage.

Howson, A. and Inglis, D. (2001) 'The body in sociology: tensions inside and outside sociological thought', *Sociological Review*, 49 (3): 297–317.

Hubler, A.E. (2000) 'Beyond the image: adolescent girls, reading, and social reality', *NWSA Journal*, 12 (1): 84–99.

Hull, G.T., Scott, P.B., and Smith, B. (eds) (1982) *All the Women are White, All the Blacks are Men, But Some of us are Brave: Black Women's Studies*. New York: The Feminist Press.

Hunter, M. (2002) '"If you're light you're alright": light skin color as social capital', *Gender and Society*, 16 (2) 175–93.

Hymowitz, C. and Schellhardt, T.D. (1986) 'The glass ceiling: why women can't break the invisible barrier that blocks them from top jobs', *Wall Street Journal*, March 24: 1, 5D.

International Institute for Population Sciences (IIPS) and ORC Macro (2000), 'Nutrition and the Prevalence of Anaemia', *National Family Health Survey (NHFS 2) 1998–99, India*. Mumbai: IIPS. http://www.nfhsindia.org/publi.html

Inter-Parliamentary Union (IPU) (2006), 'Women in parliaments' and 'Women in politics: Women's Suffrage, A World Chronology of

Women's Rights to Vote and Stand for Elections'. http://www.ipu.org/english/home.htm. Updated July 2006.

Irigaray, L. (1985) *This Sex Which is Not One*. Ithaca, NY: Cornell University Press.

Irigaray, L. (1991) 'Volume without contours', in M. Whitford (ed.), *The Irigaray Reader*. Oxford: Blackwell.

Jackson, S. (1998a) 'Telling stories: memory, narrative and experience in feminist theory and research', in C. Griffin, K. Henwood and A. Phoenix (eds), *Standpoints and Differences*. London: Sage.

Jackson, S. (1998b) 'Feminist social theory', in S. Jackson and J. Jones (eds), *Contemporary Feminist Theories*. Edinburgh: Edinburgh University Press.

Jackson, S. (1999) 'The desire for Freud: psychoanalysis and feminism', in *Heterosexuality in Question*. London: Sage.

Jackson, S. (1999) *Heterosexuality in Question*. London: Sage.

Jackson, S. and Scott, S. (eds) (1996) *Feminism and Sexuality: A Reader*. Edinburgh: Edinburgh University Press.

Jagose, A. (1996) *Queer Theory: An Introduction*. New York: New York University Press.

Jamieson, L. (1998) *Intimacy: Personal Relationships in Modern Society*. Cambridge and Oxford: Polity Press and Blackwell.

Jeffreys, S. (1996) 'Heterosexuality and the desire for gender', in D. Richardson (ed.), *Theorising Heterosexuality: Telling it Straight*. Buckingham and Philadelphia: Open University Press.

Jejeebhoy, S.J. and Sathar, Z.A. (2001) 'Women's autonomy in India and Pakistan: the influence of religion and region', *Population and Development Review*, 27 (4): 687–712.

Jones, A. and Guy, C. (1992) 'Radical feminism in New Zealand: from Piha to Newton', in R. Du Plessis (ed.), *Feminist Voices: Women's Studies Texts for Aotearoa/New Zealand*. Auckland: Oxford University Press.

Kappeler, S. (1986) *The Pornography of Representation*. Cambridge: Polity Press.

Kehler, J. (2001) 'Women and poverty: the South African experience', *Journal of International Women's Studies*, 3 (1): 1–13.

Kelly, L. (1988) *Surviving Sexual Violence*. Cambridge: Polity.

Kenny, C. (2002) North American Indian, Metis and Inuit Women Speak about Culture, Education and Work. Ottawa: Status of Women, Canada.

Kessler, S.J. and McKenna, W. (1978) *Gender: An Ethnomethodological Approach*. New York: Wiley.

Kimmel, M. (1996) *Manhood in America*. New York: Free Press.

King, M. (2003) *Penguin History of New Zealand*. Auckland: Penguin.

Kitzinger, C. and Wilkinson, S. (1993) 'The precariousness of heterosexual feminist identities', in M. Kennedy, C. Lubelska and V. Walsh (eds),

Making Connections: Women's Studies, Women's Movements, Women's Lives. London: Taylor and Francis.

Klaich, D. (1974) *Woman Plus Woman*. New York: Simon and Schuster.

Klein, Naomi (2002/2000) *No Logo: No Space, No Choice, No Jobs*. New York: Picador.

Kodoth, P. and Eapen, M. (2005) 'Looking beyond gender parity: gender inequities of some dimensions of well-being in Kerala', *Economic and Political Weekly*, July: 3278–86.

Kristeva, J. (1980a) *The Revolution in Poetic Language*. Trans. M. Waller. New York: Columbia University Press. First published in 1974 as *La Révolution du Langage Poétique*. Paris: Editions du Seuil.

Kristeva, J. (1980b) 'From one identity to another', in L. Roudiez (ed.), *Desire in Language: A Semiotic Approach to Literature and Art*. Trans. L.T. Gora, A. Jardine and L. Roudiez. New York: Columbia University Press.

Kristeva, J. (1981) 'Women's time', *Signs*, 7: 13–35.

Kristeva, Julia (1982) *Powers of Horror*. Trans. L. Roudiez. New York: Columbia University Press. First published in 1980 as *Pouvoirs de L'horreur*. Paris: Editions de Seuil.

Kuhn, A. and Wolpe, A.M. (1978) 'Feminism and materialism', in A. Kuhn and A.M. Wolpe (eds), *Feminism and Materialism: Women and Modes of Production*. London: Routledge and Kegan Paul.

Lacan, J. (1968) *The Language of the Self: The Function of Language in Psychoanalysis*. Trans. with notes and commentary, Anthony Wilden. Baltimore: John Hopkins Press.

Laclau, E. and Mouffe, C. (1985) *Hegemony and Socialist Strategy: Towards a Radical Democratic Politics*. London: Verso.

Laqueur, T. (1990) *Making Sex: Body and Gender: From the Greeks to Freud*. Boston: Harvard University Press.

Laws, S. (1990) *Issues of Blood*. Basingstoke: Macmillan.

Leonard, D. and Adkins, L. (1996) *Sex in Question: French Materialist Feminism*. London: Routledge.

Lewis, R. (1996) *Gendering Orientalism: Race, Femininity and Representation*. London: Routledge.

Lewis, R. and Mills, S. (2003) *Feminist Post-colonial Theory: A Reader*. Edinburgh: Edinburgh University Press.

Lester, A. (2002) 'British settler discourse and the circuits of empire', *History Workshop Journal*, 54: 25–48.

Lipset, D. (2003) 'Rereading *Sex and Temperament*: Margaret Mead's Sepik tryptych and its ethnographic critics', *Anthropological Quarterly*, 76 (4): 693–713.

Lloyd, G. (1984) *The Man of Reason: 'Male' and 'Female' in Western Philosophy*. London: Methuen.

Lobban, G. (1975) 'Sex-roles in reading schemes', *Educational Review*, 27: 202–10.

Lorde, A. (1984) *Sister Outsider: Essays and Speeches*. Berkeley, CA: Crossing Press.

Lorde, A. (1984) 'The master's tools will never dismantle the master's house', in *Sister Outsider: Essays and Speeches*. Berkeley, CA: Crossing Press.

McClintock, A. (1995) *Imperial Leather: Race, Gender and Sexuality in the Colonial Contest*. London: Routledge.

MacDonald, C. (1990) *A Woman of Good Character: Single Women as Immigrant Settlers in Nineteenth-century New Zealand*. Wellington: Allen and Unwin/Historical Branch.

Mac an Gahill, M. (1994) *The Making of Men: Masculinities, Sexualities and Schooling*. Buckingham: Open University Press.

MacKinnon, C.A. (1982) 'Feminism, marxism, method, and the state: an agenda for theory', *Signs*, 7 (3): 515–44.

McRae, S. (1986) *Cross-class Families: A Study of Wives' Occupational Superiority*. Oxford and New York: Clarendon Press.

MacSween, M. (1993) *Anorexic Bodies: A Feminist and Sociological Perspective*. London and New York: Routledge.

Martin, E. (1984) 'Pregnancy, labour and body image in the United States', *Social Science and Medicine*, 19: 1201–6.

Martin, P.Y. (2003) '"Said and done" versus "saying and doing": gendering practices, practicing gender at work', *Gender and Society*, 17 (3): 342–66.

Martin, E. and Martin, J.M. (1978) *The Black Extended Family*. Chicago: University of Chicago Press.

Mattel (2005) 'Barbie.com', http://barbie.everythinggirl.com/catalog/

Mauss, M. (1973) 'Techniques of the body', *Economy and Society*, 2 (1): 70–88.

Mead, G.H. (1962) *Mind, Self, and Society: From the Standpoint of a Social Behaviourist*. Chicago: University of Chicago Press.

Mead, M. (1963/1935) *Sex and Temperament in Three Primitive Societies*. New York: William Morrow.

Mead, M. (1962/1950) *Male and Female: A Study of the Sexes in a Changing World*. Harmondsworth: Penguin.

Merleau-Ponty, M. (2003/1945) *Phenomenology of Perception*. Trans. C. Smith. London and New York: Routledge.

Messner, M.A. (1997) *The Politics of Masculinities: Men in Movements*. Thousand Oaks: Sage.

Mies, M. (1982) *The Lace Makers of Narasapur: Indian Housewives Produce for the World Market*. London: Zed Books.

Millet, K. (1972/1970) *Sexual Politics*. London: Abacus.

Mills, C.W. (1959) *The Sociological Imagination*. Oxford: Oxford University Press.

Mills, S. (1998) 'Post-colonial feminist theory', in S. Jackson and J. Jones (eds), *Contemporary Feminist Theories*. Edinburgh: Edinburgh University Press.

Mitchell, J. (1973) *Woman's Estate*. New York: Vintage Books.

Mitchell, J. (1975) *Psychoanalysis and Feminism*. Harmondsworth: Penguin.

Mitchell, J. and Oakley, A. (eds) (1997) *Who's Afraid of Feminism: Seeing Through the Backlash*. London: Hamish Hamilton

Mohanty, C.T. (1991) 'Under western eyes: feminist scholarship and colonial discourses', in C.T. Mohanty, A. Russo and L. Torres (eds), *Third World Women and the Politics of Feminism*. Bloomington and Indianapolis: Indiana University Press.

Money, J. and Tucker, P. (1975) *Sexual Signatures: On Being a Man or a Woman*. Boston: Little, Brown and Co.

Morgan, D. (1993) 'You too can have a body like mine: reflections on the male body and masculinities', in S. Scott and D. Morgan (eds), *Body Matters: Essays on the Sociology of the Body*. London: Falmer Press.

Morrison, T. (1999/1970) *The Bluest Eye*. Philadelphia: Chelsea House.

Moruzzi, N.C. (2005) 'Cutting through culture: the feminist discourse on female circumcision', *Critique: Critical Middle Eastern Studies*, 14 (2): 203–20.

Mouffe, C. (1992) 'Feminism, citizenship and radical democratic politics', in J. Butler and J. Scott (eds), *Feminists Theorize the Political*. New York: Routledge.

Moyo, O. and Kawewe, S.M. (2002) 'The dynamics of racialized, gendered, ethnicized, and economically stratified society: understanding the socio-economic status of women in Zimbabwe', *Feminist Economics*, 8 (2): 163–81.

Mukhopadhyay, C.C. and Seymour, S. (1994) 'Introduction and theoretical overview', in C. Mukhopadhyay and S. Seymour (eds), *Women, Education and Family Structure in India*. Boulder, CO: Westview Press.

Naples, N.A. and Dobson, M. (2001) 'Feminists and the welfare state: Aboriginal health care workers and US community workers of color', *NSWA Journal*, 13 (3): 116–37.

Nash, K. (2001) 'The cultural turn in social theory: towards a theory of cultural politics', *Sociology*, 35 (1): 77–92.

National Science Board (2006) 'Higher education in science and engineering', in *Science and Engineering Indicators 2006*. Vol. 1. Arlington, VA: National Science Foundation. http://www.nsf.gov/statistics/seind06/c2/c2h.htm

Oakley, A. (1972) *Sex, Gender and Society*. London: Temple Smith.

Oakley, A. (1974) *The Sociology of Housework*. London: Martin Robertson.

Oakley, A. (1980) *Woman Confined: Towards a Sociology of Childbirth*. Oxford: Martin Robertson.

Oakley, A. (1985a) *Sex, Gender and Society*. Aldershot: Gower.

Oakley, A. (1985b) 'Dear Dale', in D. Spender (ed.), *For the Record: The Making and Meaning of Feminist Knowledge*. London: Women's Press.

Oakley, A. (1997) 'A brief history of gender', in A. Oakley and J. Mitchell (eds), *Who's Afraid of Feminism? Seeing Through the Backlash*. London: Hamish Hamilton.

Office for National Statistics (2001a) 'Hourly earnings differentials: 1971–2000', *New Earnings Survey*. London: HMSO.

Office for National Statistics (2001b) *Social Trends*, 31.

Office for National Statistics (2006) 'Education and training', *Social Trends*, 36: 33–48.

Oliver, K. (1997) 'Introduction: Kristeva's revolutions', in K. Oliver (ed.), *The Portable Kristeva*. New York: Columbia University Press.

Oudshoorn, N. (1994) *Beyond the Natural Body: An Archeology of Sex Hormones*. London: Routledge.

Pakenham, T (1990) *The Scramble for Africa, 1870–1912*. London: Weidenfeld and Nicolson.

Parker, G. (1992) 'Making ends meet: women, credit and debt', in C. Glendinning and J. Millar (eds), *Women and Poverty in Britain: The 1990s*. London: Harvester Wheatsheaf.

Parsons, T. and Bales, R.F. (1956) *Family Socialization and Interaction Process*. London: Routledge and Kegan Paul.

Pattel-Gray, A. (1999) 'The hard truth: white secrets, black realities', *Australian Feminist Studies*, 14 (30): 259–66.

Pateman, C. (1988) *The Sexual Contract*. Stanford, CA: Stanford University Press.

Pateman, C. (1989) *The Disorder of Women: Democracy, Feminism and Political Theory*. Cambridge: Polity Press.

Pollock, G. (1992) 'Painting, feminism, history', in M. Barrett and A. Phillips (eds), *Destabilizing Theory: Contemporary Feminist Debates*. Stanford: Stanford University Press.

Prendergast, S. and Forrest, S. (1998) 'Shorties, low-lifers, hardnuts, and kings: boys, emotions and embodiment in schools', in G. Bendelow and S. Williams (eds), *Emotions in Social Life: Critical Themes and Contemporary Issues*. London: Routledge.

Prokos, A. and Padavic, I. (2005) 'An examination of competing explanations for the pay gap among scientists and engineers', *Gender & Society*, 19 (4): 523–43.

Rahman, M. and Witz, A. (2003) 'What really matters? The elusive quality of the material in feminist thought', *Feminist Theory*, 4 (3): 243–61.

Rea, M.F., Venancio, S.I., Batista, L.E., dos Santos, R.G., Greiner, T. (1997) 'Possibilities and limitations of breast-feeding among formally employed women', *Journal of Pediatric Health Care*, 11 (1): 12–9.

Reay, D. (1997) 'Feminist theory, habitus and social class: disrupting notions of classlessness', *Women's Studies International Forum*, 20: 225–33.

Reay, D. (1998) 'Rethinking social class: qualitative perspectives on class and gender', *Sociology*, 32 (2): 259–75.

Reay, D. (2004) 'Gendering Bourdieu's concepts of capitals? Emotional capital, women and social class', in L. Adkins and B. Skeggs (eds), *Feminism After Bourdieu*. Sociological Review Monograph Series. Oxford: Blackwell.

Reay, D. (2005) 'Beyond consciousness? The physic landscape of social class', *Sociology*, 39 (5): 911–28.

Rendall, J. (1985) *Origins of Modern Feminism: Women in Britain, France and the United States*, 1780–1860. Basingstoke: Palgrave Macmillan.

Rich, A. (1986/1976) *Of Woman Born: Motherhood as Experience and Institution*. New York: W.W. Norton and Co.

Riley, D. (1988) *'Am I That Name?': Feminism and the Category of 'Women' in History*. Basingstoke: Macmillan.

Roberts, D. (1997) *Killing the Black Body: Race, Reproduction and the Meaning of Liberty*. New York: Pantheon.

Rogers, M.F. (1999) *Barbie Culture*. London: Sage.

Roseneil, S. (1995) 'The coming of age of feminist sociology: some issues of practice and theory for the next twenty years', *British Journal of Sociology*, 46 (2): 191–205.

Roseneil, S. (2000) 'Queer frameworks and queer tendencies: towards an understanding of postmodern transformations of sexuality', *Sociological Research Online*, 5 (3). http://www.socresonline.org.uk/5/3/roseneil.html

Rostow, W.W. (2000/1960) 'Stages of economic growth: a non-communist manifesto', in J. Timmons (ed.), *From Modernization to Globalization: Perspectives on Development and Social Change*. Malden: Blackwell.

Rubin, G. (1975) 'The traffic in women: notes on the "political economy" of sex', in R.R. Reiter (ed.), *Toward an Anthropology of Women*. New York and London: Monthly Review Press.

Said, E. (1978) *Orientalism*. New York: Pantheon.

Saks, M. (2001) 'Alternative medicine and the health care division of labour: present trends and future prospects', *Current Sociology*, 49 (3): 119–34.

Saliba, T., Allen, C. and Howard, J.A. (eds) (2002) *Gender, Politics and Islam*. Chicago: University of Chicago Press.

Saussure, F. de (1983) *Course in General Linguistics*. R. Harris (transl.) London: Duckworth.

Schiebinger, L. (1989) *The Mind Has No Sex? Women in The Origins Of Modern Science*. Cambridge, MA: Harvard University Press.

Schor, N. (1992) 'Feminism and George Sand: lettres à Marcie', in J. Butler and J. Scott (eds), *Feminists Theorize the Political*. New York: Routledge.

Schuller, T. and Bamford, C. (1999) 'Statistical summary, initial and continuing education in Scotland: divergence, convergence and learning relationships interim', The Scottish Council for Research in Education The University of Edinburgh, Centre for Continuing Education November 1998 and, revised January 1999. http://www.scre.ac.uk/

Scott, C. (1995) *Gender and Development: Rethinking Modernization and Dependency Theory*. Boulder, CO: Lynne Rienner Publishers.

Scottish Executive (1999) 'Examination results of first degree graduates', *Higher Education Graduates and Diplomates and their First Destinations 1986–87 to 1996–97*. Edinburgh: The Stationery Office.

Seidler, V.J. (1991) *Recreating Sexual Politics: Men, Feminism and Politics*. London and New York: Routledge.

Seidman, S. (1994) *Contested Knowledge: Social Theory in the Postmodern Era*. Oxford: Blackwell.

Seidman, S. (1996) 'Introduction', in S. Seidman (ed.), *Queer Theory/Sociology*. Oxford: Blackwell. pp 1–30.

Sennett, R. and Cobb, J. (1972) *The Hidden Injuries of Class*. New York: Knopf.

Seymour, W. (1998) *Remaking the Body: Rehabilitation and Change*. New York and London: Routledge.

Sharma, U. (1996) 'Using complementary therapies: a challenge to orthodox medicine?', in S.J. Williams and M. Calnan (eds), *Modern Medicine: Lay Perspectives and Experiences*. London: UCL Press.

Sharpe, S. (1976) *'Just Like a Girl': How Girls Learn to be Women*. Harmondsworth: Penguin.

Shildrick, M. (1997) *Leaky Bodies and Boundries*. London and New York: Routledge.

Sinha, M. (1995) *Colonial Masculinity: The 'Manly Englishman' and the Effeminate Bengali in the Late Nineteenth Century*. Manchester: Manchester University Press.

Skeggs, B. (1997) *Formations of Class and Gender: Becoming Respectable*. London: Sage.

Skeggs, B. (2004) 'Exchange, value and affect: Bourdieu and "the self"', in L. Adkins and B. Skeggs (eds), *Feminism After Bourdieu*. Sociological Review Monograph Series. Oxford: Blackwell. pp. 75–95.

Skeggs, B. (2005) 'The making of class and gender through visualizing moral subject formation', *Sociology*, 39 (5): 965–82.

Slocum, S. (1975) 'Woman the gatherer: male bias in anthropology', in R.R. Reiter (ed.), *Toward and Anthropology of Women*. New York and London: Monthly Review Press. pp. 36–50.

Smith A. (1981) *The Ethnic Revival*. Cambridge: Cambridge University Press.

Smith, L.T. (1999) *Decolonizing Methodologies: Research and Indigenous Peoples*. London, New York, Dunedin: Zed Books & University of Otago Press.

Sointu, E. (2006) 'Recognition and the creation of wellbeing', *Sociology*, 40 (3): 493–510.

Spender, D. (1982) *Invisible Women*. London: Writers and Readers' Publishing Co-operative.

Spender, D. (1985) *For the Record: The Making and Meaning of Feminist Knowledge*. London: Women's Press.

Spivak, G.C. (1990). 'Criticism, feminism and the institution: Elizabeth Gross interviews Gayatri Chakravorty Spivak', in S. Harasym (ed.), *The Post-Colonial Critic: Interviews, Strategies, Dialogues*. London: Routledge.

Stanley, L. (2001/1984) 'Should 'sex' really be 'gender' – or 'gender' really be 'sex'?, in S. Jackson and S. Scott (eds), *Gender: A Sociological Reader*. London: Routledge.

Stanley, L. and Wise, S. (1983) *Breaking Out: Feminist Consciousness and Feminist Research*. London: Routledge.

Stanworth, M. (ed.) (1987) *Reproductive Technologies: Gender, Motherhood, and Medicine*. Cambridge and Oxford: Polity/Blackwell.

Stockman, N. (2000) *Understanding Chinese Society*. Cambridge: Polity Press.

Stoltenberg, J. (2000a/1989) *Refusing to Be a Man: Essays on Sex and Justice*. London: UCL Press.

Stoltenberg, J. (2000b/1993) *The End of Manhood: Parables on Sex and Selfhood*. London: UCL Press.

Sullivan, O. (2000) 'The division of domestic labour: twenty years of change?', *Sociology*, 34 (3): 437–56.

Summers, A. (1975) *Damned Whores and God's Police*. Ringwood, Vic: Penguin.

Supreme Court of the United States (1973) 'Roe et al. v Wade' 410.U.S. 113.

Sydie, R.A. (1987) *Natural Women/Cultured Men: A Feminist Perspective on Sociological Theory*. Milton Keynes: Open University Press.

Tanner, L.B. (ed.) (1970) *Voices from Women's Liberation*. New York: Signet Books.

Taylor, J. (1979) 'Sexist bias in physics textbooks', *Physics Education*, 14: 227–80.

Thomas, H. (1997) *The Slave Trade*. Picador: London.

Thorne, B. (1993) *Gender Play: Girls and Boys in School*. New Brunswick: Rutgers University Press.

Toomey, C. (2001) 'The worst of both worlds', *Sunday Times Magazine*, October 28: 34–40.

Tseëlon, E. (1995) *The Masque of Femininity: The Presentation of Woman in Everyday Life*. London: Sage Publications.

Turner, B. (1984) *The Body in Society*. Oxford: Basil Blackwell.

Tyler, M. and Abbott, P. (1998) 'Chocs away: weight watching in the contemporary airline industry', *Sociology*, 32 (3): 433–50.

UNICEF (2006) *State of the World's Children: Excluded and Invisible*. New York: UNICEF. http://www.unicef.org/sowc06/index.php

United Nations Statistics Division (2005) 'Statistics and Indicators on Women and Men: Table 5g – Women's Wages Relative to Men's'. http//unstats.un.org/unsd/demographic/products/indwm/ww2005/tab5g.htm

United States Supreme Court (1973) 'Roe v. Wade'. 410. U.S. 113.

Uunk, W. (2004) 'The economic consequences of divorce for women in the European union: the impact of welfare state arrangements', *European Journal of Population*, 20 (3): 251–85.

Van Zoonen, L. (1995) 'Gender, representation and the media', in J. Downing, A. Mohammadi and A. Sreberny-Mohammadi (eds), *Questioning the Media*. London: Sage.

Walby, S. (1986) *Patriarchy at Work*. Cambridge: Polity Press.

Walby, S. (1990) *Theorizing Patriarchy*. Oxford: Basil Blackwell.

Walby, S. (1996) *Gender Transformations*. London: Routledge.

Walford, G. (1981) 'Do chemistry textbooks present a sex biased image?', *Education in Chemistry*, 18: 18–19.

Wallerstein, I. (1974) *The Modern World System*. New York: Academic Press.

Wandor, M. (1990) *Once a Feminist: Stories of a Generation*. London: Virago Press.

Ware, V. (1992) *Beyond the Pale: White Women, Racism and History*. London: Verso.

Waring, M. (1999/1986) *Counting for Nothing: What Men Value and What Women are Worth*. Toronto: University of Toronto Press.

Washburn, S. and Lancaster, C. (1968) 'The evolution of hunting', in R.B. Lee and I. DeVore (eds), *Man the Hunter*. Chicago: Aldine.

Waters, F. (2005) 'Physical attacks against health workers occur every two hours', *Nursing Standard*, 19 (47): 10.

Weber, M. (1968/1921) *Economy and Society*, 3 vols, Totowa, NJ: Bedminster Press.

Weber, M. (1981/1927) *General Economic History*, New Brunswick, NJ: Transaction Books.

Weeks, J. (1985) *Sexuality and its Discontents: Meanings, Myths and Modern Sexualities*. London: Routledge and Kegan Paul.

Weeks, J. (1989) *Sexuality*. London: Routledge.

Weeks, J. (2000) 'The challenge of lesbian and gay studies', in T. Sandfort, J. Schuyf, J. Duyvendak and J. Weeks (eds), *Lesbian and Gay Studies: An Introductory, Interdisciplinary Approach*. London: Sage.

Weitzman, L.J., Eifler, D., Hokada, E. and Ross, C. (1972) 'Sex-role socialization in picture books for preschool children', *American Journal of Sociology*, 77 (6): 1125–50.

West, C. and Zimmerman, D. (1987) 'Doing gender', *Gender and Society*, 1 (2): 125–51.

Whelehan, I. (1995) *Modern Feminist Thought: From the Second-Wave to 'Post-Feminism'*. Edinburgh: Edinburgh University Press.

Whitehead, A. (1994) 'Food symbolism, gender, power and the family', in H.B. White (ed.), *Food*. Oxford: Blackwell.

Whitehead, S. (2001) 'Man: the invisible gendered subject', in S.M. Whitehead and F.J. Barrett (eds), *The Masculinities Reader*. Cambridge: Polity Press.

Willis, P. (1977) *Learning to Labour: How Working Class Kids Get Working Class Jobs*. Farnborough, Hants: Saxon Ho.

Wilson, A.N. (2003) *The Victorians*. London: Arrow Books.

Wind, R. (2006) 'States enacted 52 laws restricting abortion in 2005: beyond threats to Roe v. Wade, women already face significant barriers to abortion', New York: Guttmacher Institute. http://www.agi-usa.org/media/nr/2006/ 01/20/index.html. Friday, January 20.

Wittig, M. (1992) *The Straight Mind and Other Essays*. Boston, MA: Beacon Press.

Wollstonecraft, M. (1985/1792) *Vindication of the Rights of Woman*. Harmondsworth: Penguin.

Woolf, V. (1929) *A Room of One's Own*. London: Hogarth Press.

Woollacott, A. (2006) *Gender and Empire*. Basingstoke: Palgrave.

World Bank (2006) 'Data and statistics: labor and employment', *World Development Indicators*. http://www.worldbank.org/

Yamokoski, A. and Keister, L.A. (2006) 'The wealth of single women: marital status and parenthood in the asset accumulation of young baby boomers in the United States', *Feminist Economics*, 12 (1/2): 167–94.

Yeatman, A. (1994) 'Feminism and power', *Women's Studies Journal (NZ)*, 10 (1): 70–100.

Young, I.M. (1990) 'Throwing like a girl: a phenomenology of feminine body comportment, motility, and spatiality', in *Throwing Like a Girl and Other Essays in Feminist Philosophy and Social Theory*. Bloomington: Indiana University Press.

Young, I.M. (1991) *Justice and the Politics of Difference*. New Jersey: Princeton University Press.

Young, M. and Willmott, P. (1973) *The Symmetrical Family: A Study of Work and Leisure in the London Region*. London: Routledge and Kegan Paul.

Index